The Reconfiguration of Twenty-first Century Latin American Regionalism

This cutting-edge volume brings together a diverse roster of scholars to shed light on the reconfiguration of twenty-first century Latin American regionalism. Reflecting on both the multiplicity of regional integration across Latin America (LA) and the theoretically pluralist turn in contemporary scholarship on LA politics and International Relations, this edited volume proposes an 'integrative pluralist' methodology to deciphering the complexity of regionalisation projects, from both above and below.

This book charts the contemporary evolution of older regionalisation schemes, such as the Common Market of the South (MERCOSUR), as well as more recent twenty-first century regional innovations, including the Bolivarian Alliance for the Peoples of Our America-Peoples Trade Treaty (ALBA-TCP), Pacific Alliance (AP), and the Union of South American Nations (UNASUR). Complementing this more traditional institutional perspective, this book also charts the underexplored dynamics of regionalism from below, in the context of region-wide networks of political organisation among indigenous and peasant movements. Set against the backdrop of a more critical reading of the historical origins of regionalism, this volume aims to contribute to the ever-growing conversation among scholars within and beyond Latin America on the actors, processes, contradictions, and prospects for regional cooperation.

In offering a more holistic perspective on Latin American regionalism from above and below, this volume will be of interest to both newcomers to the field and more seasoned scholars working within/across disciplinary boundaries, from International Relations and International Political Economy to Historical Sociology and Institutionalism.

The chapters in this book were originally published as a special issue of *Globalizations*.

Rowan Lubbock is Lecturer in Political Economy of Development at Queen Mary, University of London, UK. His research centres on the agrarian dynamics of International Relations, particularly within Latin America, and he has previously published in *Journal of International Relations and Development*, *New Political Economy*, *Journal of Agrarian Change*, and *Globalizations*. He is currently writing a manuscript on the politics of food sovereignty within the regional organisation of the ALBA-TCP and Venezuela.

Ernesto Vivares is Professor in the Department of International Studies and Communication at FLACSO Ecuador. He has published widely on the topic of Latin American politics, development, and regional integration, and edited two recent volumes: *Regionalism, Development and the Post-Commodities Boom in South America* (2018) and *The Routledge Handbook to Global Political Economy: Conversations and Inquiries* (2020).

Rethinking Globalizations

Edited by **Barry K. Gills**, *University of Helsinki, Finland and*
Kevin Gray, *University of Sussex, UK.*

This series is designed to break new ground in the literature on globalization and its academic and popular understanding. Rather than perpetuating or simply reacting to the economic understanding of globalization, this series seeks to capture the term and broaden its meaning to encompass a wide range of issues and disciplines and convey a sense of alternative possibilities for the future.

Globalizations from Below
The Normative Power of the World Social Forum, Ant Traders, Chinese Migrants, and Levantine Cosmopolitanism
Theodor Tudoroiu

Economics and Climate Emergency
Edited by Barry K. Gills and Jamie Morgan

Global Political Leadership
In Search of Synergy
Małgorzata Zachara-Szymańska

Post-Covid Transformations
Edited by Kevin Gray and Barry Gills

Challenging Authoritarian Capitalism
The Transformative Power of the World Social Forum
Edited by Thomas Wallgren, Uddhab Pd. Pyakurel, Catalina Revollo Pardo and Teivo Teivainen

The Reconfiguration of Twenty-first Century Latin American Regionalism
Actors, Processes, Contradictions and Prospects
Edited by Rowan Lubbock and Ernesto Vivares

Capitalism, Coronavirus and War
A Geopolitical Economy
Radhika Desai

For more information about this series, please visit:
https://www.routledge.com/Rethinking-Globalizations/book-series/RG

The Reconfiguration of Twenty-first Century Latin American Regionalism

Actors, Processes, Contradictions and Prospects

Edited by

Rowan Lubbock and Ernesto Vivares

Routledge
Taylor & Francis Group
LONDON AND NEW YORK

First published 2023
by Routledge
4 Park Square, Milton Park, Abingdon, Oxon, OX14 4RN

and by Routledge
605 Third Avenue, New York, NY 10158

Routledge is an imprint of the Taylor & Francis Group, an informa business

British Library Cataloguing-in-Publication Data
A catalogue record for this book is available from the British Library

ISBN13: 978-1-032-32992-5 (hbk)
ISBN13: 978-1-032-32993-2 (pbk)
ISBN13: 978-1-003-31765-4 (ebk)

DOI: 10.4324/9781003317654

Typeset in Minion Pro
by codeMantra

Publisher's Note
The publisher accepts responsibility for any inconsistencies that may have arisen during the conversion of this book from journal articles to book chapters, namely the inclusion of journal terminology.

Contents

Citation Information

The chapters in this book were originally published in the journal *Globalizations*, volume 19, issue 4 (2022). When citing this material, please use the original page numbering for each article, as follows:

Chapter 1
The reconfiguration of twenty-first century Latin American regionalism: actors, processes, contradictions, and prospects
Rowan Lubbock and Ernesto Vivares
Globalizations, volume 19, issue 4 (2022) pp. 519–535

Chapter 2
Capitalist geopolitics and Latin America's long road to regionalism
Rowan Lubbock
Globalizations, volume 19, issue 4 (2022) pp. 536–554

Chapter 3
The challenges of economic integration in Latin America: searching for consensus in contexts of globalization. The case of MERCOSUR (1991-2019)
Mercedes Botto
Globalizations, volume 19, issue 4 (2022) pp. 555–570

Chapter 4
The Pacific Alliance: regional integration as neoliberal discipline
Marcel Nelson
Globalizations, volume 19, issue 4 (2022) pp. 571–586

Chapter 5
Shifting tides, regional reverberations: a class-relational analysis of the ALBA-TCP
Kristin Ciupa
Globalizations, volume 19, issue 4 (2022) pp. 587–603

Chapter 6
The credibility of regional policymaking: insights from South America
Pia Riggirozzi and Matt Ryan
Globalizations, volume 19, issue 4 (2022) pp. 604–619

Chapter 7

Indigenous regionalism in the Andes
Roberta Rice
Globalizations, volume 19, issue 4 (2022) pp. 620–634

Chapter 8

Critical Latin American agroecology as a regionalism from below
Peter M. Rosset, Lia Pinheiro Barbosa, Valentín Val and Nils McCune
Globalizations, volume 19, issue 4 (2022) pp. 635–652

Notes on Contributors

Lia Pinheiro Barbosa is Professor at the Crateús School of Education (FAEC), the Graduate Program in Sociology (PPGS), and the Intercampus Master's in Education (MAIE), all at the Universidade Estadual do Ceara (UECE), Fortaleza, Brazil. Her research focuses on education, indigenous and peasant movements, processes of territorial defence and of the commons, epistemologies of knowledge in Latin America and the Caribbean, Latin American pedagogical thought, and struggles of women and feminism in Latin America.

Mercedes Botto is a sociologist and currently a member of the National Scientific and Technical Research System (CONICET) and Director in the Program of Regional Cooperation and Integration Studies (PECIR) of the Argentina office of the Latin American School of Social Sciences (FLACSO). The subjects she focuses her research and teaching activities on are regional governance and the impact of global organisations on public policies in Latin America.

Kristin Ciupa is Assistant Professor in Sociology and Social Studies at the University of Regina, Canada. With a background in Sociology, Political Science, and Law, her work is interdisciplinary and has focused on Venezuela, Latin America, Canada, and the international. Her research explores natural resource extraction through an analysis of the interrelation between local and international development processes, markets, and social relations.

Rowan Lubbock is Lecturer in Political Economy of Development at Queen Mary, University of London, UK. His research centres on the agrarian dynamics of international relations, particularly within Latin America, and he has previously published in *Journal of International Relations and Development*, *New Political Economy*, *Journal of Agrarian Change*, and *Globalizations*.

Nils McCune is a visiting researcher in the Department of Agriculture, Society and Environment of El Colegio de la Frontera Sur (ECOSUR) in San Cristóbal de las Casas, Mexico. His research focuses on the social dynamics of scaling agroecology, peasant economies, pedagogy of agroecological learning, land reform, and the autonomous peasant schools of agroecological social movements.

Marcel Nelson teaches Politics at Sheridan College, Ontario, Canada. His research interests include regionalism and the left in Latin America. His publications include *A History of the FTAA: From Hegemony to Fragmentation in the Americas* (2015) and *Walking the 'Tightrope' of Socialist Governance* (2019).

Roberta Rice is Associate Professor of Indigenous Politics in the Department of Political Science at the University of Calgary, Canada. Her research interests include comparative politics, Latin America, democracy and civil society, and indigenous politics.

Pia Riggirozzi is Professor of Global Politics at the University of Southampton, UK. She is the principal investigator on the GCRF-ESRC-funded project ReGHID and Co-Director of the Global Health and Policy Centre (GHaP). Her research focuses on the political economy of development, human rights, and regional governance in Latin America.

Peter M. Rosset is Professor and also a researcher in the Department of Agriculture, Society and Environment of El Colegio de la Frontera Sur (ECOSUR) in San Cristóbal de las Casas, Mexico. His current research focuses on the massification, scaling, and territorialisation of agroecology through social processes, on the social construction of food sovereignty and agroecology, on peasant and indigenous territorial autonomy, and in the struggle for agrarian reform and the defence of land and territory by rural social movements.

Matt Ryan is Associate Professor in Governance and Public Policy at the University of Southampton, UK. His work focuses on democratic innovations. He is Co-Director of the Centre for Democratic Futures, a collective dedicated to analysing, imagining, sustaining, augmenting, and expanding Democracy. Matt currently holds a UKRI Future Leaders Fellowship.

Valentín Val is a Ph.D. student in the Department of Agriculture, Society and Environment of El Colegio de la Frontera Sur (ECOSUR) in San Cristóbal de las Casas, Mexico. She works on social processes for the scaling of agroecology, specifically with processes from peasant to peasant in a broad sense.

Ernesto Vivares is Professor in the Department of International Studies and Communication at FLACSO Ecuador. He has published widely on the topics of Latin American politics, development, and regional integration, and edited two recent volumes: *Regionalism, Development and the Post-Commodities Boom in South America* (2018) and *The Routledge Handbook to Global Political Economy. Conversations and Inquiries* (2020).

The reconfiguration of twenty-first century Latin American regionalism: actors, processes, contradictions, and prospects

Rowan Lubbock and Ernesto Vivares

ABSTRACT

The introduction to this Special Issue reflects on both the multiplicity of Latin American (LA) regionalism and the theoretically pluralist terrain of contemporary scholarship on LA politics and international relations. The introduction will first outline the complexity of twenty-first century LA regionalism and the challenge this poses for scholars in the field. Secondly, we make the case for an 'integrative pluralism' approach to unpacking the multiplicity of regionalisation projects, from both above and below. In bringing together diverse perspectives to a common research problem, we hope to contribute to ongoing debates in IR/IPE over the 'pluralist turn', and what might be done to push this collective project forward. Thirdly, we briefly explore the multi-scalar nature of region-building, encompassing both various spaces/scales as well as political actors. Finally, we outline the contributions to the Special Issue, that span the terrain of LA regionalism from above (political institutions) and below (transnational movements).

1. Introduction: Latin America as a 'Continent of Contradiction'

Given the relative uniqueness of the Latin American region during the twenty-first century, whether in light of the changing fortunes of 'neo-developmentalism', the relative disillusionment with US influence, or the more radical strand of 'Socialism in the twenty-first century', there is no shortage of scholarly attention on these changing regional configurations (see, e.g. Briceño-Ruiz & Morales, 2017; Briceño-Ruiz & Puntigliano, 2021; Knight et al., 2016; Puntigliano & Briceño-Ruiz, 2013; Riggirozzi, 2012b; Vivares, 2014). And yet, this regional diversity underlines the deficiency of any approach that merely emphasizes one explanatory dimension over the other.

This problem has certainly not gone unnoticed. As Ronaldo Munck has argued, 'The time is ripe to (re)consider Latin America from a holistic perspective' (Munck, 2015, p. 1). Munck's comment arose in the context of Katz's (2015) dissection of Latin America in the twenty-first century. As Katz demonstrates, the current predicament facing the region lies in a series of contradictory forces acting upon it: dependency/autonomy, competition/cooperation, state/civil society power, capitalism/socialism. While many of these forces are certainty present in other world regions, it is undoubtedly in Latin America that the greatest variation of scholarly opinion has taken place, with some seeing the current configuration of LA regionalism as decisively 'post-hegemonic' (Briceño-Ruiz & Hoffman, 2015; Riggirozzi, 2012a), while others view the consolidated practice of 'extractivism' as entrenching older patterns of hegemonic dominance (Burchardt & Dietz, 2014; Petras & Veltmeyer, 2014). Moreover, the jury is still out on whether the multiplex landscape of LA's many regional bodies constitutes a fundamentally cooperative (Gürcan, 2010; Muhr, 2017) or competitive configuration (Aranda & Salinas, 2015; Tussie, 2009). What is certain, however, is that the Latin American region – and the concomitant processes of regionalization – comprises a veritable 'continent of contradiction' (Riggirozzi, 2012b).

Perhaps the most perplexing contradiction cited among scholars of LA regionalism is the proliferation of integration initiatives and regional agreements that are simultaneously structured by relatively 'thin' institutions prone to political turbulence or stagnation. Indeed, this has been the central 'puzzle' of LA regionalism over the post-war period, which Olivier Dabène sums up as 'consistency despite instability, resilience despite crises' (2009: 5). From a more pessimistic position, Malamud and Gardini see the Latin American 'quagmire' as reflective of divergent interests and ideas, leaving merely cooperation (not integration) as 'the maximum outcome to be expected'. Thus, the strong rhetorical commitment to regionalism should, they argue, be seen as a means 'to compensate for substantial failures' (2012, p. 131; cf. Gómez-Mera, 2015; Jenne et al., 2017). Puntigliano and Briceño-Ruiz, in contrast, while similarly recognising the prevalence of 'crises, institutional breakdowns or stagnation', argue for a deeper *historicization* of LA regionalism, the story of which 'should not be seen as an accumulation of failures but an aggregate of experiences' (2013, pp. 6, 4; see also Petersen & Schulz, 2018). Clearly, then, the central puzzle of Latin American regionalism – which we could call *resilient inertia* – remains a relative constant throughout the academic community; it is only its interpretation and approach that continues to divide scholarly opinion.

But this raises yet further problems. Given the relative complexity of LA regionalism/regionalization, characterised by its many 'waves' (Dabène, 2009), and increasing terminological metamorphoses – regional 'space', 'complex', 'society', 'community', or 'actor' (Riggirozzi, 2012b) – contemporary scholarship faces the unenviable task of parsing some kind of comprehension from this complexity. To shed light on this predicament, consider Philippe de Lombaerde's approach to (re)theorizing Latin American regionalism, which incorporates:

> the conceptualization of autonomy; the construction of discourses, strategies and policies pursuing autonomy; the linkages between intra-regional and extra-regional relations; the linkages between regionalism and autonomy; the domestic political economy of regionalism; the implications of inter-presidentialism for international relations; the linkages between electoral cycles, regime change, and the (dis)continuity of foreign policy; etc. (Lombaerde, 2016, p. 2)

Coupled with other long-standing criteria, such as legal fragmentation and rule ambiguity, opportunistic cross-institutional strategies, competition and associated 'feedback effects', laxity in implementation of regional commitments (Gómez-Mera, 2015; Domínguez, 2007), and we are suddenly overwhelmed with endless variables exhibiting no particular order of significance. Thus, as necessary as these criteria may be, this index of variables is as wide-ranging and complex as the regional terrain it seeks to describe. Indeed, if all these dimensions are relevant to explaining the development of Latin American regionalism (both past and present), how can scholars make sense of this complexity without falling into the trap of 'thick description'? This Special Issue seeks to meet this challenge of (re)approaching the study of Latin American regionalism from a more 'holistic' perspective (Munck, 2015). Our recourse to holism stems from a broader desire to move beyond some of the traditional practices associated with academic life characterised by disciplinary fragmentation. As a means of redressing this tendency, we engage in a theoretically pluralist perspective that attempts to incorporate several analytical dimensions: a critical historical approach to the geopolitical dynamics of regionalism, a politico-economic institutional analysis of regional organizations, and an examination of regionalism 'from below'.

2. The making of twenty-first century Latin American regionalism: global forces and local strategies

The debate surrounding the nature, origins, and future pathways of twenty-first century Latin American regionalism continues to challenge the academic comprehensions embedded within the disciplines of IR and IPE alike. The significance of this challenge is by no means trivial, since different and diametrically opposed interpretations can take us to rather different conclusions about the dynamics of development, cooperation and competition, both within the hemisphere and the wider world order. Myths and biased interpretations similarly populated the academic field, challenging scholars to critically review and rethink perspectives, approaches, and theories about surely the most significant event shaping the dynamics of development, conflict and global insertion of Latin America in the last three decades. This section engages with only a small part of the vast array of research and debates in the field that has revitalized the study of Latin American IR/IPE in a plural, historical and contextual sense. Accordingly, the following section offers a few criteria to include in research design and teaching about the Latin American Regionalism (LAR).

While new scholarly contributions come from different sources of critical thinking they maintain important common features or criteria. Firstly, they ontologically rest on, and assume, the diverse characteristics that historical world orders take in different societies and spaces (Acharya, 2014; cf. Braudel, 1977). Secondly, they epistemologically make sense of the Latin American case by unsettling traditional positivist/rationalist traditions that assume a straightforward logic of institutionalism, and instead re-situate the hemispheric configuration of the Americas in their dynamic with the wider world order, the same way used by the scholars within the Developmentalism and Dependency Theory traditions (Chodor, 2015, 2021; Di Filippo, 2019; Puntigliano & Briceño-Ruiz, 2013; Vivares & Dolcetti-Marcolini, 2016). Thirdly, new critical approaches cannot rest upon the political economy of the Europe Union as a universal benchmark for the Latin American experience. Rather, understanding the specificities of LAR, both past and present, requires a radically empiricist methodology that does not take for granted the socially situated dynamics shaping the (re)configuration of region-making (Kan & Pascual, 2013; Muhr, 2017; Vivares, 2014). Thus, these three criteria provide an ontological, epistemological, and methodological frame that distinguishes the new contributions LA regionalism, and allows us to identify, for teaching and research, key myths or conceptual cages that are commonly reproduced within the academy (see Berry, 2020; De Carvalho et al., 2011; Mathieu, 2020).

IR and IPE have developed striking myths or conceptual cages, reproduced both in the classroom and in scholarly research, defined by ahistorical and non-contextual meanings (De Carvalho et al., 2011; Vivares, 2018). Some of them have been well known, others remain to be deconstructed such as some unrevised assumptions about IR and IPE (Helleiner, 2017; Hobden & Hobson, 2002; Hobson, 2009). In that sense, the IPE of LA regionalism represents an important case of analysis, as they generally, both in the classroom and research more generally, mix Western assumptions about development and international relations with universalized and repeated conventions concerning its political economy of development (Tussie, 2020).

The LAR academic storytelling and, perhaps, its most widespread myth, generally starts with the concept that regionalism emerged from within the European Union, defining a sort of linear sequence of four regional stages marked by differentiation of development that marks out ideal types of regional spaces (e.g. Dabène, 2012; Hettne, 2005). Even some of the most important new scholars still anchor their research to the ontological assumption that regionalism in LA started after or in parallel to the European regional project (cf. Acharya, 2014, p. 654). As with other world regions, generally, the academic discourse states that LAR has gone through four major stages: 1950–1960 developmental and structuralist, 1970–1980 revisionist, 1990–2000 neoliberal, 2000–2010 progressist or neostructuralist (e.g. Dabène, 2012). There are several problems with these analytical divisions that require critical enquiry.

Firstly there is the assumption that by imitation or reflection of the Europe Union and the post-war liberal order, the global spread of regionalism tended to mirror the Western example, as if there had never been any other regional experience in other parts of the world prior to this moment (cf. Petersen & Schulz, 2018; Postel-Vinay, 2007; Puntigliano, 2011). These conceptual cages rest on the architecture of central ontological assumptions. The first is universalization of the Western experience (Acharya, 2011), and thus erasing the wider history of world regionalism (Grosfoguel, 2009). Secondly, the apolitical focus on institutions empties out the significant complexity and contestation involved in any (re)spatialization project (Lombaerde & Söderbaum, 2013). And finally, the central one, the lack of inclusion of the most important variable in the history of LA regional configurations and reconfigurations – its bounds to, and relations with, the United States (Vivares, 2014). LA is the only region in the world that lives in the same neighbourhood as the global colossus, and Washington has always persevered for itself the 'right' (and *power*) to determine the fate of the Western hemisphere, from the Monroe doctrine onwards (Livingstone, 2013). This is the central geopolitical variable that becomes important to countering naïve perspectives, since they end up either focusing on trade, institutions, or top-down elements without including hemispheric dynamics, transnational class formations, geopolitical forces, and their attendant developmental trajectories (cf. Biegon, 2017; Nelson, 2015).

The above-mentioned aspects have important implications for the academic comprehension of LAR that we must bear in mind for teaching and research. The first is that, contrary to the extensive image of LAR as mirroring the European Union, the regional experience emerged at the moment of independence in the early nineteenth century. Bolívar's dream of uniting the South American continent spoke to the common experience of anti-colonial struggle, as well as the nascent (if not contested) values of Republicanism and Liberalism (Long & Schulz, 2021; Sanders, 2014). While the regional project of Gran Colombia, comprising Colombia, Ecuador, Panama, and Venezuela, did not survive the vicissitudes of nineteenth century Latin American political geography, it laid the groundwork for a long-standing ideological and discursive trope of Latin American unity, one that was always wary of the predations of imperial power.

But the long arch of Latin American regionalism would remain overdetermined by the emergence of the US as a truly continental power. As Lubbock (2022) shows in this Special Issue, the precursor to international regional institutions was not the post-war European project but the emergence of colonial state spaces of truly continental proportions. Within the Western hemisphere, Brazil, Argentina, and the United States transformed into polities far larger than those found within the European 'core'. Yet the developmental trajectories of these (post)colonial spaces radically diverged by the turn of the twentieth century. The consolidation of a truly continent-sized industrial power within the United States paved the way for the emergence of 'continental history', in which the survival of sovereign states would rest on the agglomeration of regional-sized territories. The geopolitical pressure emanating from the scale and scope of industrial capitalism led to the strategic necessity to kick-start regionalization projects anew, in both Europe and Latin

America (Cocks, 1980; Puntigliano, 2011). Thus, post-war Latin American regionalism was not simply copied from the European experience, but rather paralleled the European project insofar as political elites on both sides of the Atlantic began to grapple with the new territorial configuration of global capitalism.

The US-led post-war order would thus leave an indelible mark on Latin American politics and the winding road to regionalism. From the Cold War and the internationalization of the state under the US hegemony emerged a series of 'bureaucratic authoritarian' states (O'Donnell, 1973), whose doctrine of national security facilitated US military and economic influence (Brands, 2010). US hegemony was therefore structured on the classical admixture of coercion and consensus, through the establishment of an 'anti-Marxist' transnational terror network, in the form of 'Operation Condor' (McSherry, 2005), as well as a series of developmentalist political-economic approaches (Kennedy's Alliance for Progress, for instance). The other side of this Cold War narrative, with the intellectual circles situated within the Economic Commission of Latin American at the UN (ECLA) under the leadership of Raul Prebisch, are not often included in the story of early post-war regionalism. The main problems concerning the ECLA centered on the strategic possibilities of autonomous development, and the potential pathways towards industrialization under the ISI model. Indeed, the project of regionalism was a relatively central concern among early ECLA thinkers, with Prebisch emphasising the necessity of scaling up regional markets through the principle of 'reciprocity' (Prebisch, 1963, p. 97f; cf. Bielschowsky, 2009, p. 174; Eder, 2019, pp. 39–41; Briceño-Ruiz et al., 2021, p. 74). And yet, as Tickner argues, '[r]egional integration was the main foreign policy application of this intellectual and practical approach to development' (2015, p. 75). Thus, early calls for regional integration in Latin America were most forcefully made by political leaders themselves, painfully aware of the geo-economic competition stemming from continental powers such as the US, Europe, USSR, and China.

With the collapse of the developmentalist project came the rise of global neoliberalism, superintended by the re-emergence of global governance institutions as key players in the increasing inter-/transnationalization of the global economy. New regional spaces such as NAFTA, MERCOSUR, ASEAN, SADC, and EU, in keeping with the broader neoliberal discourse of the 1990s, were initially referred to as 'open regionalism' schemes that could somehow reconcile the oppositional forces of closed regional blocs with open multilateral trade. Yet the increasing turbulence of the capitalist world economy rendered regional projects ever more vulnerable to systemic crisis. From the Asian financial crisis of 1997 to the global financial crisis a decade later, regional institutions struggled to manage the fallout (Haastrup & Yong-Soo, 2014). Yet each crisis presented new opportunities. The most recent phase of LAC region-building – of which we are only beginning to see the unravelling – was significantly buoyed by the resurgence of regionalism under the aegis of a 'new left'. This so-called Pink Tide era, marked by diverse forms of left-progressive governments united under a counter-hegemonic strategy against the US-led Free Trade Area of the Americas (FTAA), saw a new form of regional cooperation anchored in the expansion of social policy, complementarity and diplomacy (see Riggirozzi and Ryan, 2022, and Ciupa, 2022, in this Special Issue). Yet the Latin American left was built on shaky foundations. While expansive social programmes and new regional policies were buttressed by rising commodity prices and fiscal reserves, the ever-tighter integration into the capitalist world market rendered Pink Tide states vulnerable to the dynamics of uneven development and cyclical downturns. The sudden fall in global commodity prices, led principally by a decline in Chinese demand, unravelled the material basis of the new left's political legitimacy.

Given the complexity of region-building – the depth of which is largely lost on more traditional (and relatively apolitical) institutionalist scholarship – as well as the multiple historical phases this process takes within Latin America, it appears necessary to engage with a deeper analysis into concrete actors that historically construct the very institutional complexes that make up the terrain of 'regionness' (Hettne & Söderbaum, 2000). It is largely around these latter historical phases, as well as the social agents that forge this history, that the articles in this Special Issue converge.

3. Global complexity, disciplinary fragmentation, and the call to 'Pluralism'

As Giovanni Barbieri recently argued, '[t]he scholarly debate around regionalism and globalism has made clear how international relations (IR) as a discipline needs to be shaken from its foundations' (Barbieri, 2019, p. 424). The problem, as Barbieri sees it, stems from the increasing complexity of the international, of which the rise of regional institutions is merely one expression. In many ways, complexity was never entirely absent from the realm of world politics, only our attentiveness to it (Rosenau, 1980). Indeed, as Guzzini (1998) notes, it was Waltz's (1979) paradigm-shifting turn to scientific 'parsimony' that seemingly solved the 'identity crisis' of IR theory during the 1960s and 1970s. In seeking to tame the unruly state of IR scholarship, Waltz emphatically laid down the standards of *theory* for the sake of understanding the specificity of 'the international': 'What theories do mainly is omit things. They make bold simplifications. If they don't, they're not theories' (Waltz; cited in Halliday & Rosenberg, 1998, pp. 379–380). Almost four decades later, Waltz's 'scientifist' approach continues to influence the dominant (largely US) domain of IR theory, predicated on what Jackson and Nexon (2013, p. 549) call the 'predictable script' of mainstream scholarship: law-like processes, causal mechanisms, and hypothesis testing. As a result, the majority of mainstream IR publications tend towards 'the marginalization of alternatives and a lack of sufficient discussion about the relationship among different modes of inquiry' (Jackson & Nexon, 2013, p. 549).[1]

Yet as the proliferation of IR approaches expanded in 1990s, this trend towards theoretical isolation and insularity pervaded every corner of the discipline. As Martin Hollis and Steve Smith once noted, scholars associated with different theoretical approaches often amount to members of an 'intellectual club', replete with their own 'journals, meetings, and leaders', who simply 'see different actors, different issues, and different pieces of evidence' (Hollis & Smith, 1992, p. 61). Two decades later, the state of the field had not progressed very far beyond this morose; as Christine Sylvester (2013, p. 610) put it, 'the smoke from proliferating IR campfires makes it increasingly difficult to see even friendly neighbouring camps'. The result is an ever-expanding community of intellectual 'camps' who end up talking past each other, rather than with one another. This trend could be equally seen in the IPE realm, typically divided between the so-called American and British schools of political economy (Dickins, 2006).

In response to this disciplinary fragmentation, contemporary IR/IPE scholarship has embarked on a quest for *pluralism* among different approaches (cf. Eun, 2020; Vivares, 2020). Thus, *contra* Waltz, the complexity of world politics is to be fully embraced via the collaborative practice of inter-paradigmatic dialogue. In fact, the recent rise in 'pluralist' talk among IR practitioners was preceded by the earlier call for 'analytical eclecticism' (Katzenstein & Okawara, 2001–2002; Sil & Katzenstein, 2010; Sørensen, 2008), which sought to move past old paradigmatic boundaries for the sake of forming a more pragmatist approach to real-world problems.[2] Patrick Jackson's plea for 'methodological pluralism', on the other hand, aimed to make more explicit the methodological demarcation between approaches, 'so that when we disagree we are at least disagreeing about the same or similar things', a practice which in turn 'fosters conversation, not isolation' (2011, p. 39).

Nevertheless, both analytical eclecticism and methodological pluralism each reproduce the very fragmentation they seek to heal (Chernoff, 2013; Reus-Smit, 2013).

In taking stock of the pluralist turn, Dunne et al. (2013) note the various impasses that confront the IR community in attempting to broaden disciplinary conversations. As they argue, one cannot expect the synthesis of multiple perspectives under a general theory of explanation, nor is the turn towards a hyper-pluralist approach attractive, with the propensity for different theories to validate themselves according to their own internal standards, and thus leading to the dead end of 'disengaged pluralism' (Dunne et al., 2013, p. 416). As an alternative to these two extremes, the authors call for an 'integrative pluralism' that does not attempt to synthesise or subsume different perspectives under one framework, but also aims to assess, through sustained scholarly engagement, the relative strength and weaknesses of certain perspectives that may undergo change and modification as a result. In taking a cue from Dunne et al.'s wager for an integrative pluralism, this Special Issue aims to take a preliminary step in this direction, through an 'engagement with alternative positions where … research interests overlap' (Dunne et al., 2013, p. 417). In this case, the different contributions of the Special Issue bring a variety of perspectives to the table – Constructivism, Postcolonialism, Marxism, Institutionalism – to a common research interest in the contemporary politics of Latin American regionalism. However, our collective project can hardly put integrative pluralism to the ultimate test. Indeed, this pluralist practice 'cannot even begin unless we have some sense of its problems, possibilities and practicality' (Dunne et al., 2013, p. 417). We therefore leave the assessment of our attempt at this practice to other colleagues in the field, and to further research on both the limits and possibilities of an integrative pluralist turn.

The integrative pluralist approach in this Special Issue follows in the footsteps of two recent examples of theoretically pluralist projects on Latin American regionalism, each of which have encountered their own limits and challenges. In *Exploring the New South American Regionalism*, a diverse group of scholars were brought together via 'a critical perspective and analytical eclecticism' (Vivares, 2014, p. 3), in order to grasp the political economy of Latin American development. Though largely committed to examining regionalism from a historical perspective, the task of gathering diverse perspectives was 'not without its perils, as there was not a unique perspective and methodological approach that unified the collective effort and bridged the different perspectives involved' (Vivares, 2014, p. 3). In a subsequent edited volume, Vivares (2018) once again proposed a 'multidisciplinary and eclectic' range of approaches, but this time with a minimal grounding between participants in order to overcome previous perils. This grounding took the form of a 'critique of the mainstream stance on IPE of regionalism', to reflect upon 'the unequal and uneven structures of regional development and global insertion … within a complex world order' (Vivares, 2018, p. 2). Echoing a Coxian approach to IPE, Vivares writes of the 'importance of structures as an empirical starting point'; yet, as 'historical and contextual frameworks of action, they do not determine actions but constitute the material ideational configurations where they take place' (Vivares, 2018, p. 14).

We therefore see this Special Issue as the latest development in this wider goal to foster ever-more concrete groundings for a pluralist take on LA regionalism. Sharing relative convergence with these previous efforts – such as the need for historicist perspectives, and the material/ideational configurations of agency – this Special Issue echoes the goal of Vivares and Dolcetti-Marcolini (2016, p. 870) to specify the *normative matrices* of a given analytical framework, and to 'once more locate the "political" in the study of regionalism'. Grounding our diverse perspectives into a common research concern with the consequences of power and institutions, and the fate of Latin American peoples in the context of (re)configuring LA regionalism, the Special Issue constitutes a 'critical problem-solving' methodology, which takes seriously the real-world problems facing LA region-building, but from the perspective of 'the needs and problems of the dispossessed ... rather than with the problems of the maters of the universe' (Brown, 2013, p. 494). This methodological principle thus requires a multi-dimensional perspective to the dynamics of regionalism.

4. Regionalism from above and below

One of the challenges associated with a 'critical problem-solving' methodology is the premium placed on doing socio-relational research 'all the way down' (Hofferberth, 2018, p. 143). The topic of regionalism within the IR and IPE fields has always been skewed towards a top-down, elitist approach to the history of regional formations. No doubt this narrow focus has been shaped by the markedly un-democratic character of region-building – from the European Union to the Common Market of the South (MERCOSUR) regional institutions are rarely, if ever, built on the back of popular consensus (even if populations are given the choice to join these institutions thereafter). In light of this democratic deficit, Fioramonti (2012) argued that the time has come for a 'Regionalism 2.0', one that redresses the elitist nature of region-building by reconnecting citizens to larger institutional structures. This plea for a more bottom-up perspective to regionalism speaks to more than the glaring democratic deficit of regional institutions. Rather, closer scrutiny of big and seemingly faceless structures like 'globalization', 'international society', 'neoliberalism', and 'law' are equally produced, shaped, and critically adapted by, grassroots non-elite actors (Colás, 2002; Della Porta, 2006; Folly, 2020; Gago, 2017; Santos & Rodríguez-Garavito, 2005). In a similar vein, scholarship on regionalism has begun to reveal the often-hidden contribution made by political actors from below in the crafting, contestation and (re)production of regional institutions (Muhr, 2012a; Roncallo, 2013; Rother & Piper, 2014).

However, there is also a potential danger of over-emphasising the agency of grassroots actors, social movements, and the 'community', at the expense of more concrete insights into the lofty heights of state/regional institutions and political elites. Taking the case of social movement research – which has been a major area of scholarship on Latin American politics – most (if not all) treatments of this topic restrict the area of investigation to subaltern groups, or a politics 'from below' (e.g. Johnston & Almeida, 2006; Stahler-Sholk et al., 2014). Thus, in counter-posing subaltern actors to the amorphous structures of 'neoliberal globalization' (for example), the promise of a rigorous socio-relational approach becomes lost. Instead, it is both possible, and methodologically necessary, to analyse social movements *from above*, as well as from below. As Alf Nilson puts it,

> [a] social movement from above can be defined as the organisation of multiple forms of skilled activity around a rationality expressed and organised by dominant social groups, which aims at the maintenance or modification of a dominant structure of entrenched needs and capacities in ways that reproduce and/or extend the power of those groups and its hegemonic position within a given social formation. (2009, p. 115)

Thus, rather than looking at the question of political power through the lens of familiar but abstract categories such as 'the market', 'state', or 'neoliberalism', we need to take stock of the socially situated actors that make and remake the contours of political/economic institutions and the dominant ideas that normalise their operation (cf. Knafo, 2017). In keeping both politics from below as well as above in play, we are able to better grasp the limits and prospects of transformative politics, itself a melange of *actors, processes, and contradictions*.

This concern immediately centres on the question of space and scale within the (re)configuration of Latin American regionalism. While scholarly work on these inter-related concepts is voluminous (particularly within political/human geography), we seek only to widen our perspective to the multiple pathways to region-building that stretches across a wide variety of sites, scales, and actors. Arguably the most incisive work on the multiplicity of political scales in LAR comes from the work of Thomas Muhr, whose research into the emergence and evolution of the ALBA-TCP and related examples of left-progressive regionalism offers a more complex picture of region-building from above and below (see, e.g. Muhr, 2010, 2011, 2012b, 2013, 2017). Grounded in a critical Gramscian IPE, Muhr highlights the multiple scales across which capital operates in the contemporary global order, which necessitates the pursuit of a 'counter hegemonic pluriscalar war of position', understood as a specific counter-hegemonic spatialization strategy that 'recognizes the reconfiguration of socio-political power geometries associated with "meta-governance", through which regional and global capitalist institutions actively remake state apparatuses, governmental practices and societal institutions' (Muhr, 2013, p. 7). Thus, the strategies undertaken by ALBA states, local actors, and social movements – or, the 'state-in-revolution' and a regional 'transnational organised society' (Muhr, 2010) – reflect the diffuse and deep-seated character of capitalist globalism, embodied not merely within the state system and its attendant institutions, but throughout 'commercial society' within/across a variety of spaces and scales.

Likewise, Alejandra Roncallo reveals the organic emergence of indigenous resistance to the multi-scalar restructuring of regional political economy along neoliberal lines during the 1990s. The struggle over regional organization centred on two 'cosmologies', one produced 'from above' grounded on neo-colonial 'conquest', and one 'from below' based on 'coexistence' (Roncallo, 2013, p. 1146). Neoliberal transformation was not simply a 'global' phenomenon hovering over the realm of everyday life; rather, political-economic restructuring permeated multiple sites and institutions, from state constitutions and laws to the decentralization of municipal government and popular incorporation/adaptation to new markets and commodity networks. Thus, the resurgence of neoliberal discipline reached all the way down to the local scale, disrupting the rhythms of communal reproduction and the traditional modes of indigenous governance over lands and resources. Like the ALBA-TCP, popular resistance to neoliberal restructuring among transnational/local elites took the form of an equally heterogenous and multi-scalar form of struggle, involving 'labour, women, indigenous peoples, Afro-descendants and landless peoples' organising around local, national, and transnational scales of contention (Roncallo, 2013, p. 1150).

Taking inspiration from this critical scholarship, the contributions to this Special Issue focus on the inter-related dimensions of 'regionalism from below', the multi-scalar formation and contestation of power, and the periodic disconnect between elites and the popular classes in the (re)configuration of LA regionalism in the twenty-first century. In light of the above empirical and theoretical scope, the main objectives of the Special Issue are to address questions with respect to:

- The complexities of the *why* and *how* (explaining and understanding) of social transformation within the process of regionalism and regionalization in Latin American and the Caribbean. Where these regional spaces came from, revealing the distinctiveness of their present condition, and where are they are possibly going.
- The manner in which processes and social relations among state and non-state actors across scales beyond the international (including the local, national, regional, global) are forged, and what types of political and economic outcomes they produce.

- Uncovering the social relations of power between a variety of actors (state managers, capitalist investors, workers, peasants, urban social movements) and how specific power relations – in the form of *differential agency* – feed into the specificity of regional institutions.
- Mapping the production of new ideologies and new discourses that animate the various projects of integration across the continent. From 'neo-developmentalism' to the politics of *Pachamama*, the diversity and interaction among these discourses and political visions require careful re-examination in order to fully appreciate the complex and contested nature of Latin American region-building in the twenty-first century.
- Tracing the various challenges facing the plurality and, arguably, complexity of regionalism in the LA, the degree to which regional institutions struggle to come through on their promise for enhancing social and political welfare, and how the wide range of actors involved in the process of region-building seek to understand and overcome these challenges.
- Understanding the current conjuncture in the LA region in the context of an embattled 'Pink Tide' and the possible resurgence of neoliberal hegemony.

5. Outline of the Special Issue

In the first article in the Special Issue, Rowan Lubbock (2022) provides a wider historical context to the (re)configuration of Latin American regionalism. In moving beyond the staid narratives of mainstream IR/IPE that track the beginning of regionalism to the post-war era, Lubbock argues for a deeper understanding of regional space that emerges from the advent of 'continental history'. In departing from a Marxian historical sociology of state-formation and the production of regional space, the history of 'modern' regionalism can be traced back to the emergence of settler-colonial state spaces that achieved truly continental proportions. Yet it would be the historically specific geographical and class configurations of these spaces that determined the emergence of a new world hegemon. In taking the 'first-mover' advantage of industrialization, capitalist social property relations, and a sizeable home market, the ascendance of US power at the turn of the twentieth century unleashed a new set of geopolitical pressures emanating from this continent-sized regime of accumulation. From the concatenation of the Second World War to the post-war experiments in regional integration, the expanded reproduction of global capital would increasingly resolve into regional-sized agglomerations, from the European Community to the expansive state-spaces of the USSR, India and China. Latin American leaders were only too aware of this new geopolitical reality, and often spoke of these continental challenges as the primary rational for regional integration. While this strategic necessity has always played a residual role, Latin America's long road to regionalism has encountered a number of twists, turns, and roadblocks.

Perhaps the largest and most comprehensive regional organization remains the Common Market of the South (MERCOSUR), which finds its origins in the region-wide transition to democracy in the 1980s. In contrast to more simplistic depictions of MERCOSUR, Mercedes Botto (2022) reveals the contradictory strategies, discourses and modes of organization that have permeated MERCOSUR's operation since its inception. Rather than grafting abstract models of development onto MERCOSUR's historical trajectory – a type of either/or between 'closed' or 'open' regionalism – political and economic actors at the helm of this regional space have always embodied a contradictory mixture between these two extremes. In other words, the relative dis-organization of MERCOSUR region, which many scholars reduce to a narrow institutionalism (hyper-presidentialism), emerges from the inter-related tensions between introverted regional autonomy and extroverted export regimes. Thus, each stage of MERCOSUR's development – the 'Commercial', 'Productive', and current-ongoing phase – reveals a novel conjoining of these two developmental logics, all of which express the consensus and contestation that has accompanied the project of building a common market of the south.

While LA regionalism in the twenty-first century has be overdetermined by the 'left turn', neoliberal regional organizations were never entirely absent. As well as more familiar neoliberal projects like the North American Free Trade Association, the emergence of the Pacific Alliance (PA) constitutes the most recent expression of neoliberal discipline on a regional scale. Marcel Nelson's (2022) neo-Poulantzian analysis of the PA focuses on the social sources of elite strategy through the prism of *los técnicos*, a cadre of governmental experts steeped in the crafting of neoliberal policy. In shifting the power of economic restructuring to the unaccountable realm of technical working groups and epistemic communities divorced form democratic/electoral politics, the social transformation of the PA's four leading members – Colombia, Peru, Mexico and Chile – laid the foundation for 'scaling up' the depoliticization of neoliberal discipline. Despite 'locking in' the structural constraints of neoliberal policy-making within the institutionality of the PA, radical social forces across member states continue to place this regional institution into question.

On the other side of the political spectrum, the Bolivarian Alliance for the Peoples of Our America-Peoples' Trade Treaty (ALBA-TCP) represents a bold attempt to forge a type of socialist geopolitics in the form of a cooperative and complimentary regional grouping. Kristen Ciupa (2022) provides a critical perspective to this counter-hegemonic region through a 'Political Marxist' lens that brings to the foreground the contested nature of social property relations and their impact on the spatialization of ALBA. Expansive social policies and inter/transnational cooperation within the ALBA space represent its most notable achievements. But it has been somewhat less successful in its drive to forge a new political economy based on the principles of socialism and popular participation. Indeed, with the fate of ALBA so heavily tided to the circulation of oil rents, and the eventual decline in commodity prices and the collapse of petroleum production in Venezuela, the fate of this counter-hegemonic region remains in question.

From a broader angle, Pía Riggirozzi and Matt Ryan (2022) seek to unravel the drivers and mechanism of regional social policy in twenty-first century Latin America. While a significant part of the literature views Latin American regionalism as over-extended and/or ineffective, a more careful examination reveals a number of key policies that not only create new forms of legitimacy among regional institutions, but tangible regional public goods that benefit the broader population. From issues of medicines, health, migration to social rights and security, more recent regional fora, like UNASUR and CELAC, provide new spaces of diplomacy through which common problems are approached through mutually crafted policy. Rather than assuming an inherent 'credibility gap' among LA regional institutions, the authors urge future research to focus on what is *actually achieved*, and the social and political implications of regional social policies.

Our two final papers offer crucial insights into the often-neglected aspect of regionalism from below. Roberta Rice (2022) presents a panoramic view of indigenous regionalism across the Andean states. The rise of indigenous actors and communities has become increasingly prominent in recent years in the context of the 'Pink Tide' era. Yet less well known is the decisive role played by indigenous forms of transborder organization and governance in the making of regional space. Drawing on the constructivist and 'practice' turn in IR theory, Rice sheds critical light on the variegated strategies among two indigenous organizations – the Coordinator of Indigenous Organizations of the Amazon River Basin (COICA) and the National Council of Ayllus and Markas of Qullasuyu (CONAMAQ). Against the colonial legacies of 'modern' borders and the nation-states, indigenous movements seek to reclaim their ancestral modes of political governance collective land rights. This veritable 'coalition of sovereignties' thus intersects with other national/regional institutions, creating forms of cooperation, cooptation or marginalization.

As a complimentary form of indigenous epistemology and organization, the emergence of a transnational 'critical Latin American agroecology' constitutes a crucial vector of movement building, mutual knowledge exchange, and decolonial struggle. Peter Rosset, Lia Pinheiro Barbosa, Valentín Val, and Nils McCune (2022) provide an in-depth view of regional peasant-led epistemic networks from below, seeking to overturn the coloniality of 'modern' development and capitalist agriculture through the revalorization of peasant indigenous territory, biocultural memory and traditional knowledges, as well as the political discourse of *agroecology* that forms the edifice of 'food sovereignty' movements in Latin America and beyond. The regionalization of peasant movements/knowledges takes a variety of institutional forms, from the Latin American chapter of La Via Campesina (*Coordinadora Latinoamericana de Organizaciones del Campo* – CLOC), to the expansive regional network of agroecological schools in several Latin American countries. Through a series of participant interviews, Rosset et al. provide a rich postcolonial approach to the ongoing construction of an alternative regional mode of life grounded in the respect for nature, radical democracy, and the fusion of old and new forms of knowledge.

Notes

1. Though this should be read as a relative dominance of positivist methodology/epistemology, not Realism per se (Sterling-Folker, 2015, p. 44).
2. One could say that even this was preceded by the English School's long standing pluralist approach to IR, comprising insights from Realism (Hobbesian) Constructivism (Grotian) and Cosmopolitanism (Kantian). See, Linklater and Suganami (2006).

Acknowledgements

The guest editors would like to extend our deepest thanks to the contributors of this Special Issue for their patience and attentiveness to our many suggestions and revisions, as well as to the anonymous reviewers who offered thoughtful and insightful comments and critiques. We are grateful those participants at the FLACSO-ISA Conference in Quito (2018) who presented preliminary versions of their papers, and to the organisers at FLACSO for their generous hospitality. Special thanks goes to Thomas Muhr, who originally inspired the idea for this Special Issue all the way back in 2015. He has been a constant source of constructive critique and intellectual guidance, and we are enormously grateful for his many contributions to this project.

Disclosure statement

No potential conflict of interest was reported by the author(s).

ORCID

Rowan Lubbock http://orcid.org/0000-0002-1517-130X

References

Acharya, A. (2011). Norm subsidiarity and regional orders: Sovereignty, regionalism, and rule-making in the third world. *International Studies Quarterly*, *55*(1), 95–123. https://doi.org/10.1111/j.1468-2478.2010.00637.x

Acharya, A. (2014). Global International Relations (IR) and regional worlds. A New agenda for International studies. *International Studies Quarterly*, *58*(4), 647–659. https://doi.org/10.1111/isqu.12171

Aranda, G., & Salinas, S. (2015). 'ALBA y Alianza del Pacífico: ¿Choque de Integraciones?'. *UNIVERSUM*, *30* (1), 17–38. https://doi.org/10.4067/S0718-23762015000100002

Barbieri, G. (2019). Regionalism, globalism and complexity: A stimulus towards global IR? *Third World Thematics: A TWQ Journal*, *4*(6), 424–441. https://doi.org/10.1080/23802014.2019.1685406

Berry, C. (2020). The sick Man of IPE: The British school. In E. Vivares (Ed.), *The Routledge handbook to global political economy* (pp. 29–42). Routledge.

Biegon, R. (2017). *US power in Latin America: Renewing hegemony*. Routledge.

Bielschowsky, R. (2009). Sixty years of ECLAC: Structuralism and neo-structuralism. *CEPAL Review*, *97* (April), 171–192.

Botto, M. (2022). The challenges of economic integration in Latin America: searching for consensus in contexts of globalization. The case of MERCOSUR (1991–2019). *Globalizations*, *19*(4), 555–570. https://doi.org/10.1080/14747731.2021.1962037

Brands, H. (2010). *Latin America's Cold War*. Harvard University Press.

Braudel, F. (1977). *Afterthoughts on material civilization and capitalism*. John Hopkins University Press.

Briceño-Ruiz, J., Correa Serano, M. A., & Catalán Salgado, E. (2021). Diplomats and technocrats in the construction of Latin American regionalism: Autonomy and development as variable. In J. Briceño-Ruiz & A. R. Puntigliano (Eds.), *Regionalism in Latin America. Agents, Systems and resilience* (pp. 73–96). Routledge.

Briceño-Ruiz, J., & Hoffman, A. R. (2015). Post-hegemonic regionalism, UNASUR, and the reconfiguration of regional cooperation in South America. *Canadian Journal of Latin American and Caribbean Studies/Revue canadienne des études latino-américaines et caraïbes*, *40*(1), 48–62. https://doi.org/10.1080/08263663.2015.1031475

Briceño-Ruiz, J., & Morales, I. (2017). *Post-Hegemonic regionalism in the Americas: Toward a Pacific-Atlantic divide?* Routledge.

Briceño-Ruiz, J., & Puntigliano, A. R. (2021). *Regionalism in Latin America. Agents, systems and resilience*. Routledge.

Brown, C. (2013). The poverty of Grand Theory. *European Journal of International Relations*, *19* (3), 483–497. https://doi.org/10.1177/1354066113494321

Burchardt, H.-J., & Dietz, K. (2014). (Neo-)extractivism – a new challenge for development theory from Latin America. *Third World Quarterly*, *35*(3), 468–486. https://doi.org/10.1080/01436597.2014.893488

Chernoff, F. (2013). Science, progress and pluralism in the study of international relations. *Millennium: Journal of International Studies*, *41*(2), 346–366. https://doi.org/10.1177/0305829812464405

Chodor, T. (2015). *Neoliberal hegemony and the Pink Tide in Latin America: Breaking up with TINA?* Palgrave.

Chodor, T. (2021). The changing face of Mercosur: Legitimacy and the politics of scale in South American regionalism. *JCMS: Journal of Common Market Studies*, *59*(2), 417–431. https://doi.org/10.1111/jcms.13200

Ciupa, K. (2022). Shifting tides, regional reverberations: A class-relational analysis of the ALBA-TCP. *Globalizations, 19*(4), 587–603. https://doi.org/10.1080/14747731.2021.1991201

Cocks, P. (1980). Towards a Marxist theory of European integration. *International Organization, 34*(1), 1–40. https://doi.org/10.1017/S0020818300003957

Colás, A. (2002). *International civil society: Social movements in world politics.* Polity Press.

Dabène, O. (2009). *The politics of regional integration in Latin America: Theoretical and comparative explorations.* Springer.

Dabène, O. (2012). Consistency and Resilience Through Cycles of Repoliticization. In P. Riggirrozi and D. Tussie (Eds.), *The Rise of Post-hegemonic Regionalism: The Case of Latin America* (pp. 41–64). Springer.

De Carvalho, B., Leira, H., & Hobson, J. M. (2011). The big bangs of IR: The myths that your teachers still tell you about 1648 and 1919. *Millennium, 39*(3), 735–758. https://doi.org/10.1177/0305829811401459

Della Porta, D. (2006). *Globalization from below: Transnational activists and protest networks.* U of Minnesota Press.

Di Filippo, A. (2019). The Structuralism of Prebisch and the integration of Latin America. In V. R. Fernández & G. Brondino (Eds.), *Development in Latin America. Critical discussions from the periphery* (pp. 215–236). Palgrave.

Dickins, A. (2006). The evolution of international political economy. *International Affairs, 82*(3), 479–492. https://doi.org/10.1111/j.1468-2346.2006.00546.x

Domínguez, J. (2007). International cooperation in Latin America: The design of regional institutions by slow accretion. In A. Amitav & A. I. Johnston (Eds.), *Crafting cooperation: Regional International institutions in comparative perspective* (pp. 83–128). Cambridge University Press.

Dunne, T., Hansen, L., & Wight, C. (2013). The end of International Relations theory? *European Journal of International Relations, 19*(3), 405–425. https://doi.org/10.1177/1354066113495485

Eder, J. (2019). Integración regional y políticas de industrialización en América Latina: la historia de un amor conflictivo. *Revista de Estudios Sociales, 68*(68), 38–50. https://doi.org/10.7440/res68.2019.04

Eun, Y.-S. (2020). *Going beyond parochialism and fragmentation in the Study of International relations.* Routledge.

Fioramonti, L. (2012). Conclusion – building regions from below: Has the time come for regionalism 2.0?. *The International Spectator: Italian Journal of International Affairs, 47* (1), 151–160. https://doi.org/10.1080/03932729.2012.655015

Folly, F. B. (2020). Rethinking law from below: Experiences from the Kuna people and Rojava. *Globalizations, 17*(7), 1291–1299. https://doi.org/10.1080/14747731.2020.1783795

Gago, V. (2017). *Neoliberalism from below.* Duke University Press.

Gómez-Mera, L. (2015). International regime complexity and regional governance: Evidence from the Americas. *Global Governance, 21*(1), 19–42. https://doi.org/10.1163/19426720-02101004

Grosfoguel, R. (2009). A decolonial approach to political-economy: Transmodernity, border thinking and global coloniality. *Kult, 6*(1), 10–38.

Guzzini, S. (1998). *Realism in International Relations and International Political economy.* Routledge.

Gürcan, E. F. (2010). New Regionalisms and radical identity formation in Latin America: Towards an 'alter-global' paradigm. *Journal of Social Research & Policy, 1*(2), 19–33.

Haastrup, T., & Yong-Soo, E. (2014). *Regionalizing global crises: The financial crisis and new frontiers in regional governance.* Springer.

Halliday, F., & Rosenberg, J. (1998). Interview with Ken Waltz. *Review of International Studies, 24*(3), 371–386. https://doi.org/10.1017/S0260210598003714

Helleiner, E. (2017). What's been missing from conventional histories of Bretton woods? In G. Scott-Smith & J. S. Rofe (Eds.), *Global perspectives on the Bretton Woods Conference and the Post-War World order* (pp. 17–34). Palgrave.

Hettne, B. (2005). Beyond the 'new' regionalism. *New Political Economy, 10*(4), 543–571. https://doi.org/10.1080/13563460500344484

Hettne, B., & Söderbaum, F. (2000). Theorising the rise of regionness. *New Political Economy, 5*(3), 457–472. https://doi.org/10.1080/713687778

Hobden, S., & Hobson, J. M. (2002). *Historical sociology of international relations.* Cambridge University Press.

Hobson, J. M. (2009). Provincializing Westphalia: The Eastern origins of sovereignty. *International Politics, 46* (6), 671–690. https://doi.org/10.1057/ip.2009.22
Hofferberth, M. (2018). Get your Act(ors) together! Theorizing agency in global governance. *International Studies Review, 21*(1), 127–145. https://doi.org/10.1093/isr/viy018
Hollis, M., & Smith, S. (1992). *Explaining and understanding International relations.* Clarendon Press.
Jackson, P. T. (2011). *The conduct of inquiry in International Relations: Philosophy of Science and its implications for the study of world politics.* Routledge.
Jackson, P. T., & Nexon, D. H. (2013). International theory in a post-paradigmatic era: From substantive wagers to scientific ontologies. *European Journal of International Relations, 19*(3), 543–565. https://doi.org/10.1177/1354066113495482
Jenne, N., Schenoni, L. L., & Urdinez, F. (2017). Of words and deeds: Latin American declaratory regionalism, 1994–2014. *Cambridge Review of International Affairs, 30*(2-3), 195–215. https://doi.org/10.1080/09557571.2017.1383358
Johnston, H., & Almeida, P. 2006. *Latin American social movements: Globalization, democratization, and transnational networks.* Rowman & Littlefield.
Kan, J., & Pascual, R. (2013). Integrados (?). Debates sobre las relaciones internacionales y la integración regional latinoamericano y europea, Imago Mundi.
Katz, C. (2015). Dualities of Latin America. *Latin American Perspectives, 42*(4), 10–42. https://doi.org/10.1177/0094582X15574714
Katzenstein, P. J., & Okawara, N. (2001–2002). Japan, Asian-Pacific security, and the case for analytical eclecticism. *International Security, 26*(3), 153–185. https://doi.org/10.1162/016228801753399754
Knafo, S. (2017). A methodological turn long overdue: Or, why it is time for critical scholars to cut their losses. In S. L. Dyvik, J. Selby, & R. Wilkinson (Eds.), *What's the point of International relations?* (pp. 242–252). Routledge.
Knight, W., Andy, J. C.-R., & Ghany, H. (2016). *Re-mapping the Americas: Trends in region-making.* Routledge.
Linklater, A., & Suganami, H. (2006). *The English school of international relations: A contemporary reassessment.* Cambridge University Press.
Livingstone, G. (2013). *America's backyard: The United States and Latin America from the Monroe Doctrine to the war on terror.* Zed.
Lombaerde, P. (2016). Theorizing Latin American regionalism in the 21st century. *Fédéralisme Régionalisme, 16*, 1–6.
Lombaerde, P., & Söderbaum, F. (2013). *Reading the intellectual history of regionalism. Regionalism (four-volume set of the SAGE library of International relations)* (pp. xvii-xlviii). Sage.
Long, T., & Schulz, C. A. (2021). Republican internationalism: The nineteenth-century roots of Latin American contributions to international order. *Cambridge Review of International Affairs*, 1–23. https://doi.org/10.1080/09557571.2021.1944983
Lubbock, R. (2022). Capitalist geopolitics and Latin America's long road to regionalism. *Globalizations, 19*(4), 536–554. https://doi.org/10.1080/14747731.2021.1984733
Malamud, A., & Gardini, G. L. (2012). Has regionalism peaked? The Latin American quagmire and its lessons. *The International Spectator, 47*(1), 116–133. https://doi.org/10.1080/03932729.2012.655013
Mathieu, X. (2020). Sovereign myths in international relations: Sovereignty as equality and the reproduction of eurocentric blindness. *Journal of International Political Theory, 16*(3), 339–360. https://doi.org/10.1177/1755088218814072
McSherry, J. P. (2005). *Predatory states: Operation condor and covert war in Latin America.* Lanham, MD: Rowman & Littlefield.
Muhr, T. (2010). Counter-hegemonic regionalism and higher education for all: Venezuela and the ALBA. *Globalisation, Societies and Education, 8*(1), 39–57. https://doi.org/10.1080/14767720903574041
Muhr, T. (2011). *Venezuela and the ALBA: Counter-hegemony, Geographies of integration and development, and Higher Education for All.* VDM Verlag.
Muhr, T. (2012a). The politics of space in the Bolivarian alliance for the peoples of our America-peoples' trade agreement (ALBA-TCP): transnationalism, the organized society, and counter-hegemonic governance. *Globalizations, 9*(6), 767–782. https://doi.org/10.1080/14747731.2012.739339

Muhr, t. (2012b). (re)constructing popular power in our America: venezuela and the regionalisation of 'revolutionary democracy' in the ALBA–TCP space. *Third World Quarterly, 33*(2), 225–241. https://doi.org/10.1080/01436597.2012.666010
Muhr, T. (2013). Introduction: The enigma of socialism. In T. Muhr (Ed.), *Counter-Globalization and socialism in the 21st century* (pp. 23–52). Routledge.
Muhr, T. (2017). South-South Cooperation and the Geographies of Latin America-Caribbean Integration and Development: A socio-spatial approach. *Antipode, 49*(4), 843–866. https://doi.org/10.1111/anti.12307
Munck, R. (2015). Whither Latin America? *Latin American Perspectives, 42*(4), 52–54. https://doi.org/10.1177/0094582X15574719
Nelson, M. (2015). *A history of the FTAA: From hegemony to fragmentation in the Americas.* Springer.
Nelson, M. (2022). The Pacific Alliance: Regional integration as neoliberal discipline. *Globalizations, 19*(4), 571–586. https://doi.org/10.1080/14747731.2021.1945394
Nilsen G. A (2009). 'The authors and the actors of their own drama': Towards a marxist theory of social movements. *Capital & Class, 33*(3), 109–139.
O'Donnell, G. (1973). Modernization and bureaucratic authoritarianism: Studies in South American politic. *Institute of International Studies.*
Petersen, M., & Schulz, C. A. (2018). Setting the regional agenda: A critique of posthegemonic regionalism. *Latin American Politics and Society, 60*(1), 102–127. https://doi.org/10.1017/lap.2017.4
Petras, J., & Veltmeyer, H. (2014). *The New extractivism: A post-neoliberal development model of imperialism of the twenty-first century?* Zed Books.
Postel-Vinay, K. (2007). The historicity of the international region: Revisiting the 'Europe and the rest' divide. *Geopolitics, 12*(4), 555–569. https://doi.org/10.1080/14650040701546046
Prebisch, R. (1963). *Towards a dynamic development policy for Latin America.* United Nations.
Puntigliano, A. R. (2011). Geopolitics of integration and the imagination of South America. *Geopolitics, 16*(4), 846–864. https://doi.org/10.1080/14650045.2010.549863
Puntigliano, A. R., & Briceño-Ruiz, J. (2013). *Resilience of regionalism in Latin America and the Caribbean: Development and autonomy.* Palgrave.
Reus-Smit, C. (2013). Beyond metatheory. *European Journal of International Relations, 19*(3), 589–608. https://doi.org/10.1177/1354066113495479
Rice, R. (2022). Indigenous regionalism in the Andes. *Globalizations, 19*(4), 620–634. https://doi.org/10.1080/14747731.2021.1907734
Riggirozzi, P. (2012a). 'Re-territorializando consensos: Hacia un regionalismo post-hegemónico en América Latina'. In A. Serbin, L. Martínez, & H. Ramanzini Jr (Eds.), *El regionalismo 'post-liberal' en América Latina y el Caribe: Nuevos actors, nuevos temas, nuevos desafíos* (pp. 129–153). CRIES.
Riggirozzi, P. (2012b). Region, regionness and regionalism in Latin America: Towards a New synthesis. *New Political Economy, 17*(4), 421–443. https://doi.org/10.1080/13563467.2011.603827
Riggirozzi, P., & Ryan, M. (2022). The credibility of regional policymaking: Insights from South America. *Globalizations, 19*(4), 604–619. https://doi.org/10.1080/14747731.2021.1893530
Roncallo, A. (2013). Cosmologies and regionalisms from 'above' and 'below' in the pst-cold war Americas: The relevance of Karl Polanyi for the 21st century. *Third World Quarterly, 34*(7), 1145–1158. https://doi.org/10.1080/01436597.2013.824638
Rosenau, J. N. (1980). *The scientific study of foreign policy.* Nichols Publishing Company.
Rosset, P. M., Barbosa, L. P., Val, V., & McCune, N. (2022). Critical Latin American agroecology as a regionalism from below. *Globalizations, 19*(4), 635–652. https://doi.org/10.1080/14747731.2021.1923353
Rother, S., & Piper, N. (2015). Alternative regionalism from below: Democratizing ASEAN's migration governance. *International Migration, 5*(3), 36–49. https://doi.org/10.1111/imig.12182
Sanders, J. E. (2014). *The vanguard of the Atlantic World: Creating modernity, nation, and democracy in nineteenth-century Latin America.* Duke University Press.
Santos, B. S., & Rodríguez-Garavito, C. A. (2005). *Law and globalization from below: Towards a cosmopolitan legality.* Cambridge University Press.
Sil, R., & Katzenstein, P. J. (2010). *Beyond paradigms: Analytical eclecticism in the study of world politics.* Palgrave.
Sørensen, G. (2008). The case for combining material forces and ideas in the study of IR. *European Journal of International Relations, 14*(1), 5–32. https://doi.org/10.1177/1354066107087768

Stahler-Sholk, R., Vanden, H. E., & Becker, M. (2014). *Rethinking Latin American social movements: Radical action from below*. Rowman & Littlefield.

Sterling-Folker, J. (2015). All hail to the chief: Liberal IR theory in the new world order. *International Studies Perspectives*, *16*(1), 40–49. https://doi.org/10.1111/insp.12089

Sylvester, C. (2013). Experiencing the end and afterlives of International relations/theory. *European Journal of International Relations*, *19*(3), 609–626. https://doi.org/10.1177/1354066113494322

Tickner, A. B. (2015). Autonomy and Latin American International relations thinking. In J. I. Domínguez & A. Covarrubias (Eds.), *2014), Routledge Handbook of Latin American in the world* (pp. 74–84). Routledge.

Tussie, D. (2009). Latin America: contrasting motivations for regional projects. *Review of International Studies*, *35*(1), 169–188. https://doi.org/10.1017/S026021050900847X

Tussie, D. (2020). The tailoring of IPE in Latin America: Lost, misfit or merely misperceived? In E. Vivares (Ed.), *The Routledge Handbook to Global Political economy* (pp. 92–110). Routledge.

Vivares, E. (2014). *Exploring the New South American Regionalism (NSAR)*. Routledge.

Vivares, E. (2018). *Regionalism, development and the post-commodities boom in South America*. Palgrave.

Vivares, E. (2020). *The Routledge Handbook to Global Political Economy. Conversations and inquiries*. Routledge.

Vivares, E., & Dolcetti-Marcolini, M. (2016). Two regionalisms, two Latin Americas or beyond Latin America? Contributions from a critical and decolonial IPE. *Third World Quarterly*, *37*(5), 866–882. https://doi.org/10.1080/01436597.2015.1109438

Waltz, K. (1979). *A theory of International politics*. Addison-Wesley Publishing.

Capitalist geopolitics and Latin America's long road to regionalism

Rowan Lubbock

ABSTRACT

This article situates the current (re)configuration of Latin American regionalism within the broader history of capitalist geopolitics. I argue that modern regionalism, in the post-war period and beyond, is better understood through a deeper historicization of geopolitical dynamics that shaped, and were shaped by, global capital accumulation. From the early regional imaginaries of post-independence Latin American leaders, to the emergence of 'continental history' marked by the rise of the continent-sized island in the United States, the origins of regional institutions forms a more longer lineage than is often thought. The article provides a class-relational analysis of the ISI period, the rise (and fall) of neoliberal discipline, and the resurgence of a new Latin American left in the early twenty-first century. Through the lens of capitalist geopolitics, I offer a potential critical-theory route towards understanding the current conjuncture, and what the future portents for Latin American regionalism.

Introduction

Contemporary scholarship on international regional institutions tends to begin its historical narrative at the dawn of the post-World War II era, with the emergence of Europe's first moves towards regional integration (e.g. Paul, 2012). From the 1950s onwards, social science witnessed an explosion of theorizing on regional integration arrangements, principally centred on the European experience, but soon after evolving into a broader field of comparative regionalism (Mistry, 2003, p. 117). While the phenomenon of region-building before 1945 was sporadically acknowledged by International Relations (IR) scholars, this relative silence was largely due to the fact that 'old regionalism' (pre-1945) 'came to be judged nearly universally as negative for being constituted of closed trading blocs that led to global economic depression' (Fawn, 2009, p. 7). In contrast, regional integration/cooperation in the post-war period was generally seen to be a half-way house between national interests and the forces of globalism (van der Pijl, 2014, p. 124ff.; cf. Cooper et al., 2008; Lombaerde et al., 2012). And yet, despite the strategic goal of fostering increased geopolitical stability and international order, regional institutions have not escaped the forces of social and economic crisis permeating every layer of world society (Fioramonti, 2012; Haastrup & Yong-Soon, 2014).

The aim of this paper is to reveal the deeper forces at work in the making of regional spaces over the long twentieth century in order to properly situate the historical formation of Latin American regionalism and account for its limits and prospects. To do so, I offer a more grounded Marxian approach to international regionalism, which anchors the discursive and institutional ensemble of regional organizations to the broader dynamics of capital accumulation at the world scale. Of course, there is no shortage of academic works that incorporate political economy into the study of regionalism (e.g. Capannelli & Kawai, 2014; Manfield & Miller, 1997; Söderbaum, 2004). Yet these approaches very often rely on either heterodox or constructivist tenets of political economy, which tend to reify specific concepts, such as 'non-equilibrium' (in contrast to orthodox equilibrium theory), or the social construction of 'institutions', 'discourses', 'practices' etc. Without enquiring into deeper forces suturing these disparate features together, we run the risk of obscuring the role of capital as a social relation. In contrast, I argue that the Marxian critique of political economy, while taking seriously the discursively grounded understanding of institutions (cf. Konings, 2009), provides a common analytical register of capitalism as a global mode of production that is fragmented by the multiplicity of many states and many capitals (Davidson, 2010; Milonakis & Fine, 2009, pp. 164–165). This contradiction between the general and the particular lies at the heart of socio-economic crises that cascade through various levels of political life, insofar as the development of the productive forces and the increasing socialization of global production continues to be privatized by ruling class fractions. The struggle between and within classes, as an expression of the fundamental contradiction of capitalism (general/particular), furnishes the historical motor for the complex history of region building, in both Latin America and beyond.

To borrow from Dipesh Chakrabarty, the central tenet of this article is to 'provincialize' European integration and subsequent regional institutions, in the sense that these post-World War II spatialization projects were 'always and already modified by particular histories' (2008, p. xiv). In order to bring out the historical pre-conditions and political significance of contemporary international regions, I offer a longer view of modern region-building, beginning with the advent of 'continental history'. From the perspective of classical geographers such as Friedrich Ratzel and Rudolf Kjellén, the emergence of large-scale industrialization grafted onto continent-sized polities ushered in a new phase of geopolitics, one in which the very survival of sovereign states rested on the ability to achieve 'scale and scope' (Chandler, 1990; Puntigliano, 2011). The wars of independence across North and South America laid the groundwork for the emergence of continental history, and throughout the nineteenth century it was unclear precisely which contender in the Western hemisphere would claim the mantle of a regional-sized world power. As it turned out, the locomotive of (regional) history would arrive with the consolidation of the US 'continent-sized island' based on expansive industries across virtually ever sector. This expansive development of the productive forces, as an expression of the further socialization of production, led to entirely new possibilities for the regional spatialization of political power, of which World War II was a most painful expression.

From within this broader historical context, this article seeks to account for contemporary Latin American regionalism as the 'surface of prior layers of integration movements' (Puntigliano, 2013, p. 21). Though initially ensnared by the dictates of Cold War geopolitics, Latin American leaders had always sought to carve out a new, modern version of Simón Bolívar's nineteenth century dream of uniting the continent. Patterns of uneven development across the region, in conjunction with the contradictions of Import-Substitution Industrialisation and the over-riding dominance of US power, continually thwarted the many attempts at a comprehensive region-wide arrangement, resulting instead in a proliferation of different regionalization schemes. Yet the neoliberal onslaught would foster a new sense of rebellion throughout the Southern Cone, which in turn laid the groundwork for the rise of the new Latin American left and their reassertion of José Martí's dream of 'Our America' (*Nuestra América*) (Martí, 1977). The new Latin American left marked the latest phase of region building in the twenty-first century. And yet, this new push for a post-hegemonic regionalism was not without its own tensions and contradictions.

The rise of US hegemony and the problem of regional order

The shift of global power from British to US hegemony was, as with all such historical transitions, the manifestation of deeper socio-ecological contradictions of the capitalist state-system. The British Empire's 'extensive' regime of accumulation engendered a huge expansion in the productive forces across the globe – primarily transport infrastructures – as a response to the imperial centre's voracious appetite for food and raw materials (Collingham, 2018; Moore, 2010, p. 394). In consequence, Britain's integration of peripheral spaces into the wider circuits of global capitalism inadvertently elevated these new areas within the overall world hierarchy of grain production and supply. With the consolidation of settler colonial state-spaces, European agriculture was soon displaced by a six-fold increase in imports from these areas between 1870 and 1929 (Friedmann, 1990, p. 14; Mazoyer & Roudart, 2006, pp. 368–369).

What distinguished these spaces of accumulation – particularly the United States, Canada, Argentina and Australia – was their sheer size. And yet, this size would count for nothing as long as colonial elites remained trapped under absolutist trade regimes. Thus, in both the British colonies and the Iberian viceroyalties, the frustrated ambitions of a new strata of ruling elites crystallised around a discourse of national independence and liberal ideals (Albertone, 2016; Lubbock, 2020a). From Simón Bolívar to Andrés Bello, Latin America's independence leaders recognized their shared (anti-imperial) history, culture, language and aspirations for recognition within modern international society. However, this early regional imaginary struggled to survive beyond the tempest of post-independence politics. The federated political units envisaged by the likes of Bolívar were separated by enormous distances and a rugged geography (Deas, 1987, pp. 209–210). But political cultures, traditions and historical contingencies also played a significant part. In his address to the Congress of Angostura, which marked the birth of the idea for the federation of 'Gran Colombia' (comprising Colombia, Ecuador, Panama and Venezuela), Bolívar spoke of North Americans as 'a singular example of political virtue and moral rectitude' (Bolívar & Chávez Frías, 2009, p. 85). His admiration was no doubt shaped by the sheer survival of the US's delicate balance between federalism and anti-federalism. Yet Bolívar thought the political culture of South America's newly independent states was ill-suited to North America's 'weak and complicated' division of powers (Bolívar & Chávez Frías, 2009, p. 85). Instead, it was the British model of parliamentary democracy to which Bolívar searched for a solution. To hedge against democratic excess, a hereditary Senate (much like Britain's House of Lords) would ensure stability within a radically diverse nation. Nevertheless, the legacy of frontier sovereignty – the vast cattle ranges ruled by powerful and often rebellious *llanero* leaders, such as José Antonio Páez (Duncan Baretta & Markoff, 1978) – as well as the divisions between Bolívar and Santander over constitutional principles, led to increasing territorial fragmentation and scepticism among the constituent states of the federation, leading eventually to its demise in 1831. It is noteworthy that the newly independent states of Central America had attempted virtually the same form of federal union (1824–1838) and failed for largely the same reasons (see Chandler, 1989; Smith, 1963).

To be sure, the fledging United States encountered key moments of instability. But the reasons for why these social uprisings did not result in territorial fragmentation lies in the specific determinations of class, race, and military reform. A series of class conflicts across the Northern countryside of the US – most prominent among them being Shay's Rebellion of 1786 – catalysed the centralization of the previously frayed federal militia system. Merchants and land speculators across the Northern states faced a hostile class of independent farmers seeking to hold onto their lands and resist the predations of creditors and tax collectors. But ruling elites failed to quell these uprisings, with local rural militias often siding with the rebels rather than fight against then. The class (and racial) solidarity uniting significant sections of the then small federal army and independent farmers led to a tactical alliance between the Northern bourgeoisie and Southern planters, with the latter fearful of what might come without a large, consolidated army corps. Some years later, in 1789, the newly expanded federal army, comprised mostly of urban poor, crushed the Whisky Rebellion in Pennsylvania (Post, 2011, pp. 188–191). Thus, unlike their counterparts in North America, those at the helm of the Gran Colombia project faced an altogether different problem: rather than elites seeking horizontal class unity in the face of an increasingly united rural underclass – as with the case of state-formation in Mexico and Brazil (Mazzuca, 2021, p. 371) – in Gran Colombia class unity was regionally specific through vertical lines of clientelistic control over land and people (Duncan Baretta & Markoff, 1978, p. 601f.).

When comparing the trajectory of state formation across North and South America, one should not forget the prominent, if not inconvenient, role played by sheer chance. The survival of the Constitutional Settlement in the US was based on the most radical contingencies and shaped by an unimaginable number of compromises and deliberations (for a voluminous study of this chaotic process, see Klarman, 2016). The eventual expansion of the Western frontier was essentially beyond the reach of the sovereign American state, and while deeper norms of popular sovereignty and racial hierarchies kept the process of state-formation on a stable, if not winding, path (Billington & Ridge, 2001), the expansion of the frontier brought with it an endless number of class conflicts among farmers, cowboys, ranchers and merchants (Boatright, 1941). Territorial expansion created new tensions within the regime of slave labour, as new states decided independently on the question of slavery, leading eventually to the American civil war which brought to the surface a long standing contradiction between industrial capitalism in the North and territorially expansive slave economies in the South. The survival of the United States was thus far from assured.

By the end of the nineteenth century, the consolidation of the US 'continent-sized island' reflected the fundamental contradiction of the capitalist mode of production – between the geographical expansion and socialization of the productive forces, and their organization by private/national interests (Mandel, 1986, p. 20) – culminating in a new spatial form seemingly adequate to the immanent development of large-scale industrial capitalism. Precisely why the United States eventually became the territorial powerhouse of global capitalism cannot simply be put down to its size; indeed, as noted above, the expansion of the capitalist world system created new colonial state-spaces that were far larger than anything seen in Europe, and largely similar in their export-oriented economies.

The Portuguese colony of Brazil, the largest political space in South America, is comparable to the size of the US yet contains a geographical anomaly. The Brazilian rainforest presented a significant challenge to the expansion of both political and economic frontiers. Even by the mid-nineteenth century, the Amazon Valley 'remained virtually a sealed book to the world' (Martin, 1918, p. 146). Although partly a result local elites' fierce desire to keep foreigners out, the sealed space of the Amazon was largely a reflection of its ungovernability; well into twentieth century, development institutions struggled to carry out their projects due to immense distances and natural physical barriers (Bunker, 1988, p. 160). In contrast, North America's temperate open plains offered easy access to new lands and resource frontiers. And while Brazil's coffee boom in the mid-nineteenth century helped to consolidate financial and industrial development, early moves towards diversification were mortgaged by the Brazilian ruling class' tight integration into British-dominated circuits of trade, credit, and debt (Salgado, 2017, p. 161; cf. Topik, 1985, pp. 227–228). Ultimately, the fusion of landowner interests (based on free trade principles) and the patrimonial state undermined industrial policy based on protective import tariffs.

The case of Argentina is even more striking, given the relative similarities in initial conditions compared to North America. Indeed, as Rocchi (2006, p. 4) contends, the pace of economic growth from 1860 to 1930 'was so impressive that [Argentina] was expected eventually to become the United States of South America'. And yet, that moment never arrived. In terms of rural development, despite the steady importation of North Atlantic technologies (Pineda, 2018), a combination of labour regimes and tight credit markets led to a less intense use of capital on the Argentine pampas. The prevalence of lease-holding tenants over independent owner-occupiers disincentivised the adoption of capital-intensive production (though smaller farms, even if owner-occupied, tended to employ less machinery) (Adelman, 1994, p. 253). And in contrast to the quite similar agricultural conditions in Canada, it was credit that was scarce in Argentina, not labour. Thus, financing new fixed capital was increasingly out of reach of the mass of medium-sized owner-occupiers.

While Argentina's industrialization occurred far earlier than usually assumed (the last decades of the nineteenth century), it remained relatively hampered by two key aspects. Firstly, the expansion of the frontier was more intense relative to the non-resource (industrial) economy. Having increased its total farmland by 319% between 1870 and 1910 (the most rapid expansion of all frontier development states), the eventual closure of the frontier was not followed by a compensatory push from industry (Barbier, 2010, p. 381; di Tella, 1982, p. 222). And secondly, the simple fact of *timing* placed Argentina in a significant disadvantage compared to its northern neighbour. To use one simple proxy, the turning point from 'extensive' to 'intensive' growth in the US and Argentina occurred in 1830 and 1860, respectively (Barbier, 2010, p. 393).[1] Thus while Argentina went through many of the developmental phases seen in the US, by the 1920s, it was US corporations investing in Argentina, not vice versa (cf. Chandler, 1990; Rocchi, 2006, p. 236).[2]

Expansive industrialization in the US was ultimately underwritten by enormous resource frontiers capable of creating forward and backward linkages with industry, and thus leading to a truly diversified national economy and sizeable home market (Arrighi, 2006, p. 300; Barbier, 2010, p. 395ff.; Moore, 2002). Yet the driver of national accumulation stemmed from the increasing subsumption of small farmers under the power of commercial capital. By the end of the eighteenth century, the transformation of cheap and open land into legally constituted private property forced yeoman farmers in the North-East to increase their output in order to service debts and maintain their plots, while farmers in the North-West went through a similar process almost a century later (Post, 2011, pp. 231–233). With the proliferation of vertically integrated firms from the late nineteenth century – supplying everything from farm tools to petro-chemicals – capital accumulation was now embedded within truly continental-sized agglomerations, providing considerable power over labour, as well as other national (and international) competitors (Bauerly, 2017, p. 56ff.; Moore, 2002, p. 188; cf. Barkan, 2013, p. 44).

The preceding comparisons between the developmental trajectories of colonial state-spaces help to bring focus to the socio-economic and geopolitical determinations of 'continental history'. As noted previously, the colonial conquest of the Western hemisphere brought into being vast political territories that dwarfed the polities of Europe. In a sense, these were indeed 'regional' configurations, but only in the most general terms. In themselves, these territorial expanses were not the true precursors to regionalism as we know it today, in so far as the advent of modern regionalism was the result of *geopolitical pressures mediated through the rise of industrialism*. As we saw from the comparison of the Brazil, Argentina and the US, it is not simply a question of size and industry – characteristics that all three states shared together. It is rather a question of *relative competitiveness* and the intensity of accumulation which determines the eventual pre-eminence of one state over the others. Thus, the Swedish geographer, Rudolf Kjellén, envisaged a new world of continental states ordered into a tripartite system of industrial autarky centred on the United States, Germany, and Japan (Holdar, 1992).

From this broader historical context, it becomes possible to view the entire World War II conflagration, precipitated by German and Japanese regional expansionism, as a global instance of geopolitical strategy attempting to adapt to the extensity and intensity of capitalist accumulation within the US continent-sized island (cf. Nolan, 1994; Samuels, 1994). Friedrich Ratzel, a key geopolitical thinker in late nineteenth century Germany, emphasized the importance of carving out ever larger 'living space' (*Lebansraum*) for a given people (*Volk*) (Heffernan, 2003, p. 45). Though he was not resistant to commercial trade expansion, Ratzel believed that '[o]nly with a secure agricultural foundation and an adequate Lebensraum could permanent commercial expansion take place' (Smith, 1980, p. 61). The German political theorist and legal scholar, Carl Schmitt, would later translate the notion of living space into a political programme of absolute strategic necessity – from *Lebensraum* to Großraum (pan-region) – which 'challenge[d] Lockean governance in the name of sovereign equality' (van der Pijl, 2014, p. 84). What took place during this transformation in political geography, therefore, was the reproduction of sovereign equality (the hardening of borders between insiders and outsiders, or in Schmitt's terms, 'friends' and 'enemies') but on a much larger scale (legal recognition between *regional* sovereigns). Thus, for Schmitt, '[t]he age of (nation-)states and the post Versailles *Kleinstaaterei* (mini-state proliferation) was irretrievably over. The future, he argued, belonged to a different type of political unit, for which the Monroe Doctrine provided the historical and legal precedent' (Teschke, 2011, p. 76).

On the other side of the Eurasian continent, Japanese intellectuals were also beginning to experiment with the idea of regional spheres of influence. In response to the post-World War I context of overproduction across the capitalist world economy, Japanese leaders sought to avert post-war recession (and the rise of socialism) through the creation of an autarkic regional economic space (Matsumura, 2016, p. 153). The imperative of national development, which always has a symbiotic relationship with industrial militarization, fundamentally hinged on the number one staple crop of Japanese society: rice. With a general migration of capital from the countryside and into the urban-industrial sectors, the creation of an imperial space centred around Asia would help to ease the burden of raw material constraints in a geographically small and resource poor nation such as Japan (Brandt, 1993; Macpherson, 1995, p. 53).

The evolution of regional spaces among fascist states should not be taken as simply the territorial expression of dictatorship, standing in supposed contrast to the regime of liberal democracy. Indeed, the geopolitical imaginaries circulating among German and Japanese intellectuals found fertile ground within the epistemic networks of US empire. In the early 1940s, the publisher of *Life* magazine, Henry Luce, proclaimed that 'Tyrannies may require a large amount of living space … [but] [f]reedom requires and will require far greater living space than Tyranny' (cited in Smith, 2003, p. 319). The American geographer, Isaiah Bowman, took to Ratzel's concept of *Lebensraum* as the cornerstone of US primacy within a world of regions: '*Lebensraum* for all is the answer to *Lebensraum* for one' (Bowman; cited in Smith, 2003, p. 319). And yet, for Bowman and US planners, the question of *Lebansraum* was not based on territorial expansion; rather, American *Lebensraum* was 'an economic question' (Smith, 2003, p. 319). In substituting economics for territory, the American *Lebensraum* would, in effect, encompass the entire world under a system in which regional space would lean towards liberalism's goal of open doors, rather than a series of closed regional blocs that ran the risk of heighted geopolitical competition (McCormick, 1989, p. 31).

However, Roosevelt's notion of the regional 'Four Policeman' (US, USSR, Britain, China) eventually lost out to the State Department's preference for universal multilateralism in the shape of the UN General Assembly (the Security Council, wielding the monopoly of legitimate force, was the basic compromise between these two extremes). Yet the rapidly escalating antagonism between the US and USSR – including the victory of communist forces in China that required the entrance of Japan as the regional ally in Asia (Katzenstein, 2005, p. 48) – simply increased the necessity of regional forms of governance. The emergence of 'integration theory' was not only premised on seeking adequate spatial complexes for the continental scale of capital accumulation (Cocks, 1980, p. 27; McCormick, 1989, pp. 79–80), it was also a fundamental tool in the Atlantic heartland's quest for hegemony throughout the international system (Murphy, 2005, p. 92).

Thus, the post-war project of regional integration was, like the inter-war period, premised on the exigencies of specific accumulation regimes and their spatial-agglomeration effects, yet this time refracted through US 'imperium' (Katzenstein, 2005; van der Pijl, 2014, p. 123ff.). And yet, both superpowers tolerated regional formations only to the extent that they satisfied their short-term security interests (Hurrell, 1995, p. 341). The signing of Latin America's regional security Rio Pact in 1947 would set the trend for other regional security regimes, from the North Atlantic Treaty Organisation to the Southeast Asia Treaty Organization (Grandin, 2007, p. 39).[3] The very fact that US policy makers favoured regional security regimes so early on revealed the underlying role that the Global South was supposed to play within the post-war order: as pliant spaces of raw material supplies or open markets to the three regional nodes of global capitalism (US, Western Europe and Japan). Economic integration among weaker states, by definition, dilutes this subordinate position in the international division of labour through the establishment of collective tariffs and common markets. This was the central premise of post-war integration initiatives throughout Latin America, which fundamentally aimed to challenge the continued dependency of national economies on the dynamics of accumulation within the Global North (Puntigliano, 2011, p. 854). And as we will see below, it continues to inform contemporary region-building, from MERCOSUR to the ALBA-TCP.

However, it was soon realized that the limited role assigned to the Global South would be the undoing of US influence throughout the non-Western world. As the prominent policy advisor Walt Rostow remarked at the time, 'Even if Marx and Lenin did not exist, we would still have a problem' (cited in Peck, 2010, p. 36). For all the intensity of Washington's bid to portray the communist 'menace' as some international conspiracy, the fact remained that the continuation of US imperialism throughout the Global South would simply do the USSR's biding by fostering continual subaltern rebellions that challenged the dominance of the Atlanticist West.

Creating (and containing) class struggle in Latin America: between imperium and regional autonomy

The post-World War II order, spearheaded by the US's 'Fordist' hegemonic project (Rupert, 1995), witnessed the establishment of a world-wide productivist paradigm of Import-Substitution Industrialisation (ISI) that applied directly to those states in the Global South which for so long depended on foreign markets for their primary commodity exports and imported consumables. Yet it seemed clear to Latin American leaders that the ISI strategy could not solve foreign exchange constraints if left within the frontiers of the nation-state (Nogués & Quintanilla, 1993, p. 281). Early geopolitical imaginaries of integration among Latin American figures consistently centred on the advent of continental history in relation to industrialization and development. President of the Inter-American Bank, Felipe Herrera, foresaw the geopolitical pressures emanating from 'continental states', and the need to unite the region's states in order to achieve true sovereignty (Puntigliano, 2011, p. 854). In his *Foreign Affairs* article of 1959, then ex-president of Ecuador, Galo Plaza, similarly argued for the establishment of a 'regional market' in order to further stimulate Latin America's push into the producer goods and consumer durables sectors. In Plaza's view, the territories of the US, USSR, China and India were already 'regional markets of enormous magnitude. Only Latin America remains divided into 20 separate economic units' (Plaza, 1959, pp. 609–610). Some years later, at a conference held in 1966 at Georgetown University, Gustavo Lagos, a Chilean intellectual and later Minister of Justice under the Frei administration, noted the structural necessity of moving towards a larger politico-economic space for the South American nations. Like Herrera and Plaza, he noted that the sheer scale of capital accumulation during the second half of the twentieth century (marked primarily by the 'continental federations' of the US and USSR) necessitated a concerted push towards tighter political and economic cooperation between the smaller South American states (Milenky, 1973, pp. 10–11).

In light of this long-held strategic goal, the *Tratado de Montevideo* (Treaty of Montevideo) was signed in 1960 by Argentina, Brazil, Uruguay and Chile, and later joined by Paraguay, Peru and Mexico, creating the Latin American Free Trade Association (LAFTA), which reached eleven member states by 1968. The idea behind LAFTA was to institute a negotiated and gradual elimination of trade barriers (buffeted with countless clauses and concessions for particular countries on particular commodities), and the eventual formation of the Latin American Common Market (LACM) within 12 years (Phillips, 2004, p. 48; Puntigliano, 2011, p. 854).

The Association produced some notable results, but perhaps not those envisaged by Latin American leaders: agriculture and primary products accounted for 70% of intra-LAFTA trade, rather than manufactures. By 1967, the push for the LACM was all but abandoned. The principal reasons for LAFTA's disappointing career was due to the sheer diversity in size, structure and socio-ecological basis of its member states, the low levels of physical and communicative integration between them, and the concomitant concentration of trade between the biggest players, Argentina, Brazil and Chile (Phillips, 2004, pp. 49–50; cf. Haas & Schmitter, 1964, p. 721).

Yet these developmental bottlenecks merely stumped the LAFTA space, not the integrationist project itself. The spatial divisions that expressed the continent's differential development patterns re-emerged in subsequent integration initiatives, which brought together groups of states that were closer in both geography and levels of development, such as the Central American Common Market, the Andean Pact and The Caribbean Community (Fawcett, 2005, p. 39).

The lost decades: economic liberalization and neoliberal discipline

The decline of the ISI-boom was more than just the result of erroneous economic policy on behalf of Latin American leaders. Embedded within the wider circuits of global accumulation, the transition from ISI to neoliberalism was a result of much broader crisis of the capitalist world system. With the overaccumulation of capital and falling rates of profit within the core states (US, Germany and Japan), the US essentially changed the rules of the global game in order to stave off unbearable competition and ensure its continued dominance (Kiely, 2005, pp. 56–64). The world economy was now linked to the US dollar, instead of gold, as measure of value and (for many commodities) the *de facto* medium of exchange. Concurrent with the oil crisis in 1973 which sent world petroleum prices skyrocketing, cash-flushed oil states became new sources of credit to Latin American governments via US banks operating within the less-regulated Eurodollar markets (Selva, 2017). The subsequent 'Volcker shock' of 1980, which hiked US interest rates in the battle against inflation and domestic class conflict, put enormous pressure on states in the Global South with respect to their debt repayment values, which correspondingly increased.

Contrary to economic orthodoxy, neoliberal economic reforms, which aimed to solve Latin America's debt crisis through the elimination of social security, state support, and labour protections, led to slow growth and sluggish economic performance. In the agricultural sector, growth reached around 2% in the 1980s and 2.6 in the 1990s, compared to 3.5% between 1950 and 1980 (Kay, 2004, p. 234). Lower domestic output was compensated for through increased food imports during the 1970s, with the food import-export ratio reaching 40% in the 1980s, and 60% in the 1990s (Kay, 2004, p. 235). As a result, rural production became skewed in favour of niche commodities favouring urban tastes and foreign consumers (e.g. fruits, livestock, and sorghum) (Ortiz, 2014). Under these conditions, rural populations underwent a 'semi-proletarianization' in which peasants devoted more of their time to off-farm activities, either in urban centres or from seasonal wage-labour on larger farms (Kay, 2004, p. 241). In sum, the consolidation of neoliberal discipline resulted in the generalization of weak growth, rising under- or unemployment, poverty and inequality, as well as a decrease in total population (Hermann, 2016, p. 530), entering what would soon be known as 'the lost decade'.

As with the challenges faced by Latin American states during the closure of the ISI boom, the systemic pressures of neoliberalism were met with a wider push towards regionalization. Gustavo Lagos' prophetic remarks concerning the continent sized confederations of the US and USSR were now borne out by the increasing regionalization of the global trade regime, seeking to economize on geographical distance and transaction costs (Rugman & Verbeke, 2004). Nevertheless, there remained important differences across Latin America's regional landscape. NAFTA and MERCOSUR, for instance, are perhaps the most significant as well as qualitatively different cases. NAFTA's accumulation strategy is premised on a specific economic division of labour between its three members (with Canada and Mexico as low-cost raw material/semi-assembled supply 'spokes' to the US manufacturing 'hub') facilitated through iron-clad free-trade legal commitments, and ideological appeals to 'market rationality' (Ciccantell, 2001; Kühnhardt, 2010, pp. 28–29). The US-led construction of NAFTA ultimately stemmed from concerns for increased regional competitiveness over the rival blocs led by Germany in the European Community and Japan's regional 'flying geese' model. Yet US designs for the western hemisphere went far beyond the mere trilateralisation of cross-border flows. The Miami Summit in 1994 became the diplomatic platform for the US's proposed Free Trade Area of the Americas (FTAA), which would stretch from Alaska to Tierra del Fuego (with projected completion by 2004). For Latin America's biggest economy, Brazil, the FTAA threatened to subsume the region under an expanded NAFTA-type configuration, which would have threatened the possibility for diversification. The solution to this challenge was found in a more autonomous regional market in South America.

Latin America's most developed regional project, the Southern Common Market (MERCOSUR), dates back to the earlier round of regional integration agreements in 1986 between the two largest players, Argentina and Brazil (Gardini, 2010). It finally came to fruition as the 'Southern Cone Common Market' in 1991, signed by Brazil, Argentina, Paraguay and Uruguay. In its early phase, the economic content of the MERCOSUR space was not radically different from the neoliberal pattern, yet its institutional ensemble was 'located somewhere between NAFTA and a common market' (Katzenstein, 2005, p. 231; see also Carranza, 2006; Botto, 2021). Thus, MERCOSUR has always positioned itself as an inherently *integrationist* project, aiming towards a common external position as a protection against the wider world market. Trade levels among member states grew significantly, from 4.1 to 20.3 billion USD (1990–1997), with the percentage of intra-MERCOSUR trade relative to members' global trade at 14–25% (1992–1997) (Muñoz, 2001, p. 83).

However, MERCOSUR has always engendered a continuing (if not varied) democratic deficit at the regional level. Indeed, MERCOSUR's origins can be found within epistemic networks of political elites – from diplomats to economists – with little to no input from civil society (Patomäki & Teivainen, 2002, p. 57). Even more established sectors, such as trade unions, were at best 'second order' actors within the formation of this regional project. While their participation was largely limited to lobbying national governments, several regional MERCOSUR forums were eventually created for the participation of organized labour (Phillips, 2004, p. 141). Nevertheless, such channels were essentially consultative in nature, with no real scope for concrete participation in policymaking. Only after several years of concerted regional coordination from below among a variety of national unions did labour's influence over MERCOSUR's social and economic policy increase by the close of the 1990s (Phillips, 2004, p. 173). Beyond organized labour, radical social forces across the continent – from indigenous groups and informal workers, to peasants and non-recognized labour unions – began to push for a 'social agenda', and for 'another integration' within MERCOSUR that would hedge against the US-sponsored FTAA (Chodor, 2021, p. 423). Despite this push from below, participation within MERCOSUR among regional social forces (outside of officially recognized trade unions) remained virtually closed off (Jacobs & Maldonado, 2005, pp. 168–169; Riggirozzi, 2014, p. 440).

In terms of regional development, MERCOSUR has not moved substantially towards an integrated regional market. Rather, it is principally structured around an externally protected bloc within which resides a series of inter-state agreements on trade balances. Thus, exporting to the MERCOSUR market is inherently restrictive, limiting the scale of production that would bring lower unit costs, and thereby restricting the development of technological frontiers that contribute towards upgrading regional production as a whole (Fitzsimons & Guevara, 2016). As a result, the relative fragmentation within and across MERCOSUR's policies can be seen as a reflection of executive elites seeking to protect and accommodate nationally constituted sectoral interests (Carranza, 2006, pp. 817–818; Pezzola, 2018).

Given the turbulence MERCOSUR has had to endure with Brazil's devaluation of the real in 1999, and the Argentine economic collapse of 2001, it became increasingly clear that member states' cooperation had to ensure the stability of its social fabric. With the ascension of Lula da Silva to the Brazilian presidency in 2003 from a 'developmentalist front' coalition within the Workers' Party (PT), a new social compact between the 'grand bourgeoisie' and the subaltern classes would enable Brazil to endure the strains of region building and insertion into the world market on a potentially more solid (and popular) footing (Boito & Berringer, 2014; van der Pijl, 2006, p. 198). And yet, the rise of Lula was merely reflective of a much deeper fissure that began to emerge between Latin America and the Atlantic core.

Reclaiming '*Nuestra América*': contradictions of the new Latin American left

The eventual challenge against neoliberal discipline would emerge from a confluence of different social forces. The politico-economic transformations wrought by externally imposed structural adjustment policies, and internally imposed authoritarian repression, led to a rapid expansion of informal employment and social insecurity (Portes, 1985; Portes & Hoffman, 2003; see also Fuentes

& Durán, 2018). With the waning of traditional political institutions (unions and political parties), the rise of 'new social movements' throughout the region filled the void, mobilizing around issues of 'justice', 'dignity', 'identity', 'solidarity' and traditional cultures (Silva, 2009).

During this time, Latin American social movements increasingly organized through forms of 'transnational activism' (Silva, 2013; Tarrow, 2005), such as the Hemispheric Social Alliance founded in 1997, and the Foro Mesoamericano network in 2001, which sought to challenge the neoliberal Free Trade Area of the Americas (FTAA) and Plan Puebla-Panama (PPP), respectively (Saguier, 2010; Spalding, 2008). Yet this new spatialisation strategy among the region's social movements, as a type of *regionalism from below* (see Rice, 2021; Rosset et al., 2021), also engendered a contradictory co-mingling with a resurgent discourse on sovereign independence (Silva, 2009). In bringing the state back in, anti-neoliberal social movements, which for so long had eschewed traditional institutions as vehicles for popular demands, found themselves in close partnership with progressive political parties and state institutions that came to prominence at the turn of the century.

Thus, with the emergence of the 'new left' in the early twenty-first century, regional organizations saw a relative transformation towards a 'post-hegemonic' or 'post-liberal' regionalism (Riggirozzi & Tussie, 2012; Sanahuja, 2008-9). Underwritten by the 'commodity consensus' (Svampa, 2015), progressive governments were afforded greater fiscal capacity to finance social and developmental projects at home, and greater incentive for cooperation with regional partners abroad. However, this 'second incorporation' of the popular sectors within state/regional institutions (Rossi, 2018) tended to take shape through uneven relations of power and knowledge among state/civil society actors.

This period witnessed an increasing focus on the establishment of a 'Social MERCOSUR' during the *pro tempore* regional presidency of Uruguay's Tabaré Vazquez. This new phase of region-building gave much greater emphasis on the participation of civil society actors and social policy, under the banner *Somos MERCOSUR* (We Are MERCOSUR), which subsequently held the First Encounter of the Social and Productive MERCOSUR in 2006 bringing together some 500 regional organizations (Vázquez, 2008, pp. 146–147). Yet this broader inclusion of civil society was entirely engineered from the elite level, while some of the most prominent transnational social movements, such as the HSA, remained (quite self-consciously) outside MERCOSUR's formal institutions (Briceño Ruiz, 2012). This relative exclusion of non-state actors from the policymaking process has in turn severely curtailed the progress of regional social policy, which is often hostage to inter-governmental decision making that tends to filter social policy through economic logics (Riggirozzi, 2014, p. 439).

Other prominent examples include the Union of South American Nations (UNASUR, 2008), and the Community of Latin American and Caribbean States (CELAC, 2011). While the origins of UNASUR can be traced to the previous South American Free Trade Area, proposed by former Brazilian President Itamar Franco in 2003, the subsequent rise of Hugo Chávez, Evo Morales and Rafael Correa helped to shift this regional body away from neoliberal trade-related issues, and towards a more socially-oriented cooperative institution (Briceño-Ruiz & Hoffmann, 2015, p. 55). Interestingly, UNASUR later went on to incorporate the South American Regional Infrastructure initiative (IIRSA) in 2010. With its proposal for extensive investments in regional infrastructures (transport, energy, communications), the IIRSA represents the long sought-after solution to establishing a region-wide economic space of continental proportions (Van Dijck, 2008). And yet, somewhat paradoxically, IIRSA is geared less towards the consolidation of a continental market, and more towards the further subsumption of Latin American economies within the broader international division of labour (Kanai, 2016; Zibechi, 2006, pp. 24–25). The radical territorial transformations brought about by these region-wide 'axes' of development have also elicited some marked resistance among ecological movements and local populations suffering negative externalities of such projects (cf. Pieck, 2015)

Perhaps the most remarkable example of Latin America's post-hegemonic regionalism is the Bolivarian Alliance for the Peoples of Our America-Peoples Trade Treaty (*Alianza Bolivariana para los Pueblos de Nuestra América* – ALBA-TCP). Born from the general antipathy to the Bush administration's unilateralism, and the rejection of the FTAA, ALBA was formed in 2004 through bi-lateral agreement between Cuba and Venezuela, eventually growing to eleven member states at its peak. Based on the principles of cooperation, solidarity and economic complementarity, the ALBA-TCP would go on to forge a number of regional policies focusing on healthcare, education, trade, and food security/sovereignty (Lubbock, 2020b; Muhr, 2011; Pearce, 2013). While the ALBA-TCP represents the most novel re-configuration of twenty-first century Latin American regionalism, it is also shaped by a number of contradictory forces. First and foremost, the ALBA bloc is fundamentally underwritten through a 'reprimarization' of natural resource rents, as a function of the 'commodity super-cycle' of the early twenty-first century (Estay, 2018, pp. 60–61). Just as the conjectural shifts in global capital during the 1970s and beyond had radically shifted regional patterns of development, the ascendance of China as a new centre of accumulation created a strategic opportunity for the valorization of primary commodities. As Higginbottom (2013, p. 200) notes, ALBA states have been far more successful in their struggle over the capture of ground-rent relative to private capital, either through nationalizations or more favourable contracts with foreign firms. And yet, the specific composition of ground-rent within the ALBA space, particularly that of Venezuelan oil production, gives rise to two inter-related determinations. Firstly, much of ALBA's regional policies are dependent upon either the magnitude of ground-rent, or the volume of oil produced (particularly with respect to the parallel PETROCARIBE initiative). With the collapse of global commodity prices from around 2012, as well the general contraction in Venezuelan oil production, the material foundation of ALBA's regional policies began to crumble; and with the resurgence of right-wing governments in Ecuador and Bolivia, its membership declined.[4] Secondly, the centrality of Venezuelan oil rent has placed the Bolivarian state at the centre of the region's organizational architecture (see Ciupa, in press). One consequence of this is the relative lack of regional coordination and institutionalization across the ALBA-TCP, which partially reflects the general complexity and institutional fragmentation of the Venezuelan state itself (cf. Cusack, 2018; Lubbock, 2020b). Finally, while ALBA's creation of the 'Council of Social Movements' (CSM) within the top echelons of its institutional architecture reflected the second reincorporation of social movements at the regional scale, the reality of the CSM – much like *Somos MERCOSUR* – reveals a more tepid relationship between political elites and social movement representatives, relegating the latter to merely symbolic or consultative roles (Lubbock, 2017, p. 105ff.).

Thus, while the era of post-hegemonic regionalism reflected a new geopolitical conjuncture, characterized by increased autonomy as a function of rising commodity prices and the formation of new geo-economic axes (particularly across the Pacific), the limits and contradictions of the Latin American left can be traced to the legacies of neoliberal restructuring, as well as the structural limitations imposed by the nature of the capitalist state itself. Quite apart from the lingering market-oriented policies within MERCSOUR and UNASUR (particularly around the IIRSA), the landscape of post-hegemonic regionalism assumes a tense co-existence with ongoing neoliberal projects, particularly the newly formed Pacific Alliance (see Nelson, 2021). Finally, with respect to the ALBA-TCP, the reproduction of resource dependence, as well as the relative disorganization of regional institutions, brings to the foreground the immense challenges faced by radical social forces seeking to challenge the power of elite privilege in order to realize Martí's dream of *Nuestra América*.

Conclusion

This article offered a historical reconstruction of Latin America's long road to regionalism in the context of the changing material and territorial configurations of global capitalism. Capital's continued revolution in the productive forces, and the spatial complexes these engendered, eventually gave rise to the advent of continental history, and the material possibility for the creation of regional societies.

With the defeat of early regional contenders in the first half of the twentieth century, the US-led world order would eventually consecrate the regionalization of world politics. As with much else during the early Cold War years, US geopolitical strategy was refracted through containing the communist 'menace', which more often than not appeared in the active formation of regional 'security communities'. Yet neglect of development diplomacy would simply stoke the fires of subaltern resistance against the new global order. It was precisely this danger of subaltern insurgency that informed the economic and geopolitical strategies of the US Fordist compact.

The systemic crisis of the capitalist world economy beginning in the late 1960s ushered in a transition away from discourses of national development and political inclusiveness (however fleeting these may have been in practice) and towards a new form of social discipline and regional integration based on the invisible hand of the (global) market. The inter- and trans-national class offensive against subaltern groups in Latin America launched by the US and fractions of Latin American ruling classes led to a reorganization of the region's class structures. Yet the severity of neoliberal discipline had merely ensured its own downfall. The myriad social struggles that wracked the Latin American continent laid the foundations for a renewed left-wing insurgency in both the streets and the ballot box.

While the emergence of post-hegemonic regionalism signalled a new phase in Latin America's long road, the various projects it spawned – from UNASUR to the ALBA-TCP – were caught within a contradictory bind of furthering the accumulation of ground-rent for the sake of social development. And the regional expression of the second incorporation of the popular sectors into political channels of power and decision making were often more symbolic than real. Instead, incorporation embodied a top-down process of social redistribution, one that was always tied to the health of extractive capital. With the resurgence of the Latin American right in recent years, the reconfiguration of Latin American regionalism is now at a crossroads (cf. Serbin et al., 2016), leading either to a regressive return to neoliberal orthodoxy or a renewed postliberal regionalism that may yet overcome the limitations of progressive politics of the early twenty-first century.

Notes

1. The 'turning point' of intensive growth refers to the initial moment of a sustained rise in per capita output.
2. This timing also helps to account for the importation of Atlantic (British/US) farm technology into Argentina during its turning point (Pineda, 2018).
3. The Rio Pact of 1947 and the subsequent Bogotá summit of 1948 would culminate in the Organization of American States (OAS), which effectively embodied the institutional expression of US imperial domination within the region (van der Pijl, 2006, p. 180).

4. However, the recently elected left-wing president, Luis Arce, has proclaimed Bolivia's intention to re-join the ALBA-TCP (*ATB Digital*, 2021).

Acknowledgements

I would like to extend my deepest thanks to Laleh Khalili and the three anonymous reviewers for their helpful comments and feedback. The usual disclaimers apply.

Disclosure statement

No potential conflict of interest was reported by the author(s).

ORCID

Rowan Lubbock http://orcid.org/0000-0002-1517-130X

References

Adelman, J. (1994). *Frontier development: Land, labour and capital on the wheatlands of Argentina and Canada, 1890–1914*. Clarendon Press.
Albertone, M. (2016). *National identity and the agrarian republic: The transatlantic commerce of ideas between America and France (1750–1830)*. Routledge.
Arrighi, G. (2006). *The long twentieth century: Money, power, and the Origins of Our times*. Verso.
ATB Digital. (2021, Febrero 2). Bolivia retoma su participación plena en el ALBA-TCP, CELAC y UNASUR. https://www.atb.com.bo/sociedad/bolivia-retoma-su-participación-plena-en-el-alba-tpc-celac-y-unasur
Barbier, E. B. (2010). *Scarcity and frontiers: How economies have developed through natural resource exploitation*. Cambridge University Press.
Barkan, J. (2013). *Corporate sovereignty: Law and government under capitalism*. University of Minnesota Press.
Bauerly, B. (2017). *The agrarian seeds of empire: The political economy of agriculture in US state building*. Brill.
Billington, R. A., & Ridge, M. (2001). *Westward expansion. A history of the American frontier*. University of New Mexico Press.
Boatright, M. C. (1941). The myth of frontier individualism. *The Southwestern Social Science Quarterly*, *22*(1), 14–32.
Boito, A., & Berringer, T. (2014). Social classes, neodevelopmentalism, and Brazilian foreign policy under presidents Lula and Dilma. *Latin American Perspectives*, *41*(5), 94–109. https://doi.org/10.1177/0094582X14543790
Bolívar, S., & Chávez Frías, H. (2009). *The Bolívarian revolution*. Verso.
Botto, M. (2021). The challenges of economic integration in Latin America: Searching for consensus in contexts of globalization. The case of MERCOSUR (1991–2019). *Globalizations*. Advance online publication. https://doi.org/10.1080/14747731.2021.1962037

Brandt, L. (1993). Interwar Japanese agriculture: Revisionist views on the impact of the colonial rice policy and the labor-surplus hypothesis. *Explorations in Economic History, 30*(3), 259–293. https://doi.org/10.1006/exeh.1993.1011
Briceño Ruiz, J. (2012). New left governments, civil society and constructing a social dimension in Mercosur. In B. Cannon & P. Kirby (Eds.), *Civil society and the state in left-led Latin America: Challenges and limitations to democratization* (pp. 173–186). Zed Books.
Briceño-Ruiz, J., & Hoffmann, A. R. (2015). Post-hegemonic regionalism, UNASUR, and the reconfiguration of regional cooperation in South America. *Canadian Journal of Latin American and Caribbean Studies, 40* (1), 48–62. http://dx.doi.org/10.1080/08263663.2015.1031475
Bunker, S. G. (1988). *Underdeveloping the Amazon: Extraction, unequal exchange, and the failure of the modern state.* University of Chicago Press.
Capannelli, G., & Kawai, M. (Eds.). (2014). *The political economy of Asian regionalism.* Springer.
Carranza, M. E. (2006). Clinging together: Mercosur's ambitious external agenda, its internal crisis, and the future of regional economic integration in South America. *Review of International Political Economy, 13*(5), 802–829. https://doi.org/10.1080/09692290600950662
Chakrabarty, D. (2008). *Provincializing Europe. Postcolonial thought and historical difference.* Princeton University Press.
Chandler, A. (1990). *Scale and scope: The dynamics of industrial capitalism.* Harvard University Press.
Chandler, D. (1989). Peace through disunion: Father Juan José de Aycinena and the fall of the Central American Federation. *The Americas, 46*(2), 137–157. https://doi.org/10.2307/1007080
Chodor, T. (2021). The changing face of Mercosur: Legitimacy and the politics of scale in South American regionalism. *JCMS: Journal of Common Market Studies, 59*(2), 417–431. https://doi.org/10.1111/jcms.13200
Ciccantell, P. (2001). NAFTA and the reconstruction of US hegemony: The raw materials foundations of economic competitiveness. *Canadian Journal of Sociology, 26*(1), 47–65. https://doi.org/10.2307/3341511
Ciupa, K. (in press). Shifting tides, regional reverberations: A class-relational analysis of the ALBA-TCP. *Globalizations.*
Cocks, P. (1980). Towards a Marxist theory of European integration. *International Organization, 34*(1), 1–40. https://doi.org/10.1017/S0020818300003957
Collingham, L. (2018). *The hungry empire. How Britain's quest for food shaped the modern world.* Vintage.
Cooper, A. F., Hughes, C. W., & Lombaerde, P. (Eds.). (2008). *Regionlisation and global governance: The taming of globalization.* Routledge.
Cusack, A. K. (2018). *Venezuela, ALBA, and the limits of postneoliberal regionalism in Latin America and the Caribbean.* Palgrave.
Davidson, N. (2010). Many capitals, many states: Contingency, logic or mediation? In A. Anievas (Ed.), *Marxism and world politics* (pp. 77–93). Routledge.
Deas, M. (1987). Venezuela, Colombia and Ecuador. In L. Bethell (Ed.), *Spanish America after independence, c. 1820–1870* (pp. 207–238). Cambridge University Press.
di Tella, G. (1982). The economics of the frontier. In C. P. Kindleberger & G. di Tella (Eds.), *Economics in the long view. Essays in honour of W. W. Rostow* (pp. 210–227). Macmillan.
Duncan Baretta, S., & Markoff, J. (1978). Civilization and barbarism: Cattle frontiers in Latin America. *Comparative Studies in Society and History, 20*(4), 587–620. https://doi.org/10.1017/S0010417500012561
Estay, J. (2018). Past and present in Latin American regionalisms, in the face of economic reprimarization. In E. Vivares (Ed.), *Regionalism development and the post-commodities boom in South America* (pp. 47–76). Palgrave.
Fawcett, L. (2005). The origins and development of the regional idea in the Americas. In L. Fawcett & M. Serrano (Eds.), *Regionalism and governance in the Americas: Continental drift* (pp. 25–51). Palgrave.
Fawn, R. (2009). "Regions" and their study: Wherefrom, what for and whereto? *Review of International Studies, 35*(S1), 5–34. https://doi.org/10.1017/S0260210509008419
Fioramonti, L. (Ed.). (2012). *Regions and crises: New challenges for contemporary regionalisms.* Palgrave.
Fitzsimons, A., & Guevara, S. (2016). Transnational corporations and the "restructuring" of the Argentine automotive industry: Change or continuity? In G. Charnock & G. Starosta (Eds.), *The new international division of labour. Global transformation and uneven development* (pp. 183–214). Palgrave.
Friedmann, H. (1990). The origins of third world food dependence. In H. Bernstein, B. Crow, M. Mackintosh, & C. Martin (Eds.), *The food question: Profits versus people?* (pp. 13–31). Earthscan.

Fuentes, L., & Durán, G. (2018). Cities in the South American development: Bogota, Lima, Quito, and Santiago in regional frame. In E. Vivares (Ed.), *Regionalism development and the post-commodities boom in South America* (pp. 217–242). Palgrave.
Gardini, G. L. (2010). *The origins of MERCOSUR: Democracy and regionalization in South America*. Palgrave.
Grandin, G. (2007). *Empire's workshop: Latin America, the United States, and the rise of the new imperialism*. Holt.
Haas, E. B., & Schmitter, P. C. (1964). Economics and differential patterns of political integration: Projections about unity in Latin America. *International Organization*, *18*(4), 705–737. https://doi.org/10.1017/S0020818300025297
Haastrup, T., & Yong-Soon, E. (Eds.). (2014). *Regionalizing global crises: The financial crisis and new frontiers in regional governance*. Palgrave.
Heffernan, M. (2003). Fin de siecle, fin du monde? On the origins of European geopolitics, 1890–1920. In K. Dodds & D. Atkinson (Eds.), *Geopolitical traditions. A century of geopolitical thought* (pp. 27–51). Routledge.
Hermann, C. (2016). Another "lost decade?" Crisis and structural adjustment in Europe and Latin America. *Globalizations*, *14*(4), 519–534. https://doi.org/10.1080/14747731.2016.1236464
Higginbottom, A. (2013). The political economy of foreign investment in Latin America: Dependency revisited. *Latin American Perspectives*, *190*(3), 184–206. https://doi.org/10.1177/0094582X13479304
Holdar, S. (1992). The ideal state and the power of geography. The life-work of Rudolf Kjellén. *Political Geography*, *11*(3), 307–323. https://doi.org/10.1016/0962-6298(92)90031-N
Hurrell, A. (1995). Explaining the resurgence of regionalism in world politics. *Review of International Studies*, *21*(4), 331–358. https://doi.org/10.1017/S0260210500117954
Jacobs, J. E., & Maldonado, M. (2005). Civil society in Argentina: Opportunities and challenges for national and transnational organisation. *Journal of Latin American Studies*, *37*(1), 141–172. https://doi.org/10.1017/S0022216X04008557
Kanai, J. M. (2016). The pervasiveness of neoliberal territorial design: Cross-border infrastructure planning in South America since the introduction of IIRSA. *Geoforum; Journal of Physical, Human, and Regional Geosciences*, *69*, 160–170. https://doi.org/10.1016/j.geoforum.2015.10.002
Katzenstein, P. J. (2005). *A world of regions: Asia and Europe in the American imperium*. Cornell University Press.
Kay, C. (2004). Rural livelihoods and peasant futures. In R. N. Gwynne & C. Kay (Eds.), *Latin America transformed: Globalization and modernity* (pp. 232–250). Hodder.
Kiely, R. (2005). *The clash of globalisations: Neo-liberalism, the third war and anti-globalisation*. Brill.
Klarman, M. J. (2016). *The framers' coup: The making of the United States constitution*. Oxford University Press.
Konings, M. (2009). The construction of US financial power. *Review of International Studies*, *35*(1), 69–94. https://doi.org/10.1017/S026021050900833X
Kühnhardt, L. (2010). *Region-building. Volume I: The global proliferation of regional integration*. Berghahn Books.
Lombaerde, P., Baert, F., & Felício, T. (Eds.). (2012). *The United Nations and the regions: Third world report on regional integration*. Springer.
Lubbock, R. (2017). *Spaces of agrarian struggle: ALBA, La Via Campesina and the politics of "food sovereignty"* [PhD thesis]. Birkbeck, University of London.
Lubbock, R. (2020a). Rights, recognition and norms in the making of Latin American International Society: An historical materialist interpretation. *Journal of International Relations and Development*, *23*(2), 237–261. https://doi.org/10.1057/s41268-018-0142-4
Lubbock, R. (2020b). The social contradictions of regional development in the ALBA-TCP: The case of food production. *New Political Economy*, *25*(2), 213–230. https://doi.org/10.1080/13563467.2019.1586863
Macpherson, W. J. (1995). *The economic development of Japan 1868–1941*. Cambridge University Press.
Mandel, E. (1986). *The meaning of the Second World War*. Verso.
Manfield, E. D., & Miller, H. V. (Eds.). (1997). *The political economy of regionalism*. Colombia University Press.
Martí, J. (1977). *Nuestra américa*. Ayacucho.

Martin, P. A. (1918). The influence of the United States on the opening of the Amazon to the world's commerce. *Hispanic American Historical Review, 1*(2), 146–162.

Matsumura, W. (2016). The expansion of the Japanese empire and the rise of the global agrarian question after the First World War. In A. Anievas (Ed.), *Cataclysm 1914. The First World War and the making of modern world politics* (pp. 144–173). Haymarket.

Mazoyer, M., & Roudart, L. (2006). *A history of world agriculture: From the Neolithic age to the current crisis.* Earthscan.

Mazzuca, S. (2021). *Latecomer state formation. Political geography and capacity failure in Latin America.* Yale University Press.

McCormick, T. J. (1989). *America's half-century. United States foreign policy in the cold war.* John Hopkins University Press.

Milenky, E. S. (1973). *The politics of regional organization in Latin America: The Latin American Free Trade Association.* Praeger.

Milonakis, D., & Fine, B. (2009). *From political economy to economics: Method, the social and the historical in the evolution of economic theory.* Routledge.

Mistry, P. S. (2003). New regionalism and economic development. In F. Soderbaum & T. M. Shaw (Eds.), *Theories of new regionalism. A Palgrave reader* (pp. 117–139). Palgrave.

Moore, J. W. (2002). Remaking work, remaking space: Spaces of production and accumulation in the reconstruction of American capitalism, 1865–1920. *Antipode, 34*(2), 176–204. https://doi.org/10.1111/1467-8330.00235

Moore, J. W. (2010). The end of the road? Agricultural revolutions in the capitalist world-ecology, 1450-2010. *Journal of Agrarian Change, 10*(3), 389–413.

Muhr, T. (2011). *Venezuela and the ALBA: Counter-hegemony, geographies of integration and development, and higher education for all.* VDM.

Muñoz, H. (2001). Good-bye U.S.A.? In J. S. Tulchin & R. H. Espach (Eds.), *Latin America in the new international system* (pp. 73–90). Lynne Rienner.

Murphy, C. (2005). *Global institutions, marginalization, and development.* Routledge.

Nelson, M. (2021). The pacific alliance: Regional Integration as neoliberal discipline. *Globalizations.* Advance online publication. https://doi.org/10.1080/14747731.2021.1945394

Nogués, J., & Quintanilla, R. (1993). Latin America's integration and the multilateral trading system. In J. D. Melo & A. Panagariya (Eds.), *New dimensions in regional integration* (pp. 278–313). Cambridge University Press.

Nolan, M. (1994). *Visions of modernity: American business and the modernization of Germany.* Oxford University Press.

Ortiz, R. J. (2014). Agro-industrialization, petrodollar illusions and the transformation of the capitalist world economy in the 1970s: The Latin American experience. *Critical Sociology, 42*(4–5), 599–621. https://doi.org/10.1177/0896920514540187

Patomäki, H., & Teivainen, T. (2002). Critical responses to neoliberal globalization in the Mercosur region: Roads towards cosmopolitan democracy? *Review of International Political Economy, 9*(1), 37–71. https://doi.org/10.1080/09692290110101144

Paul, T. V. (Ed.). (2012). *International relations theory and regional transformation.* Cambridge University Press.

Pearce, S. (2013). *Twenty-first century countertrade: The case of Venezuela, 2004–2011* [PhD thesis]. Queen Mary University.

Peck, J. (2010). *Ideal illusions: How the U.S. government co-opted human rights.* Metropolitan Books.

Pezzola, A. A. (2018). The deep roots of protectionism in the southern cone: Constituent interests and Mercosur's common external tariff. *Latin American Politics and Society, 60*(4), 69–92. https://doi.org/10.1017/lap.2018.42

Phillips, N. (2004). *The southern cone model: The political economy of regional capitalist development in Latin America.* Routledge.

Pieck, S. K. (2015). "To be led differently": Neoliberalism, road construction, and NGO counter-conducts in Peru. *Geoforum; Journal of Physical, Human, and Regional Geosciences, 64*, 304–313. https://doi.org/10.1016/j.geoforum.2013.06.011

Pineda, Y. (2018). Farm machinery users, designers, and government policy in Argentina, 1861–1930. *Agricultural History, 92*(3), 351–379. https://doi.org/10.3098/ah.2018.092.3.351
Plaza, G. (1959). For a regional market in Latin America. *Foreign Affairs, 37*(4), 607–616. https://doi.org/10.2307/20029382
Portes, A. (1985). Latin American class structures: Their composition and change during the last decades. *Latin American Research Review, 20*(3), 7–39.
Portes, A., & Hoffman, K. (2003). Latin American class structures: Their composition and change during the neoliberal era. *Latin American Research Review, 38*(1), 41–82. https://doi.org/10.1353/lar.2003.0011
Post, C. (2011). *The American road to capitalism: Studies in class-structure, economic development and political conflict, 1620–1877*. Brill.
Puntigliano, A. R. (2011). "Geopolitics of integration" and the imagination of South America. *Geopolitics, 16*(4), 846–864. https://doi.org/10.1080/14650045.2010.549863
Puntigliano, A. R. (2013). Geopolitics and integration: A South American perspective. In A. R. Puntigliano & J. Briceño-Ruiz (Eds.), *Resilience of regionalism in Latin America and the Caribbean* (pp. 19–52). Palgrave.
Rice. R. (2021): Indigenous regionalism in the Andes. *Globalizations*. Advance online publication. https://doi.org/10.1080/14747731.2021.1907734
Riggirozzi, P. (2014). Regionalism through social policy: Collective action and health diplomacy in South America. *Economy and Society, 43*(3), 432–454. https://doi.org/10.1080/03085147.2014.881598
Riggirozzi, P., & Tussie, D. (2012). *The rise of post-hegemonic regionalism*. Springer.
Rocchi, F. (2006). *Chimneys in the desert: Industrialization in Argentina during the export boom years, 1870–1930*. Stanford University Press.
Rosset, P. M., Barbosa, L. P., Val, V. & McCune, N. (2021). Critical Latin American agroecology as a regionalism from below. *Globalizations*. Advance online publication. https://doi.org/10.1080/14747731.2021.1923353
Rossi, F. M. (2018). Social movements and the second wave of (territorial) incorporation in Latin America. In E. Silva & F. M. Rossi (Eds.), *Reshaping the political arena in Latin America. From resisting neoliberalism to the second incorporation* (pp. 23–31). University of Pittsburgh Press.
Rugman, A. M., & Verbeke, A. (2004). A perspective on regional and global strategies of multinational enterprises. *Journal of International Business Studies, 35*(1), 3–18. https://doi.org/10.1057/palgrave.jibs.8400073
Rupert, M. (1995). *Producing hegemony: The politics of mass production and US global power*. Cambridge University Press.
Saguier, M. I. (2010). The hemispheric social alliance and the free trade area of the Americas process: The challenges and opportunities of transnational coalitions against neo-liberalism. *Globalizations, 4*(2), 251–265. https://doi.org/10.1080/14747730701345267
Salgado, P. L. D. (2017). *The peculiarity of Brazilian state-formation in geopolitical context: The challenge of eurocentrism in international relations and political Marxism* [PhD thesis]. University of Sussex.
Samuels, R. J. (1994). *"Rich nation, strong army": National security and the technological transformation of Japan*. Cornell University Press.
Sanahuja, J. A. (2008-9). "Del regionalism abierto" al "regionalismo post-liberal". Crisis y cambio en la integración latinoamericana. In L. Martínez Alfonso, L. Peña & M. Vazquez (Eds.), *Anuario de la Integración Regional en América Latina y el Gran Caribe* (No. 7, pp. 11–53). CRIES.
Selva, S. (2017). *Before the neoliberal turn: The rise of energy finance and the limits to US foreign economic policy*. Palgrave.
Serbin, A., Martínez, L., Ramanzini, H., & Pont, A. S. (Eds.). (2016). *América Latina y el Caribe frente a la encrucijada actual de la globalización: Anuario de la Integración Regional de América Latina y el Caribe, No. 13*. CRIES.
Silva, E. (2009). *Challenging neoliberalism in Latin America*. Cambridge University Press.
Silva, E. (Ed.). (2013). *Transnational activism and national movements in Latin America. Bridging the divide*. Routledge.
Smith, N. (2003). *American empire: Roosevelt's geographer and the prelude to globalization*. University of California Press.
Smith, R. S. (1963). Financing the Central American Federation, 1821–1838. *Hispanic American Historical Review, 43*(4), 483–510.

Smith, W. D. (1980). Friedrich Ratzel and the origins of Lebensraum. *German Studies Review, 3*(1), 51–68. https://doi.org/10.2307/1429483
Söderbaum, F. (2004). *The political economy of regionalism: The case of Southern Africa*. Palgrave.
Spalding, R. J. (2008). Neoliberal regionalism and resistance in Mesoamerica: Foro Mesoamericano opposition in plan Puebla-Panama and CAFTA. In R. Stahler-Sholk, H. E. Vanden, & G. D. Kuecker (Eds.), *Latin American social movements in the twenty-first century* (pp. 323–336). Rowman and Littlefield.
Svampa, M. (2015). Commodities consensus: Neoextractivism and enclosure of the commons in Latin America. *South Atlantic Quarterly, 114*(1), 65–82. https://doi.org/10.1215/00382876-2831290
Tarrow, S. (2005). *The new transnational activism*. University of Cambridge Press.
Teschke, B. (2011). Decisions and indecisions: Political and intellectual receptions of Carl Schmitt. *New Left Review, 67*(2), 61–95.
Topik, S. (1985). The state's contribution to the development of Brazil's internal economy, 1850–1930. *Hispanic American Historical Review, 65*(2), 203–228.
van der Pijl, K. (2006). *Global rivalries: From the cold war to Iraq*. Verso.
van der Pijl, K. (2014). *The discipline of western supremacy: Modes of foreign relations and political economy, volume III*. Pluto Press.
Van Dijck, P. (2008). Troublesome construction: The rationale and risks of IIRSA. *Revista Europea de Estudios Latinoamericanos y del Caribe/European Review of Latin American and Caribbean Studies, 85* (85), 101–120. https://doi.org/10.18352/erlacs.9621
Vázquez, M. (2008). Los escenarios de participación social en el Mercosur. In G. Jaramillo (Ed.), *Los nuevos enfoques de la integración: más allá del regionalismo* (pp. 137–148). FLACSO.
Zibechi, R. (2006). IIRSA: la integración a la medida de los mercados. *Ecología política, 31*, 19–26.

The challenges of economic integration in Latin America: searching for consensus in contexts of globalization. The case of MERCOSUR (1991–2019)

Mercedes Botto

ABSTRACT

This paper analyses the trajectory of MERCOSUR from a critical historical perspective. This interpretation presents an alternative to more Eurocentric approaches to regionalism, which tends to view MERCOSUR as a failed integration process due to the inability of governments to build supranational institutions in the image of the European Union. In contrast, I analyse MERCOSUR as a field of contestation between visions of autonomy or dependence. Consensus between national actors with different visions, material capacities and institutions varied over time with direct effects on the correlation of political forces. However, the results of this dispute remain strongly tied to the international division of labour. To demonstrate this idea, this article moves through three stages of MERCOSUR, identifying the changes in terms of consensus and dissent between national governments around the regional institutional framework and its external realignment.

1. Introduction

Latin American regionalism emerges from a political project spanning all the way back to the early nineteenth century as an outcome of the struggle from independence. In the 1960s this idea reappeared economically, promoting the integration of expanded markets with high tariff barriers with respect to third countries, and strengthening trade in industrial manufactures produced in the region. In this way, economic regionalism echoed the idea that, through equal cooperation, it was possible to break the situation of dependence that bound Latin American economics with the fate of developing countries more generally (Prébisch, 1963; cf. Sunkel, 1995).

MERCOSUR takes up this integrationist aspiration, but it does so in an international and regional context very different from the previous one. The end of the Cold War and the great technological advances of the late 1980s fuelled the expectation that economic globalization would bring benefits for all. Accompanying this expectation was the creation of new modes of economic interdependence, deregulation, new global governance institutions (such as the World Trade Organisation), and proliferation of Regional Integration Agreements (Bergsten, 1997; Stallings, 1995). Rather than promoting states' freedom of action, as had occurred with protected or closed integration, open regionalism carves out new spaces of accumulation for the benefit of transnational capital seeking investment markets and flexible terms of production and export (Cox & Sinclair, 1996; Robinson, 2008).

The southern cone governments' decision to join this wave was not only motivated by the promise of greater economic growth and Foreign Direct Investment (FDI), but through the changing balance of political forces within domestic contexts (see inter alia Carranza, 2003; Doctor, 2013; Kaltenthaler & Mora, 2002). These included the necessity to consolidate democratic regimes in the face of attempts at destabilization by outgoing military governments, and the reform processes that were being carried out simultaneously, which severely weakened protectionist lobbies. However, when deciding their scope and governance model, governments departed from the global paradigm cantered on a free trade area, and opted instead on the creation of a common market, where national states would commit to intervene more actively in the regional governance model through common external tariffs (Bid, 2002; Phillips, 2003; Gomez-Mera, 2008).

The results of this decision were initially successful: prime tariff liberalization and the creation of an external tariff led to rapid growth in trade, FDI and productive integration of the automotive sector (see Tables 1 and 2). However, by 1998 growth slowed, and after unilateral currency devaluations by Brazil and Argentina, MERCOSUR entered a deep political crisis that threatened its continuity over time. Since then, MERCOSUR has undergone a process of institutional deconstruction in which the initial commitments to achieve a customs union and joint external position have not been fulfilled. On the contrary, commitments have been made more flexible in practice with the implicit consent of the parties on their non-compliance, while trade negotiations with third countries are carried out bilaterally by each member country and subsequently validated at the regional level (Botto, 2015, p. 20).

The 'crisis or integration', and the successive attempts to revive it, has generated a proliferation of works that analyse the performance of MERCOSUR from a 'problem-solving' perspective and from top-down logic, according to which the success or failure of an integration is measured by its ability to build institutions (see Cox, 1981). For these authors, the history of Latin American regionalism begins and ends with European integration and the institutional schemes formulated around this experience (see Vivares & Dolcetti-Marcolini, 2015). Some of these works stress the role of agency, focusing on the concentration of power in the executive and the hyper-presidential style of the governments of the region (Carranza, 2003; Kaltenthaler & Mora, 2002; Malamud, 2013),[1] others, such as Pezzola (2018) highlight the importance of national lobbies and other domestic groups in defining or shaping national positions.[2] Finally, authors such as Caichiolo (2017) centre on the need to promote civil society participation in regional decision-making processes, which, like the MERCOSUR parliament, would help generate regional interests and preferences beyond the national interest.

A second area of scholarship sheds light on the factors linked to MERCOSUR's social and economic structure. Burges (2008), for instance, speaks of the low level of productive interdependence between the region's economies, measured in trade, investment and/or physical interconnection, while others, such as Doctor (2013), point to the broader structural and competitive asymmetries that separate member countries. Finally, authors such as Blyde (2006) show that this initial

Table 1. Intra-regional trade in MERCOSUR (1991–1998).

Countries	1994–1998 (%)	1999–2002 (%)	2003–2010 (%)	2011–2015 (%)
Argentina	34	28	22	24
Brasil	15	11	10	10
Paraguay	55	79	61	42
Uruguay	50	41	28	26

Source: Botto (2017).

Table 2. Foreign investments flows (1990–2006).

Years	Argentina (%)	Brasil (%)	Paraguay (%)	Uruguay (%)	MERCOSUR (%)
1990–1994	64.3	32.3	2.0	1.4	100
1995–1998	31	67	0.9	0.6	100
1999–2002	27.6	71.5	0.2	0.7	100
2003–2006	19.7	76.3	0.4	3.6	100

Source: Botto (2017).

asymmetry, measured in income distribution, was expanded throughout MERCOSUR and was largely a consequence of measures taken or omitted by governments at the regional level.[3]

In contrast, this article offers a more critical historical perspective on the formation and evolution of MERCOSUR. Firstly, I frame the analysis of MERCOSUR as part of a broader and longer-term collective construction process, recognizing the importance of the global context in its current trajectory. Secondly, I use the concept of regionalism (and not regional integration) because it allows to capture more flexible forms of regional cooperation, in which economic and political logics that feed each other coexist, without necessarily prevailing over each other (Riggirozzi, 2012).

However, I recognize, as with previous studies, MERCOSUR's relative failure in terms of becoming a more equal regional development instrument. This failure is not linked to the type of institutionality *per se*, but to the difficulty of governments reaching minimum consensus on national and regional development models.[4] In this sense, as I will demonstrate in this article, MERCOSUR has been (and continues to be) a contested regional space between major national actors, which becomes further complicated by both the re-configuration of private actors shaping the strategic choices of policy-makers, as well as broader global dynamics and forces (cf. Phillips, 2003).

To demonstrate this idea, I will analyse MERCOSUR's trajectory from its origins until 2019, dividing it into the three stages of ideological convergence among national leaders. In each stage, I identify the main consensus and dissent of governments around the construction and scope of the customs union. As Pezzola (2018) notes, the customs union is a key element on which regional governance is structured and MERCOSUR's international strategy is defined.

The work is divided into two parts. The first characterizes the two paradigms or ideological visions that have flowed over the history of economic regionalism in Latin America and which maintain a contradictory presence in MERCOSUR. The second outlines how these models were reflected in the discussions and decisions that MERCOSUR was taking on its institutional construction.

2. Competing models of Latin American regional integration

Broadly speaking, there are two opposite regional development paradigms in Latin America. They are not abstract models, but rather choices that evolved from ideas embedded in Latin American historical experience and the region's insertion into global capitalism (Vivares, 2018).

2.1. A 'closed' regional model

The first model known as 'Closed Regionalism' focuses on production diversification through a process of industrialization based on the substitution of imports in order to ensure better domestic employment levels and income distribution. Led by Raúl Prebish working within the United

Nations Economic Commission for Latin America (ECLA) devised and promoted this model, ECLA economists believed that Latin America's fundamental problem originated from external disequilibrium and pressure due to the persistent disparate tendencies of international demand and their consequences on exports, as well as the relative prices of traded goods (Prébisch, 1963). The industrialized states established their economies through the supply of cheap resources extracted from the less-industrialized states. This latter group of states is thus forced to buy industrial products at higher relative prices in order to stimulate their own industrial development.

The rationale behind this theory is that this external disequilibrium is neither situational nor transitory but structural (hence the name 'structuralism'). For the ECLA, the only way to reverse this situation is to modify the traditional approach: Latin America should abandon the classical development strategy based on the export of primary products with static comparative advantages, and replace it with an autonomous development model based on import-substitution industrialization (ISI).

In order to achieve this structural transformation, national governments had to initiate a process of industrialization in which the national state would become a key actor (cf. Grigera, 2015). Their participation was indispensable both in planning tasks and in public investment in national public and private companies. It also required a significant concentration of public power in strategic areas, such as science and technology, and in income distribution policies, whether through employment or land ownership. Only through these reforms could continuous development and well-being for the population be achieved.

In this ISI process, regional strategies play a crucial role, since the creation of a common market would allow national governments to resolve new obstacles as ISI eventually deepens (Briceño-Ruiz, 2017). Even though the first phase of ISI, focusing on consumption goods, appears to be simple and easily attainable by increasing import tariffs, the extension of this to durable goods and capital goods in the following phases requires larger production and consumption markets. Therefore, regional coordination and the creation of supranational institutions are necessary in order to ensure the formation of a regional market, ensure public well-being and distribute costs and benefits more equitably among member states (Prébisch, 1963).

2.2. An 'open' regional integration model

In light of the relative failure of regional ISI,[5] the 1980s saw the introduction of a new paradigm in the form of 'Open Regionalism'. This regional development model suggests that states should open their economy and participate in the global market, by enhancing domestic firms' competitiveness and improving the country's production capacity in global commodity chains. In order to achieve this competitive development model, the Washington Consensus broke down the strategy into three levels. At the national level, it recommends (1) fiscal discipline; (2) redirecting public expenditure; (3) tax reform; (4) financial liberalization; (5) adoption of a single, competitive exchange rate; (6) trade liberalization; (7) elimination of barriers to foreign direct investment; (8) privatization of state-owned enterprises; (9) deregulation of market entry and competition; and (10) secure property rights (Williamson, 1990).

At the regional level, the open regional integration model supports the creation of a free trade area, as a flexible and non-bureaucratized organization. A free trade area meets two requirements from global corporations to invest in the region: to ensure the elimination of constraints and tariff barriers, which would reduce intraregional transaction costs, and also guarantee an externally oriented investment strategy for the member states, in proportion to their size. Unlike closed integration schemes, like customs unions or common markets, this model does not require strong commitments for the future in terms of regional policies or bureaucratic capacity. Thus, the largest economies are freer to exert their regional leadership role, including financing structural compensation instruments that would reduce the intra-regional asymmetry generated by the uneven distribution of costs and benefits amongst member states.

Finally, at the global level, open regionalism was expected to contribute to the multilateral liberalization process promoted from the WTO. In this sense and in opposition to open regionalism, external economic relations do not presuppose a joint action plan with third countries; this model suggests that each country defines its own policy with extra-regional. Yet, according to the IDB's recommendations on this matter, each one should prioritize closer economic linkages with developed countries (BID/IADB, 2002). In the specific case of Latin America, it argues that North–South free trade agreements are more attractive for FDI than South-South agreements. In the first place, they could ensure the conditions for 'natural' production complementarity, where the developed countries provide investment and technology and peripheral countries supply cheap labour, a consumption market, and/or natural resources. Secondly, these North–South agreements are more effective at the time of consolidating unilateral structural reforms, because, on the one hand, they include new regulatory subjects (such as investments, intellectual property, or labour), and on the other hand, strong penalties for noncompliance that discourage breaches of agreement or backtracking.

In Latin America, the implementation of the open regionalism model was 'successful' only in the case of the North American Free Trade Agreement (currently known as USMCA) in which Mexico joined the United States and Canada.[6] And yet, in the case of MERCOSUR states, it has become the hegemonic approach to region-building in recent decades (IADB/BID, 2002, pp. 46–47). Indeed, unlike the previous ISI paradigm, the 'Open Regionalism' development model was devised and promoted by the Global North, and arrived in the Global South through regional actors and organizations, such as the Inter-American Development Bank in the Latin American case. But it quickly found its way into the ECLAC, revamped under a new document, *Changing Production Patterns with Social Equity* (ECLAC, 1990). The text criticized the insufficient development of the ISI period and proposed a more selective model of industrialization that could participate in global commodity chains in order to capture more value-added. The starting point of this 'neostructuralist' development model also begins at the national level, identifying industrial sectors with comparative advantages in sectors like electronics, metalworking, chemicals, energy infrastructure, transport, and telecommunication. These endogenous focal points for 'technological specialization hubs' would make it possible to create more supply chains with new sectors and new countries (Bielschowsky, 1998; Sunkel, 1995). In this scheme, the state played a fundamental role in facilitating social and infrastructure projects through social policies, institutional reforms, and investment in research and development. The precepts of neostructuralism became the defining feature of the Latin American left in the early twenty-first century, based on the reincorporation of the popular sectors and a larger role for state coordination within the economy. And yet, as we will see during MERCOSUR's 'productive' phase, neostructuralist development dovetailed with the hegemonic paradigm of open regionalism, in attempting to 'take the high road to globalization' by balancing social equity with regional insertion into the capitalist world economy (ECLAC, 1994; cf. Leiva, 2008).

3. The contested construction of MERCOSUR

To what extent were these competing ideas and theoretical proposals for Latin American integration carried out within MERCOSUR? Which one of the two models was chosen by the governments of member states? I argue that neither one of these two approaches *entirely* prevailed; elements of both merged their practices and institutions, accumulating incoherencies and inconsistencies over time. To demonstrate this contention, MERCOSUR's regional development policies will be analysed, revealing how these models combined in each period, identifying internal (in)coherence between the different dimensions and the type of consensus reached among them.

The historical trajectory of MERCOSUR will be divided into three periods, in which there were changes to national executives that generated ideological convergence, at least at the discursive level over the necessity to transform regional policy (Prieto Corredor & Betancourt Vélez, 2014). In practical terms, this shift is evident in the ongoing debate among member states over the extent of the customs union.

3.1. Commercial MERCOSUR (1991–2002)

Regarding national development, this first period was characterized by strong consensus between the regional leaders concerning domestic needs and emergencies, such as the consolidation of democratic regimes and ongoing structural reforms (see, *inter alia*, Kaltenthaler & Mora, 2002). At the regional level, however, the divergence of interests and preferences became more visible. Despite the shared understanding concerning the benefits of open integration, member states did not limit the design of the newly created institution to a free trade area. Rather, they agreed upon establishing a customs union, with a view to the creation of a common market. This founding moment also created 'the original sin of the MERCOSUR', on the grounds that the governments committed themselves to a substantive regionalization project without adequate conditions for minimum consensus on how to move forward (Botto, 2015). For instance, transnational social organizations, such as trade unions and governments of smaller economies – Paraguay and Uruguay – expected to emulate the European experience – namely, that the MERCOSUR would, over time, include macroeconomic coordination and regional production policies mediated through supranational institutions, so that regional development would be equitable (Meissner, 2017, p. 154). For semi-industrialized economies, in contrast, the expectation was focused on a common external tariff. It would not only protect the regional industry from global competition, but would also set up a captive market for the production and consumption of regionally manufactured goods. There was neither agreement nor explicit acknowledgement regarding the expected level of intraregional coordination (Malamud, 2013). By way of illustration, progress was made in signing three sectoral protocols related to investment and services under pressure from asymmetric negotiations; but none of them have been launched thus far (Botto & Bianculli, 2011; Botto & Peixoto, 2010). [7]

Likewise, there was no distributive policy for the costs and benefits of common tariffs amongst different countries, while the external tariff was hastily drawn up. There were highly unequal levels of material capacities and institutional resources between the four-member states. Indeed, the tariff nomenclature was tailored to Brazil's national development interests, shaped largely by domestic private interests (Botto, 2009; Pezzola, 2018). The automotive industry, which involved Argentina and Brazil, was exempt from the common external tariff and was protected under a special regime of 35%, which is equivalent to the consolidated tariff of the region in the WTO. The sugar sector was also excluded from tariff liberalization and target for special treatment due to the powerful lobby of local elites (Botto & Quiliconi, 2010; Pezzola, 2017). At the end of this period, the elimination of intraregional tariffs allowed the member states to immediately increase intraregional trade and FDI flows. Still, these results were short-lived, as they could not lay the foundation for continuous and equitably distributed growth in the region.

For Argentina, blanket commercial liberalization followed by the customs union had an adverse effect on its production activities, such as the deindustrialization and economic concentration within a few competitive sectors such as petrochemicals and steel, which benefited from privatization (Sanchez Bajo, 1999). In contrast, others with more resources and options, like Brazil, could use integration to strengthen and diversify their manufacturing industry for investments, with FDI flows concentrated towards low-risk assets, particularly the privatized utility sectors. The only production sector that reaped benefits from the customs union was the automotive sector, because it could obtain commodities and labour at low costs while selling their highly protected products against imports from extra-regional countries. Nonetheless, this had less to do with a regional production chain than with comparative advantages in terms of labour, commodities, and consumption markets. Apart from the lack of macroeconomic coordination and adjustment of the production structure, this uneven distribution of costs and benefits led to practices that, in the short-term, jeopardized the initial commitment (Blyde, 2006; Doctor, 2013).

Early dissents and conflicts between governments arose as a result of timing and commitments to trade liberalization. Smaller countries, as well as Argentina, resorted to non-compliance with deadlines or unilateral protection measures to defend those sectors with entrenched vested interests among local elites (Gomez-Mera, 2008). Nonetheless, it was the decisions taken by the larger economies that put integration in check.

In 1999, on the back of the global financial crisis, Brazil decided unilaterally to devalue its currency. This decision generated an uneven crisis throughout the bloc: FDI and Multinational Corporations (MNCs) were moved to Brazil to the detriment of Argentina. Intra-regional trade slowed between 1998 and 2003 and interdependence fell to 1991 levels (13%)

The consequences were expressed in institutional terms: trade conflicts multiplied, while tariff commitments were broken unilaterally. On foreign trade policy, the collective negotiations that

MERCOSUR was conducting, such as with the Andean community, were stopped. In their absence, Uruguay and Paraguay started a bilateral free trade agreement with the United States in view of a bilateral, which would lead to a rupture with MERCOSUR.

MERCOSUR's crisis could only be overcome with a political solution: the informal agreement sealed by Presidents Cardoso (1995–2002) and Menem (1989–1999) on the need to keep the region together in order to put a brake on to the advance of the US Free Trade Area of the Americas (FTAA) (Genna & Hiroi, 2007, pp. 49–51; Phillips, 2001). Finally, at the Buenos Aires summit, decision 32/00 was signed in which governments ratified the commitment to jointly negotiate trade agreements.

3.2. The productive MERCOSUR (2002–2015)

At the beginning of the twenty-first century, state forms across Latin America underwent a significant transformation, which subsequently re-shaped the ideas of region-building and its positioning within the prevailing world order (Chodor, 2015). Two facts marked this change of vision. At the domestic level, progressive governments came into power – Lula da Silva (2003–2010) in Brazil, Nestor Kirchner (2003–2007) in Argentina, Tabaré Vazquez in Uruguay (2005–2010) and Fernando Lugo (2008–2012) in Paraguay – shifting the ideological orientation of MERCOSUR. At the global level, the ideological hegemony of neoliberalism and trade liberalization came into serious question by both anti-globalization movements and the emergent group of Latin America's progressive governments (Silva, 2009). In this direction, MERCOSUR, in alliance with the Venezuelan President, Hugo Chávez, broke the negotiation for the Free Trade Area of the Americas (FTAA) with the United States in Mar del Plata summit (2004), as well as the negotiation agreement with the European Union (Nelson, 2015).

With the idea of breaking the initial profile of a commercial openness, and to bring back the idea of state intervention to promote industrialization and social development (as in closed regional integration) new governments defined this stage as the social and productive MERCOSUR (at the Cordoba Summit, 2006). In the first place, formal procedures were reformed, including: (1) the creation of a permanent court for commercial disputes, which unlike the previous dispute system was permanent and handled by regional judges; (2) the creation of a MERCOSUR's structural fund in order to reduce intraregional asymmetries; (3) adjustments were made to the timelines and mechanisms of implementation of the MERCOSUR provisions by member countries (Malamud, 2013). In the second place, priorities within the regional scheme were modified: instead of focusing solely on commercial policies, the scope was extended to coordination and integration of production. In this direction, there were talks concerning the inclusion of small and medium-sized enterprises (SMEs) into regional production chains with concerted assistance to regional firms through a guarantee fund. The rationale behind these initiatives was that the SMEs, not the large regional corporations (the so-called '*multilatinas*'), are both the essential source of employment and contributors to the internal regional market.

However, these initiatives were neither sufficient nor effective to change the established regional patterns of production/reproduction of the commercial MERCOSUR. One of several reasons was the lack of material resources and financial support, mainly from Brazil. Brazil was not only the strongest economy in the region, but it had also become its main beneficiary, especially post-2002 when trade had grown at an even higher rate than in the early days of MERCOSUR (Doctor, 2013).[8]

Between 2003 and 2010 intraregional trade grew by 15% but it never managed to recover to the previous level of 25% during the previous stage (see Table 1). The recovery was both in intra-regional exports (70%) composed of primary products, which grew even more than extra-regional exports (75%). The main beneficiary of this recovery was Brazil, which concentrated 60% of intra-zone exports, increasing structural asymmetries, this time to the detriment of Argentina (Table 1). MERCOSUR's productive integration was hindered by the inability or disinterest of governments, especially Brazil, to jointly develop competitive advantages through cross-sectoral specialization. In its absence, cross-sectoral trade was restricted to protected sectors, such as automobiles (Costa et al., 2018; Mecham, 2003).

Nonetheless, in this new context, Brazil's priorities were not centred on MERCOSUR, but refocused towards the global level (Phillips, 2001). In this vein, Lula faced a dual leadership strategy. In commercial terms, he focused on cooperation with developing countries from Africa, Asia, and the Middle East (Muhr, 2016); while in political terms, he prioritized its links within Latin America through the creation of the Union of South American Nations (*Unión de Naciones Suramericanas* – UNASUR in 2008) and the Community of Latin American and Caribbean states (*Comunidad de Estados Latinoamericanos y Caribeños* – CELAC, in 2010).

The second reason for the difficulty in implementing MERCOSUR's regional production policies is linked to the enhanced divergences within MERCOSUR around distinct development models. On the one hand, there were countries that sought to enhance the production of primary goods, where they had competitive advantages: such as the export of meat and cellulose in the case of Uruguay; *maquilas* (low value-added production) in Paraguay, and (after its incorporation in 2006) oil in Venezuela (cf. Burchardt & Dietz, 2014, pp. 471–472). On the other hand, there was Brazil, which continued its national development model based on regional ISI of the previous stage, with the Lula and Rousseff administrations significantly strengthening the scope of public enterprises and social inclusion (Boito & Berringer, 2014). Indeed, Argentina shared several features characteristic of Brazil's neo-developmentalist policies. The Kirchner administrations (2003–2016) revived the concept of state economic intervention and attempted to change their development orientation towards re-industrialization. To make this ideological turn possible, Argentina and Brazil once again reached an informal agreement, which in this case allowed Argentina to recover shares in the domestic consumer market through trade measures such as temporary safeguard mechanisms, the renewal of exception lists, and the implicit acceptance of unilateral violation of the common external tariff (Gezmis, 2018, p. 78).

The third reason for MERCOSUR's challenges during its productive phase is external in nature and is linked to the emergence of China as a global economic power. After joining the WTO in 2002, China became the first importer of MERCOSUR grains and minerals. While in the short term, increased exports to China guaranteed resources for leftist governments to carry out active policies for economic and social development; in the long term, it generated an early- de- industrialization process of MERCOSUR, which was strongly influenced by lobbies in the finance and commodity export sectors (Salama, 2012, p. 249).

Given the increase in demand for soybean, and its subsequent price hike, many MERCOSUR member states, particularly Brazil and Argentina, radically expanded their mono-crop production (Soria & García, 2015). Though this largely resulted from private sector strategies in search of higher profitability, this massive redirection essentially generated a change in the production structure of MERCOSUR states towards a development model based on comparative advantages. This was not a new phenomenon, given that production dualism was the characteristic of the MERCOSUR since its very creation, as we saw in the previous section.

What is new is the impact of China in the primarization of Brazil's economy. In 2009, China became Brazil's main trading partner. The intensification of this trade relationship caused rapid changes in the aggregate results and profile of Brazilian trade. On the one hand, it allowed an expansion of Brazilian exports, but highly concentrated in low-tech products, such as agricultural raw materials and minerals. Only two products accounted for 63% of Brazilian to Chinese exports: iron ore, soybeans and their derivatives. Far from showing diversification, this mono-export profile increased from 57.5% in 2010 to 82.6% in 2010 (Mansor de Mattos & Dias Carcanholo, 2012, p. 120) On the other hand, it produced a strong expansion of the share of Chinese manufactured products in the Brazilian domestic market, affecting Brazil's industrial production and its share of the domestic and regional market. The products that Brazil imports from China are low-tech and high-tech industrial goods.

Finally, this Chinese-Brazilian exchange led to changes in the balance of payments. Thanks to MERCOSUR, the Brazilian economy began to generate vigorous trade surpluses from the late 1990s, reaching its peak in 2006 with almost $46.5 billion. By 2007 this surplus began to deteriorate due to the trajectory of imports (which doubled between 2006 and 2010), with export growth registering 46% over the same period. The effects on MERCOSUR were immediate. However, Brazil's institutional advantages in MERCOSUR has allowed it to avoid or slow the further expansion of Chinese imports into the regional market; by 2008, for example, Chinese exports to the wider Latin American Integration Association (LAIA) were 34% higher than Brazilian exports, whereas within MERCOSUR, Chinese exports were 18% higher (Mansor de Mattos & Dias Carcanholo, 2012, p. 139).

4. Projection: the current MERCOSUR (2016–present day)

By 2016, the regional setting had changed once more, due to the resurgence of neoliberal state forms, as the four-member states saw the emergence of more right-leaning governments, with Mauricio Macri (2015–2019) in Argentina, Tabaré Vázquez (2015–2020) in Uruguay, Mario Abdo Benitez (2013–2018) in Paraguay, and Temer (2016–2018) in Brazil. In spite of personal differences, all new MERCOSUR leaders shared the same orientation to orthodox neoliberalism.

In this context, the idea of returning to the commercial MERCOSUR once again became the centre of attention. For the first time in MERCOSUR's history, there was among the member states complete agreement regarding the national development model, the regional integration model, and the external relations strategy.

Every member state shared the same vision: regional integration should be a platform for each country to promote its exports of primary products (raw materials) – those with static comparative advantages. Accordingly, they undertook a series of joint actions. First, the idea of political integration against the hegemony of the United States was discarded, and simultaneously renouncing their UNASUR membership. Second, Venezuelan membership of MERCOSUR was indefinitely suspended. Thus, member countries aligned themselves geopolitically with the United States and the European Union.

Third, the idea of 'flexibilizing' MERCOSUR's initial commitments around external negotiations was discussed. This was a historic demand from Uruguay and Paraguay in favour of expanding countries' autonomy to negotiate free trade agreements bilaterally, which was now supported by all. However, instead of advancing this reform, the four countries agreed on the need to move forward with the signing of a free trade agreement with the EU and to start further negotiations with developed countries in addition to the Pacific Alliance (created in 2012). They also agreed on the need to deepen the process of trade liberalization, with the removal of non- tariff barriers, to re-establish the Common External Tariff (CET), to implement investment and services agreements and to move forward on new trade agreements.

As for external relations, these new governments shared the conviction concerning the need to create closer ties with China and the US. This was expected not only to improve access to consumer markets but also to attract FDI flows, which would alleviate the fiscal pressure handed down to them by previous administrations within a context of declining global commodity prices and relative paralysis of the WTO.

Taking account of the progress in this agenda, the principal advance up to this point materialized in terms of successful implementation of international policies among member states, led by Argentina, concerning free trade with the European Union. While this agreement was initiated in 1995, negotiations encountered both internal and external resistance over the successive steps of MERCOSUR's evolution. It was only at the recent G20 Summit, held in Buenos Aires in 2018, when the parties signed the first accord via a referendum within the national congress. To that end, countries such as France do not seem favourable to this accord, given the opposition from environmental organizations as well as European protectionists, which rejected the idea of ratifying the accord while President Jair Bolsonaro's environmental policy remains unchanged (Greenpeace, 2019).

5. Conclusions

In bringing the analysis of MERCOSUR under a critical-historical lens, this article has offered a deeper understanding of economic regionalization as part of a much longer process of international relations within Latin America.

MERCOSUR's trajectory is analysed under the lens of ideas and discourses that inspired the processes of economic regionalism in Latin America. On the one hand, we have the closed regionalism paradigm, which in the 1950s proposed the creation of regional markets to strengthen and expand industrialization; and on the other hand, open regionalism promotes the creation of free trade areas to attract FDI and participation in global production chains, on the part of multinational companies that, in the context of globalization, seek to settle in territories with competitive advantages, be it the size of the market, cheap labour, or natural resources. South America's competitive advantages in the global market are linked to the production and export of raw materials, such as mining, agriculture and livestock.

And yet, a critical examination of MERCOSUR's short track record shows us the presence and overlap of aspects of both paradigms, without one ever becoming entirely dominant over the other. Thus, in the first stage characterized by the hegemony of the 'open regionalism' paradigm in the global context, MERCOSUR opts for institutional construction closer to the principles of closed regionalism. This decision to move towards a customs union was based upon both economic and political motivations. Through the Common External Tariff (CET), MERCOSUR would be able to unify and increase the voice of all countries in the different international fora and in turn protect local industry and especially the automotive industry, ensuring privileged access to regional production and consumption markets.

However, when defining their scope, contestation arose between the larger economies over trade coordination, and with the smaller states calling for further productive integration and compensatory policies to reduce structural asymmetries However, the negotiation between governments to define a CET showed strong asymmetry in terms of technical capabilities and institutional resources among governments, in which the main beneficiary was the Brazilian industrial sectors which exerted enormous leverage and lobbying power at the national level. Intraregional trade and FDI grew steadily during the early years of this stage; but towards the end of 1988 it began to show a slowdown resulting from non-compliance with deadlines and commitments by smaller economies that saw a great imbalance in terms of costs and benefits in favour of Brazil.

The most critical moment came with Brazil's unilateral decision to devalue its currency, something Argentina would repeat years later. While these unilateral decisions are justified by causes of external origin – such as global financial crises – their effects on MERCOSUR were devastating: investments and enterprises were concentrated in Brazil and trade conflicts multiplied, generating a negative balance of intraregional trade and the paralysis of MERCOSUR's governing bodies. However, the main threat to the continuity of the bloc came from one of the smaller economies and manifested itself in Uruguay's decision to negotiate a bilateral free trade agreement with the United States.

In the second stage of MERCOSUR, initiated in 2003, the idea or paradigm of closed regionalism reappears strongly and authentically in a regional and global context, characterized by a challenge to the ideas of the Washington consensus. The new progressive governments of MERCOSUR agreed on the need to strengthen the implementation of the Mercosur External Tariff; but their consensus ran deeper and sought to correct the debts and omissions of the previous stage. In terms of economic integration, they launched the social and productive MERCOSUR, with two important innovations: first, to advance regional distributive policies through the creation of a structural convergence fund (FOCEM) that reduced the financial asymmetry among smaller members; secondly, to advance productive policy, by generating value chains with the participation of small and medium-sized enterprises (SMEs). In terms of political integration, they decided to reinforce the rejection of the US Free Trade Area of the Americas (FTAA), a decision that would then be reflected by Venezuela's incorporation into the bloc. However, this policy consensus failed to move forward successfully. The main problem was Brazil's resistance to funding the resources necessary to carry this policy forward. In this second stage, Brazil's priorities were not to strengthen a regional integration process as such, but to project itself as a global regional leader within the BRICs, G20 and United Nations Security Council. With this achievement of political regionalism, Brazil managed to expand its projection at the regional level as one of the most prominent leaders of UNASUR, a forum of political regionalism to which it gave significant financial, technical and political support.

Changes in the global scenario – with the waning of US hegemony following the failure of the FTAA and China's accession to the WTO – changed the balance of forces in the region and contributed to the construction of this new political regionalism. However, China's leading presence in the region as the main trading partner and supplier of FDI had contradictory effects on MERCOSUR. On the one hand, the increase in the price of commodities allowed governments in the region to invest in active policies of productive, technological and social development. On the other hand, it started a process of repressing the Brazilian economy that ended up weakening the material and political bases of support for the Brazilian industrialist model.

It is only in the third and final stage that the idea of open regionalism reappears on the agenda of the new governments, and with greater possibilities for implementation. While the proposal to make the Common Market more flexible had been raised by smaller economies at the end of the first stage, it is under a new regional context (characterized by neoliberal economic governments) that the idea captures the consent of the largest countries, especially Brazil.

The results of this initiative are still uncertain at the national level, the Brazilian government attempted to embark on a unilateral tariff reduction path to incentivize the competitiveness of its companies on a global scale. However, this attempt found resistance from the chambers of business which, with parliamentary representation, rejected the initiative to introduce flexibility in labour markets in return. At the regional level, governments succeeded in signing the bi-regional customs agreement with the EU for the establishment of a free trade area (via referendum of the legislatures themselves). The reason for this progress is justified in the gap generated by this agreement within the automotive sector, among European brands that, thanks to the agreement, will be enhanced by their competitiveness with respect to brands of Asian and/or North American origin. If this agreement is accepted, the common union's flexibility will in fact be by expanding preferential access to more competitive outside industries. Once again, however, the decision does not go through national actors, but remains tied to an external logic, this time on the part of European environmental groups that are reluctant to endorse an agreement with Bolsonaro.

Notes

1. 'Presidential intergovernmentalism' creates problems in decision-making, as it requires first the unanimity of the partners and then the internalization of what is decided by each of them. Added to this decision-making inefficiency is the execution, since the authority to implement regional policies resides in national bureaucracies that lack incentives to prioritize them(Malamud, 2013).
2. In his work on how to define the MERCOSUR External Tariff (CET), he demonstrates how subnational entrepreneurs, especially those in Brazil, who had parliamentary representation ended up imposing their needs and demands on regional negotiation (Pezzola, 2018).
3. Had a gradual freeing of trade been accompanied by the free mobility of persons across borders been implemented (expressed in the Treaty of Asunción), the gaps between countries would have narrowed and interdependence deepened (Blyde, 2006).
4. As a counterpoint to mainstream/Eurocentric approaches to MERCOSUR, the relative sophistication of the European Union, in the form of *supranationalism*, does not exempt this regional space from socio-economic crisis and relative disintegration, as the Eurozone crisis and recent exit of Great Britain has shown (see Lapavitsas et al., 2012; Jessop, 2017).
5. Only smaller countries in Central America and the Andean region integrated their markets for consumption and production, such as the Central American Common Market (CACM), created in 1961; and the Andean Community (AC) in 1969. Progress in CACM and AC were obstructed by inter-state conflicts, in addition to physical barriers which were impossible to be overcome without infrastructure projects (Sunkel, 1995).
6. As with much scholarship on the EU, 'success' in the case of NAFTA is very much dependent on the perspective taken. From the perspective of transnational capital, NAFTA created a virtual gold mine in the form of the 'maquiladora' complex of low-cost (sweatshop) labour, while, from a different perspective, both labour and the environment became over-exploited resources with devastating consequences to both (Robinson, 2008, pp. 106–107; Ciccantell, 2001).
7. In 1997, three protocols were signed, those being the Protocol of facilitation and cooperation of intra-MERCOSUR investment (in force); Montevideo Protocol on MERCOSUR trade and services (in force).
8. There is a widespread confusion in the IR literature around the leadership of Brazil (e.g. Vigevani & Ramazzini, 2009). This paragraph is not intended to discuss the existence or not of (regional) political leadership, but rather Brazilian *economic* leadership. During the first years, Brazil received few benefits of intra-regional trade. While after the crisis, it became the regional economic leader not only as a provider of industrial manufactures but also as a significant importer of intra-regional commodities (Burges, 2008; see also Figure 1).

Acknowledgements

The author is grateful for comments from the reviewers, and especially the collaboration with Ernesto Vivares and Rowan Lubbock.

Disclosure statement

No potential conflict of interest was reported by the author(s).

ORCID

Mercedes Botto http://orcid.org/0000-0003-4368-2374

References

Banco Interamericano de Desarrollo/IADB. (2002). El nuevo regionalismo en América Latina. En *Más allá de las fronteras: el nuevo regionalismo en América latina*, Informe 2002, cap. 2, cap.9.

Bergsten, F. (1997). Open regionalism. *The World Economy*, *20*(5), 545–565. https://doi.org/10.1111/1467-9701.00088

Bielschowsky, R. (1998). Cincuenta años del pensamiento de la CEPAL: una reseña. En CEPAL: *Cincuenta años de pensamiento de la CEPAL. Textos seleccionados*. Volumen I. Santiago de Chile, FCE-CEPAL.

Blyde, J. S. (2006). Convergence dynamics in Mercosur. *Journal of Economic Integration*, *21*(4), 784–815. https://doi.org/10.11130/jei.2006.21.4.784

Boito, A., & Berringer, T. (2014). Social classes, neodevelopmentalism, and Brazilian Foreign Policy under Presidents Lula and Dilma. *Latin American Perspectives*, *41*(5), 94–109. https://doi.org/10.1177/0094582X14543790

Botto, M. (2009). The role of epistemic communities in the makability of Mercosur. In M. Schulz & P. De Lombaerde (Eds.), *The makability of regionanlism* (pp. 171–187). Ashgate Publishing.

Botto, M. (2015). La política comercial en el Mercosur y la deconstrucción de una idea: de mercado común sudamericano a una pragmática área de libre comercio. En M. Botto (Ed.), *La Integración Regional en América: Quo Vadis? El Mercosur desde una perspectiva sectorial y comparada* (pp. 45–110). Eudeba.

Botto, M. (2017). El Mercosur y sus crisis: análisis de interpretaciones sobre el fracaso de la Integración regional sudamericana. *Revista: Estado & comunes, revista de políticas y problemas públicos*, *2*(5), 132–155. https://doi.org/10.37228/estado_comunes.v2.n5.2017

Botto, M., & Bianculli, A. (2011). Comparative asymmetric trade negotiations in the Southern Cone: FTAA and UE-Mercosur. En B. Sanoussi, P. De Lombaerde, & D. Tussie (Eds.), *Asymmetric trade negotiations* (pp. 98–116). Ashgate.

Botto, M., & Peixoto, J. (2010). The impact of academia on the negotiations on health and education services in Argentina: Challenges and opportunities. In M. Botto (Ed.), *Research and international trade policy negotiations. Knowledge and power in Latin America* (pp. 175–210). Routledge.

Botto, M., & Quiliconi, C. (2010). The influence of academia on Mercosur's tariff policy. In M. Botto (Ed.), *Research and international trade policy negotiations. Knowledge and power in Latin America* (pp. 144–174). Routledge.

Briceño-Ruiz, J. (2017). Raúl Prebisch and the theory of regional economic integration. In M. E. Margulis (Ed.), *The global political economy of Raúl Prebisch* (pp. 61–77). Routledge.
Burchardt, H.-J., & Dietz, K. (2014). (Neo-)extractivism – a new challenge for development theory from Latin America. *Third World Quarterly*, *35*(3), 468–486. https://doi.org/10.1080/01436597.2014.893488
Burges, S. W. (2008). Consensual hegemony: Theorizing Brazilian Foreign Policy after the Cold War. *International Relations*, *22*(1), 65–84. https://doi.org/10.1177/0047117807087243
Caichiolo, C. (2017). The Mercosur experience and theories of regional integration. *Contexto Internacional*, *39*(1) Jan/Apr. https://doi.org/10.1590/S0102-8529.20173901000
Carranza, M. (2003). Can Mercosur survive? Domestic and international constraints on Mercosur. *Latin American Politics and Society*, *45*(2), 67–103. https://doi.org/10.1111/j.1548-2456.2003.tb00241.x
Chodor, T. (2015). *Neoliberal hegemony and the pink tide in Latin America: Breaking up with TINA?* Routledge.
Ciccantell, P. (2001). NAFTA and the reconstruction of US hegemony: The raw materials foundations of economic competitiveness. *Canadian Journal of Sociology / Cahiers Canadiens de Sociologie*, *26*(1), 57–65. https://doi.org/10.2307/3341511
Costa, A., Bembi, M., & Bianco, C. (2018). El trilema del MERCOSUR. Políticas nacionales, integración económica y relacionamiento externo. En M. Vázquez (Ed.), *El Mercosur. Geografía en disputa* (pp. 97–167). Editorial Cicus.
Cox, R. (1981). Social forces, states and world orders: Beyond international relations theory. *Millennium: Journal of International Studies*, *10*(2), 126–155. https://doi.org/10.1177/03058298810100020501
Cox, R. W., & Sinclair, T. J. (1996). *Approaches to world order*. Cambridge University Press.
Doctor, M. (2013). Prospects for deepening Mercosur integration: Economic asymmetry and institutional deficits. *Review of International Political Economy*, *20*(3), 515–540. https://doi.org/10.1080/09692290.2012.671763
ECLAC. (1990). *Changing production patterns with social equity*. United Nations.
ECLAC. (1994). *Open regionalism in Latin America and the Caribbean. Economic integration as a contribution to changing production patterns with social equity*. United Nations.
Genna, G. M., & Hiroi, T. (2007). Brazilian regional power in the development of Mercosul. *Latin American Perspectives*, *34*(5), 43–57. https://doi.org/10.1177/0094582X07306237
Gezmis, H. (2018). From neoliberalism to neo-developmentalism? The political economy of post-crisis Argentina (2002-2015). *New Political Economy*, *23*(1), 66–87. https://doi.org/10.1080/13563467.2017.1330877
Gomez-Mera, L. (2008). How 'new' is the 'new regionalism' in the Americas? The case of MERCOSUR. *Journal of International Relations and Development*, *11*(3), 279–308. https://doi.org/10.1057/jird.2008.14
Greenpeace. (2019). Greenpeace denuncia que el acuerdo comercial UE-Mercosur agravará la destrucción ambiental. https://es.greenpeace.org/es/sala-de-prensa/comunicados/greenpeace-denuncia-que-el-acuerdo-comercial-ue-mercosur-agravara-la-destruccion-ambiental/
Grigera, J. (2015). Conspicuous silences: State and class in structuralist and neostructuralist thought. In J. R. Webber & S. Spronk (Eds.), *Crisis and contradiction: Marxist perspectives on Latin America in the global political economy* (pp. 193–210). Brill.
Jessop, B. (2017). The organic crisis of the British State: Putting Brexit in its place. *Globalizations*, *14*(1), 133–141. https://doi.org/10.1080/14747731.2016.1228783
Kaltenthaler, K., & Mora, F. O. (2002). Explaining Latin American economic integration: The case of Mercosur. *Review of International Political Economy*, *9*(1), 72–97. https://doi.org/10.1080/09692290110101108
Lapavitsas, C., Kaltenbrunner, A., Labrinidis, G., Lindo, D., Meadway, J., Michell, J., Painceira, J. P., Pires, E., Powell, J., Stenfors, A., Teles, N., & Vatikiotis, L. (2012). *Crisis in the Eurozone*. Verso.
Leiva, F. I. (2008). Toward a critique of Latin American neostructuralism. *Latin American Politics and Society*, *50*(4), 1–25. https://doi.org/10.1111/j.1548-2456.2008.00028.x
Malamud, A. (2013, noviembre). El Mercosur: misión cumplida Revista SAAP. *Publicación de Ciencia Política de la Sociedad Argentina de Análisis Político*, *7*(2), 275–282. http://hdl.handle.net/10451/10209
Mansor de Mattos, F., & Dias Carcanholo, M. (2012). Amenazas y oportunidades del comercio brasileño con China lecciones para Brasil. *Revista Problemas del Desarrollo*, *168*(43), enero-marzo. https://doi.org/10.22201/iiec.20078951e.2012.168.28640

Mecham, M. (2003). Mercosur: A failing development project? *International Affairs*, *79*(2), 369–387. https://doi.org/10.1111/1468-2346.00313

Meissner, K. L. (2017). MERCOSUR. In S. Krapohl (Ed.), *Regional integration in the global south: External influence on economic cooperation in ASEAN, MERCOSUR and SADC* (pp. 147–178). Palgrave.

Muhr, T. (2016). Beyond 'BRICS': Ten theses on south-south cooperation in the twenty-first century. *Third World Quarterly*, *37*(4), 630–648. https://doi.org/10.1080/01436597.2015.1108161

Nelson, M. (2015). *A history of the FTAA: From hegemony to fragmentation in the Americas*. Palgrave.

Pezzola, A. A. (2017). Cooperación diacrónica para intereses diversos.intereses y lealtades provinciales en la formulación de políticas en argentina. *Política y gobierno*, *XXIV*(1 I semestre), 125–156. http://hdl.handle.net/11651/1511

Pezzola, A. A. (2018). The deep roots of protectionism in the Southern Cone: Constituent interests and Mercosur's common external tarif. *Latin American Politics and Society*, *60*(4), 69–92. https://doi.org/10.1017/lap.2018.42

Phillips, N. (2001). Regionalist governance in the new political economy of development: 'Relaunching' the Mercosur. *Third World Quarterly*, *22*(4), 565–583. https://doi.org/10.1080/01436590120071786

Phillips, N. (2003). The rise and fall of open regionalism? Comparative reflections on regional governance in the Southern Cone of Latin America. *Third World Quarterly*, *24*(2), 217–234. https://doi.org/10.1080/0143659032000074565

Prébisch, R. (1963). Las disparidades de la demanda y sus efectos sobre el desarrollo económico. En Prébisch *Hacia una dinámica del desarrollo latinoamericano* (pp. 81–106). Fondo de Cultura Económica.

Prieto Corredor, G., & Betancourt Vélez, R. (2014). Entre la soberanía, la autonomía y la innovación: un marco conceptual para el análisis de la Alianza del Pacifico. En E. Paltrana Buelvas & H. Gerhing (Eds.), *Alianza del Pacifico: Mitos y Realidades* (pp. 75–115). Editorial Universidad de Santiago de Cali.

Riggirozzi, P. (2012). Region, regionness and regionalism in Latin America: Towards a new synthesis. *New Political Economy*, *17*(4), 421–443. https://doi.org/10.1080/13563467.2011.603827

Robinson, W. I. (2008). *Latin American and global capitalism: A critical globalization perspective*. John Hopkins University Press.

Salama, P. (2012). China-brasil: industrialización y 'desindustrialización temprana'. *Cuadernos de economía*, *31*(56), 253–272. Disponible en: https://revistas.unal.edu.co/index.php/ceconomia/article/view/35841 (Accedido: 9 agosto 2021).

Sanchez Bajo, C. (1999). MERCOSUR's open regionalism and regulation focusing on the petrochemical and steel sectors. *Iberoamericana – Nordic Journal of Latin America and Caribbean Studies*, *29*(1–2), 67. https://doi.org/10.16993/ibero.364

Silva, E. (2009). *Challenging neoliberalism in Latin America*. Cambridge University Press.

Soria, A. B., & García, P. M. (Eds.). (2015). *China en América Latina y el Caribe: Escenarios estratégicos subregionales*. FLACSO-CAF.

Stallings, B. (1995). *Global change, regional response: The new international context of development*. Cambridge University Press.

Sunkel, O. (1995). Del desarrollo hacia adentro al desarrollo desde dentro. En O. Sunkel (Ed.), *El desarrollo desde dentro. Un enfoque neoestructuralista para la América Latina* (Primera reimpresión, pp. 35–79). Fondo de Cultura Económica.

Vigevani, T., & Ramazzini, H. (2009). Brasil en el centro de la integración. *Revista Nueva Sociedad*, *219*, 76–96.

Vivares, E. (ed.). (2018). *Regionalism, development and the post-commodities boom in South America*. Palgrave.

Vivares, E., & Dolcetti-Marcolini, M. (2015). Two regionalisms, two Latin Americas or beyond Latin America? Contributions from a critical and decolonial IPE. *Third World Quarterly*, *37*(5), 866–882. https://doi.org/10.1080/01436597.2015.1109438.

Williamson, J. (1990). *Latin American adjustment: How much has happened?* Institute for International Economics. November 2002.

The Pacific Alliance: regional integration as neoliberal discipline

Marcel Nelson

ABSTRACT

This article examines how the Pacific Alliance constitutes a multilevel state project to lock-in neoliberal reforms in each member country. Using a strategic relational approach to institutions that emphasizes the interconnection between institutional and social dynamics, it demonstrates that the AP is a state project that is both a regional market access strategy and a domestic disciplinary mechanism. Notably, it represents an attempt to reinforce the neoliberal economic export models that predominate in each member country: Chile, Mexico, Peru, and Colombia. Buttressed by dominant domestic and transnational social forces in each country, technocrats in each member countries seek to reproduce institutional strategies of depoliticization that were successfully employed in their countries at a regional level in the AP in view of growing political instability and discontentment with neoliberalism.

Introduction

Latin America is arguably unique among the world's regions in terms of its diversity, complexity, and polarization. From the explicitly anti-neoliberal *Alianza Bolivariana para los Pueblos de Nuestra América* (Bolivarian Alliance for the Peoples of Our America – ALBA), to the more interventionist *Mercado Común del Sur* (Southern Common Market – MERCOSUR), and the more recent neoliberal *Alianza del Pacífico* (Pacific Alliance – AP), Latin America's regional landscape sharply reflects the divergent ideological orientations among its states and peoples. Much of the scholarship has narrowly focused on these ideological divisions (see, e.g. Gómez-Mera & Barrett, 2012; Martínez-Castillo, 2016; Quiliconi & Salgado Espinoza, 2017), less attention has been paid to the concrete social forces that create spatialisation strategies geared towards the consolidation of a given class project. And as more critical approaches to Latin American regionalism have largely focused on the ALBA-TCP (e.g. Lubbock, 2020; Muhr, 2011; see also Ciupa (2022) in this Special Issue), or MERCOSUR (Carranza, 2006; Guevara, 2016), there has been less focus on the unique case of the AP, arguably the most neoliberal regional formation in twenty-first century Latin America.

While very much oriented towards the Asia-Pacific region as the name suggests, the AP is also a neoliberal domestic 'state project' shaped by social forces within each of its member states: Chile, Mexico, Peru, and Colombia. It is only in adjoining both dynamics that the AP begins to make sense in view of its very low levels of intra-regional trade, poor prospects for greater intra-regional trade, and differential trade complementarity with Asian economies (for more on the AP's regional economic prospects see Briceño-Ruiz, 2019; Sauvé et al., 2019). In other words, the potential constraints to economic domestic policy that comes with membership in the AP is just as important as its potential benefits in areas such as market access. Once fully realized, the AP would constitute an institutional mechanism that can be leveraged by specific domestic actors to reproduce neoliberal economic policies based on export led growth.

Drawing upon (neo)Poulantzian scholarship on the capitalist state and regional institutions, I argue that the AP represents an extension of the strength of technocratic actors in charge of national economic ministries buttressed by the relative cohesion of different fractions of capital.[1] In this sense, trade agreements, function as a mechanism to 'lock-in' reforms implemented by economic ministries at the domestic level and to reinforce their influence within the national state apparatus (Gill & Cutler, 2014; Vergara & Encinas, 2016, pp. 171–172). Not only does the AP promote the policy priorities of the economic ministries of each country, it also seeks to replicate their institutional forms and strategies that were largely influenced by the neoliberal Washington Consensus promoted by the United States in the region during from the 1980s into the 2000s.[2] As Eduardo Dargent notes, the technocrats or *los técnicos* of Latin America, where successful as in the four AP member countries, entrenched their political power within the state by forming networks within and across different national state agencies that reinforced their autonomy vis-à-vis the governments of the day and more politicized state agencies. This was part of a strategy to depoliticize economic policy-making (Dargent, 2014, pp. 4–5), which sits in marked contrast with the post-neoliberal regional projects that sought to repoliticise decision-making by rejecting the neoliberal policies of the Washington Consensus with its 'excessive marketization' and the 'technocratic democracies that accompanied market reforms' (Grugel & Riggirozzi, 2012, p. 3). If the AP were to be fully negotiated and implemented, it would constitute a significant coil in the armature of a state project to ensure the interests of transnational and dominant fractions of domestic capital that seek to deepen and protect neoliberal accumulation strategies across multiple scales. Indeed, the mass mobilisations and political instability that has beset three of the core member states in South America since 2019 attests to the need for class projects such as the AP to exist to ensure the persistence of neoliberal accumulation strategies in the region. The mobilisations also affirm the precarity of such a project.

The AP in context

The AP is a wide-ranging regional integration project with four core members and over fifty-nine observer members from around the world as of 2021. It is ambitious in its scope with its 25 technical and working groups that range from issue areas as diverse as gender and environmental protection (Angeles Villareal, 2016, p. 5). Nevertheless, the AP is primarily intergovernmental organization that is an heir of the open regionalism that predominated the region in the 1990s by virtue of its making trade a central component of integration and by providing the private sector with an important role in the process (Malamud, 2015, pp. 100–101). In its Framework Agreement, accordingly, the AP announces that it has three major goals that include (i) the creation of a 'deep integration area' that would facilitate the circulation of 'goods, services, capital and persons', (ii) to increase the economic performance of member states to ameliorate social indicators, and (iii) to become a 'platform' for political and economic integration and projection into the rest of the world with an 'emphasis' on the Asia Pacific region (Palacio Valencia, 2019, pp. 5–7). It is very much a work in progress often characterized as being 'pragmatic' by virtue of its gradualist approach. Significant achievements, as we will see, have mostly been limited to trade liberalization within the bloc and the establishment partially integrated common stock market. Nevertheless, if it were to achieve its goal of 'deep integration' on all of its negotiating fronts, it would essentially lock-in the economies of member states into a neoliberal framework.

With regard to its overall weight within South America and the Caribbean, the economies that participate in the AP represent '36% of GDP, concentrates 50% of total trade, and absorbs 41% of foreign investment flows directed to the region' (Sauvé et al., 2019, p. ix). However, in relation to integration, trade and investment among AP members themselves is low due to the fact that the three members located in South America have similar production profiles except for Mexico, which is nonetheless located at a distance from them. In fact, the United States, the European Union, and China are the principle trading partners of AP member states; and Mexico and Chile, in fact, export more to *Mercado Común del Sur* (Southern Common Market, MERCOSUR), the AP's regional rival, than to the other AP countries. The architects of the AP were nevertheless aware of this reality and designed its institutional infrastructure to be flexible enough to work as a long-term integration project (Sauvé et al., 2019, p. ix).

In terms of its constituting a platform to project the interests of member states into different regions, the AP constitutes both change and continuity with regard to its strategic orientation. A factor that unites member states is their generally positive orientation and alignment with the United States in the hemisphere (Morales Castillo et al., 2016, p. 141). In fact, the AP's member states were some of the strongest proponents of the failed Free Trade Area of the Americas (FTAA), which sought to integrate the entire hemisphere into a single economic zone. Nevertheless, the AP is by no means an initiative that originated in Washington and imposed on its core members. In fact, the AP emerged in 2011 just as American trade flows began to wane globally and in Latin America in the wake of the 2008 financial crisis; and as those of the Asia Pacific region, especially China, began to increase (Oyarzún Serrano, 2017, p. 141; World Bank, 2019). Moreover, the AP emphasizes the importance of increasing economic links with one of the United States' greatest geopolitical rival: China (Palacio Valencia, 2019, p. 18).

Conversely, the AP represents continuity and alignment with the United States in terms of its institutional strategy. Notably, that the AP constitutes a state project that relies on the institutional strategy of depoliticization that is a key component of the neoliberal Washington Consensus. As Tickell and Peck explain, 'while the 'Washington Consensus' clearly reflects the geo-economic interests of the global North, as a policy programme, it has been forged, adapted and reshaped in a wide variety of global contexts' (2003, p. 164–165). Thus, while the American state's interest in Latin America may wax and wane, the AP ensures the interests of more transnationalized fractions of American capital by contributing to a more harmonized and open global economy. Therefore, it is a project that is premised ideologically on unity of the global capitalist economy that skirts the growing geopolitical rivalry between China and the United States.

The evolution of the Pacific Alliance

The origins of the AP can be found in the Latin American Pacific Arc (APL) initiative that was launched in 2006 at the behest of the Peruvian government (Ovando Aldana et al., 2017, p. 179). Incidentally, the states that came to form the AP were the most steadfast supporters of the FTAA. The Peruvian government's decision to launch the initiative was precipitated by the crisis caused by Venezuelàs decision to leave the *Comunidad Andina* (Andean Community – CAN) as well as the election of governments critical of neoliberalism in Bolivia and Ecuador (Ruiz, 2010, pp. 50–51). More broadly, impetus was also generated by the failure of the FTAA negotiations the previous year. The APL sought greater integration and cooperation among Latin American states with a coastline on the Pacific in order to increase access to Asian markets and especially China (CEPAL, 2008, p. 11). The following year, Peru's Foreign Minister announced his country's intention to create a Latin American Pacific Association (LAPA) that would span from Mexico to Chile, with the aim of reincorporating Chile into the CAN. As a result of gathering momentum, Mexico signalled its interest in the initiative (Ruiz, 2010, p. 52).

The LAPA initiative faced hostility from other Latin American countries, particularly those within the ALBA-TCP (Martínez-Castillo, 2016, pp. 486–487). Nonetheless, a subsequent meeting in Cali for the region`s ministers of commerce from Mexico, Guatemala, El Salvador, Honduras, Panama, Peru, Chile and Colombia resulted in the creation of the Basin Initiative of the Latin American Pacific as a forum to further discuss the matter of integration, trade promotion, investment, market access, and competitiveness (Ruiz, 2010, p. 53). The meeting in Cali also launched a High Level Technical Working Group charged with, among other things, proposing initiatives that would augment the economic convergence among member states. Through the forum of the Basin Initiative, several other meetings took place over the years as work proceeded in the technical working groups. Meanwhile, the integration project shed several more members as Ecuador and Nicaragua opted to engage the ALBA-TCP and other Central American states decided to prioritize different integration projects. With the four core members and consensus in place, the ground was set for the formal launch of the AP.

At a presidential meeting held in Lima in 2011, the AP was inaugurated. The following year at Antofagasta in Chile, a Framework Agreement was launched that formally brought the alliance into existence. As stated previously, the overall goal of the AP is to facilitate the economic integration through the free goods, people, capital, and services. To that end, in 2014 an Additional Protocol was signed in Colombia, which committed member countries to reduce tariffs by 92% and came into effect in 2016 with a plan to further reduce them in the future (OAS, 2018). A further concrete feat included the creation of the *Mercado Integrado Latinoamericano* (MILA) in 2011 as a financial regulatory framework with the goal of harmonizing policies across the financial markets of all four member states (Malamud, 2015, pp. 100–101). In 2014, when Mexico joined the MILA, bourses from all four countries were integrated into one thus making it the largest stock exchange in Latin America (Duarte, 2020). The financial regulatory harmonization between countries has been significant, but the number of operations running through the MILA has remained limited (Perry, 2016, p. ix). Member countries are also negotiating a tax information exchange agreement as well as greater harmonization of intellectual property rights (Angeles Villareal, 2016, p. 6). The AP is quite clear with its policy goals though it very much remains a work in progress.

More recently, AP members invited four countries to apply to become associate members in 2017 including Canada, Singapore, Australia, and New Zealand (Stephens & Navarro, 2018, p. 1). Since then, it has initiated negotiations in 2018 for further cooperation with MERCOSUR at a meeting in Puerto Vallarta in Mexico as more members of that block were governed by right-leaning governments with a more positive outlook on the AP's project than their predecessors. More recently, at the 2019 Lima Summit, member countries signed 'declarations of cooperation with Japan, the Eurasian Economic Union, and the Organization for Economic Cooperation and Development, launched negotiations to upgrade Ecuador to full membership' (Foster, 2020). Despite this flurry of activity and plaudits regarding its pragmatic strategy to integration, it remains to be seen whether AP will emerge untroubled in view of mass mobilisations in three of its member states and manage to expand the number of concrete measures negotiated under its aegis.

A strategic relational approach to the state and governance

To get at the heart of what the AP is and aspires to be, it is important to examine the institutional infrastructure of the integration project and the discern its interconnection with the institutions of its member of states. The strategic relational theory of the state, largely influenced by Nicos Poulantzas' work, provides a useful analytical framework through which to understand these elements. The theory is marked by its conception of the state as a *strategic field of struggle* emanating from the relations of production as the main driver of changing state configurations. In this way, the 'institutional materiality' of the capitalist state is not conceived of as a direct reflection of the capitalist mode of production or a simple instrument of the bourgeoisie, as in more reductionist Marxist approaches to the state, but more as a 'material condensation of a relationship of forces' (Poulantzas, 2014, p. 136). In other words, the institutional materiality of the state apparatus, and different formal and informal networks therein, are shaped, in a refracted form, by class struggle. Social classes and their relationships are thus present within the state by the representation of their interests within its various apparatuses. The specificity of the *capitalist state*, meanwhile, is its tendency to promote the interests of dominant classes, while keeping the dominated classes at a 'critical distance' from the centres of decision-making (Poulantzas, 2014, p. 136).

The antagonistic nature of class relations promotes a continual tendency towards inter-institutional competition and divergence (Poulantzas, 2014, p. 194). The policies that emerge out of this 'strategic field and process of intersecting power networks' shaped by class struggle is typically the result of coordination and/or the aggregation of micro-policies (Poulantzas, 2014, p. 136). This does not mean that state personnel, who they themselves are imbricated within class relations, have no agency when it comes to developing policy. Nevertheless, this agency must move through the contradictory strategic field, in which policy becomes 'constructed out of the accelerations and breakings, about-turns, hesitations, and changes of course' (Poulantzas, 2014, pp. 135–136). Though the state is not inherently coherent, it exhibits a 'fissiparous' unity and coherence *post facto* via the agency of actors representing the 'hegemonic class or fractions' through the deployment of a 'state project' of coordination (Poulantzas, 2014, p. 136). These complex processes thus amount to a 'strategic selectivity' vis-à-vis policies that favour the interests of powerful social forces (Jessop, 2007, p. 31).

Among these complex social relations arrayed across several political scales, different class projects become refracted through the 'internationalization of policy regimes'. On the one hand, domestic policy is increasingly shaped by the '"interiorization" of international constraints' generated by them to limit the scope of policy options at the domestic level. On the other hand, state actors are themselves involved in shaping the 'nature of international regimes, their interrelations, and their local implementation' (Jessop, 2004, p. 66). This leads to what Jessop calls 'tangled hierarchies and complex interdependence' whereby governance mechanisms are re-scaled to 'orchestrate economic and social policy' (Jessop, 2004, p. 58). Consequently, due to their relational nature, regional policy regimes or projects that seek to coordinate institutions and harmonize policies across scales are not exempt from contradictions and contestation as they themselves continue to be shaped by the relations of production (Brand et al., 2011)

'Los Técnicos' and the depoliticisation of state policy

While hegemonic class fraction attempt to unify the dominant classes both institutionally and ideologically, such unity emerges from 'technical intellectuals and experts' (i.e. 'state personnel') that translates this broad orientation into specific policies (Jessop, 2016, p. 114). Translation by these epistemic networks – for example, *los técnicos* in the case of Latin America – can take several forms, one of which is 'collibration', which actively 'alter[s] the weight' and 'arrangements' of different modes of governance to achieve certain objectives (Jessop, 2016, p. 171). In other words, it is the manner in which experts organize the institutional environment in which social forces operate such as, for example, determining what issues are considered 'public', what strategies or forums are deemed relevant for addressing them, as well as shaping the identities of different actors.

Particularly in light of neoliberal class projects, these collibrations tend towards the steady depoliticization of policy, in which capital-favouring policies are increasingly distanced from public scrutiny and contention. Depoliticization, of course, does not occur in a vacuum. Such a strategy has to traverse networks of power relations that crisscross the state/civil society nexus. *Los técnicos* in Latin America have not universally been successful in asserting their influence over national state institutions. Indeed, one of the characteristics of the electoral Pink Tide that swept Latin America during the early twenty-first century has been the *repoliticization* of economic policymaking (Chodor, 2015). Furthermore, even where relatively successful, as in the cases of the AP countries, the process of depoliticization did not follow the same pattern in every national context and are subject to very different social forces. Nevertheless, what the AP countries have in common was the important role played by economic agencies – typically ministries of finance – in successfully imposing state projects in highly volatile political contexts.

It is nevertheless important to also note that the state projects of depoliticization in question were not always consistent with the interests of transnational and large domestic capital in every instance – for example, by putting in place tariffs or subsidies that may have benefitted their narrow interests, but overall they were supported by these sectors as they come to appreciate *los técnicos*' ability to manage their overall long-term interests and come to 'prefer technocratic independence to the control of economic policy by a competing actor' (Dargent, 2014, p. 325). In other words, it is by way of state projects coordinated by these central agencies that leading fractions of capital in all of the countries in question are able to universalize their interests through the elaboration of mechanisms such as the AP. The next section will examine the application of this type of strategy in the four founding members of that project.

Chile

Under the cover of Pinochet's dictatorship, an epistemic network of neo-classical economists (the so-called 'Chicago Boys') used their positions within Chile's National Planning Office (ODEPLAN) to launch their goal of reforming the entire Chilean state as well as launch themselves into the central economic agencies, such as the Ministry of Finance. Although the Chicago Boys lost some of their influence because of a financial crisis in 1982–1983 (Clark, 2017, pp. 3–7), their structural reforms to the state remained in place and they retained their control over the Ministry of Finance. These neoliberal reforms within the state and the economy transformed a fractious economic elite into 'arguably the most powerful, ideologically coherent and organized capitalist elite in Latin America, whose values and vision permeated across Chilean society and its principal institutions' (Clark, 2017, p. 9). With the advent of democracy in 1989 and the election of Concertación government, the strategic selectivity of the state established during the dictatorship remained largely in place (Silva, 1996, p. 314). Business support for democracy was buttressed by constitutional mechanisms that limited the potential for state intervention in the economy, as well as an electoral system that favoured more conservative parties close to business interests, and a general cross-party consensus on the 'new extractivist consensus' (Leiva, 2019, p. 135; cf. Fisse & Thomas, 2014, p. 319).

In terms of the Chilean power bloc, financial capital and mining capital (both foreign and domestic) are central to the country's political economy. While Chile hosts a relatively competitive financial sector attracting transnational finance capital, the most important sector for Foreign Direct Investments (FDI) has consistently been its mining sector reaching as high as an average of 57% between 1990 and 1995 (Du et al., 2018, p. 167; cf. Santander, n.d.). As the world's leading copper exporter, this sector comprises over 30% of Chile's GDP since 2000, rising to 50% if one includes copper byproducts. Moreover, primary products, constituted between 50–90% of its exports since 1990 (Dubé, 2019, p. 43). As of 2018, the main destinations for Chile's exports include China (33%), the United States (13.8%), Japan (9.2%), South Korea (5.7%), and Brazil (4.4%). Meanwhile, the three other AP members represent just under 5% of total exports, with Peru making up the most important share with 2.2% (Observatory of Economic Complexity, 2018a). As a capital-intensive sector of the national economy, mineral export sectors provide little employment; at the start of the decade in the midst of the resource boom micro and small firms in the manufacturing and service sectors represent approximately 64 percent of all employment (Solimano, 2012, p. 130). This highlights the importance of the AP for Chile, not only as a platform for intraregional trade, but also as an internal disciplinary mechanism to ensure continued competitiveness and stability in order to maintain its market share in Asia for its mining sector.

This consensus came to be challenged in 2010 on the eve of the formation of the AP after the decrease in commodity prices, including copper, that brought the 2004–2012 commodity boom to an end. This launched a drive to deepen the Chile's model and to expand mining projects, which encountered both social protests in 2011 and more effective local resistance mining projects. These protests were not effectively managed by the political system: 'for the first time since the negotiated transition to civilian rule in 1990, Chile's business elites felt their hegemony openly questioned' (Leiva, 2019, p. 136). As a response to this challenge, state personnel deployed a strategy of obtaining 'social license' for new mining projects at the local level with the help of center-left civil society and political actors (Leiva, 2019, p. 137). However, Chile's model was hit with another wave of protests beginning in October 2019 that shook the political system to its foundations. The protests are a direct rejection of the neoliberal state and it remains to be seen whether *los técnicos* will be able to retain their structural power in light of the constituent assembly process and how this will shape Chile's participation in the AP.

Mexico

Mexico's participation in the AP was also part of a wider project of neoliberal consolidation that began in the 1980s. Similar to the Chicago Boys in Chile, *los técnicos* in the Mexican state came to prominence as part of a broader transformation of Mexico's political regime, though without recourse to a military coup. Auraujo describes this transition as being one between a corporatist 'Old Regime' and a neoliberal 'New Regime' (Araujo, 2010, p. 41). The former was grounded in an Import-Substitution Industrialisation (ISI) economic model organized around a national power bloc composed of domestic capital and organized labour. Tension between the different forces in Mexico's corporatist framework came to a head with President Lopez Portillo's (1976–1982) decision to nationalize the banking sector in 1982 in view of the debt crisis. The government essentially socialized the foreign-debt obligations of Mexican commercial banks to the benefit of creditors and the American state (Marois, 2014, p. 315). As a result, the Mexican banking sector, as well as the wider business sector, began to push for greater autonomy and to demand a larger role in policymaking. Domestic pressure to dismantle the ISI model converged with the structural adjustment programmes (SAPs) implemented by the International Monetary Fund (IMF) and the World Bank. This combination of factors helped *los técnicos* consolidate their control over the Ministry of Finance, the Ministry of Planning and Budgeting, and the Bank of Mexico. Buttressed by SAPs, *los técnicos* were able to push through a programme of liberalization, privatization, and austerity, and supported by large domestic and transnational financial capital who profited off the privatization of banks and the liberalization foreign investment at the expense of already weakened trade unions (Hogenboom, 2014, p. 298; see also Araujo, 2010, pp. 42–43; Kleinberg, 1999, pp. 74–75).

These changes were consolidated and furthered by a group of technocrats within the Ministry of Planning and Budgeting (Secretaría de Programación y Presupuesto, SPP) during the presidency of Carlos Salinas de Gortari (1988–1994) (León-Manríquez & Alvarez León, 2019, pp. 123–124). Along with a group centred in the Ministry of Finance, these technocrats favoured greater integration with the US, which led to Mexico joining the North American Free Trade Agreement (NAFTA) in 1993 (León-Manríquez & Alvarez León, 2019, pp. 123–124). Mexico's exports to the US grew exponentially, reaching 77% of total exports in 2018 while Canada represented its second most important destination with 4.14% (Observatory of Economic Complexity, 2018c). NAFTA represented *los técnicos'* a successful attempt to consolidate the neoliberal transformation of the Mexican state through the rescaling of authority (Ramírez, 2014, p. 18). Neoliberal reforms were continued during the Ernesto Zedillo presidency (1994–2000) that sought to further 'chileanize' the Mexican economy and state (Kleinberg, 1999, p. 82). These different changes ensured that the interests of, transnational capital, and financial capital entered into a power bloc within the Mexican state. New social movements, such as the Zapatista uprising in Chiapas, emerged as a reaction to the neoliberal reforms of the period. However, overall, Mexican civil society overall had been weakened by decades of corporatist rule and was not able to successfully block the reforms (Hogenboom, 2014, p. 299). Importantly, neoliberal reforms weakened the corporatist framework that sustained the PRI's grip on power to the degree that it unravelled and opened the way for the election of Vincent Fox (2000–2006) from the *Partido Acción Nacional* (National Action Party – PAN).

With Fox's victory, some *técnicos* associated with the PRI were replaced by actors that had been operating in the private sector (Hogenboom, 2014, p. 298). Yet the strategic selectivity of the state did not change significantly during the two PAN presidencies. Although the PRI had lost, neoliberal technocracy 'had guaranteed 'its' model' (Araujo, 2010, p. 50). Their neoliberal state project was not put into question when the PRI retook the presidency in 2012 with the election of Enrique Peña Nieto. With regard to regionalism, Nieto's political rival, Lopez Obrador (AMLO), had a record of criticizing free trade agreements such as NAFTA. Nevertheless, in the latter stages of the 2018 presidential campaign that saw the election of Lopez Obrador, he began softening his tone towards business interests. Though AMLO has been lukewarm in embracing the AP itself – his absence from Lima Presidential Summit in 2019 caused some consternation among other regional partners – he has remained unobtrusive. This is likely due to his aim to diversify exports away from the US and towards South America and Asia (Foster, 2020).

Peru

The consolidation of technocratic powers along neoliberal lines within the Peruvian state occurred in a delayed fashion and was mediated by economic crisis. Alberto Fujimori won the 1990 presidential election amid hyperinflation and growing difficulty in accessing international credit. The economic crisis reinforced the political strength of economic sectors that were supportive of neoliberal reforms and austerity, which facilitated their implementation in coordination with the World Bank and IMF. Not satisfied by the constraints of the existing constitution, Fujimori carried out an *auto-golpe* in 1992 that allowed him to 'rule by decree' while he supervised the elaboration of a new constitution. Keeping in line with the reforms that had been passed, the new constitution that was adopted consecrated free enterprise and private property while guaranteeing the equal treatment of domestic and foreign investment (Avilés & Rosas, 2017, pp. 165–166).

The changes implemented by the Fujimori government elided the established bureaucracy and was guided by a mix of newly minted *técnicos* and 'non-political' ministers from the private sector. Armed by the protection of the authoritarian regime during the 1990s, this nexus of actors was able to extend their influence throughout the Peruvian state. The new class of technocrats centred their influence in the central economic agencies of the state; notably the Ministry of the Economy and Finance, the Central Bank, and a series of newly minted economic agencies such as the *Superintendencia de Banca y Seguros*. Key policies emerging from this technocratic network centred on the reduction of tariffs and increased interest rates to bring inflation under control, all of which adversely affected domestic industry as the importation of consumer goods increased by 27.4% annually between 1990 and 1996 (Lust, 2019, pp. 57–58).

This network of neoliberal *técnicos* were able to survive the collapse of the Fujimori regime in 2000 by participating in the rearticulation of democracy by focusing on transparency and cracking down on clientelism. Significantly, all of Fujimori's presidential successors up until Pedro Pablo Kuczynski (2016–2018), a former *técnico*, all campaigned on platforms that touched upon anti-neoliberal themes, yet all ended up conforming to it in view of significant pressure from Peru's right-oriented state/society complex (Cannon, 2016, p. 79). Indeed, Fujimori's first elected successor, Alejandro Toledo (2001–2006) rapidly lost the support of the popular sectors by failing to carry out promised reforms, and instead relying on *técnicos* for day-to-day governance (Vergara & Wantanabe, 2016, pp. 150–151; Vergara & Encinas, 2016, pp. 166–167). The overall weakness of political parties and an export boom during the 2000s led to a strategic selectivity that played to the interests of technocratic state fractions well into the subsequent Garcia presidency (2006–2011). These reforms, nonetheless, generated political instability in the period leading up the creation of the AP.

Precipitating social dislocation and instability was the expansion of the mining sector, which went from 45.1% of exports in 1990–61.2% in 2010, helped by the commodity price boom of the 2000s (Lust, 2019, p. 66). As a result of these changes, 'transnational extractive Capital' became the 'hegemonic fraction within the bloc in power' in conjunction with the 'financial fraction of the bourgeoisie' reinforced by the policies of subsequent presidents (Lust, 2019, 120). Yet the expansion of this sector created little employment, leading to a decline in real wages, increasingly informal employment, and systematic encroachment into indigenous territories (Lust, 2019, pp. 69–74). As a result of these factors, 2003 saw a major strike wave on the basis of increased wage demands, ending privatisations, and protection for agriculture; which forced Toledo to declare a state of emergency. Even in the face of renewed social protest over austerity, indigenous rights and environmental protection, Garcia launched the negotiation of the AP. Even Garcia's successor, Ollanta Humala, finalized the AP accord despite having criticized free trade agreements and who, like his predecessors, refused to challenge the sway of the *técnicos* over economic policy (Avilés & Rosas, 2017, p. 173). Notwithstanding some initial uncertainty from traditional economic elites accustomed to clientelistic relations with the state, *los técnicos* eventually gained support from the private sector by consulting peak business organizations and ensuring the long-term interests of domestic capital as a whole (Dargent, 2014, p. 323).

In line with the South American partners of the AP, Peru shifted towards an economy largely focused on mineral exports focused on the Asia-Pacific region. In 2018, China was the primary destination for its exports (27.3%) with Korea (5.1%) and Japan (4.5%) also constituting important markets(Observatory of Economic Complexity, 2018c). Peru's orientation towards Asian markets was deepened by a series of bilateral trade agreements with Asian countries right before, during, and after the AP was being negotiated. In fact, during the period in question, Peru signed over twenty bilateral investments agreements and eleven free trade agreements, all of which imposed legal constraints on the ability of incoming governments to change Peru's economic policy (Vergara & Encinas, 2016, pp. 171–172; cf. Reinoso, 2019, p. 73).

The Odebrecht disclosures of political corruption in 2016 presented a major challenge Peru's political system. Notably, Kuczynski was forced to resign as president due to another corruption case. His replacement, Martín Vizcarra (2018–2020), pursued an anti-corruption campaign that embroiled former presidents and put him at loggerheads with the Peruvian Congress. Tensions came to a head when Vizcarra was removed from power by the Congress in November 2020 in what has been described as a legislative coup. Mass protests against Vizcarra's removal from power forced his immediate successor to resign and the current president, Francisco Sagasti, is tasked with managing a persistent crisis amid demands by protesters for a new constitution as in Chile (Nestor Pastor, 2020). The question remains as in Chile, and as we will see in Colombia, whether technocratic forces within the Peruvian state will be able to maintain that country's neoliberal orientation domestically and regionally in view of these challenges.

Colombia

The Colombian case presents somewhat of an exception as a result of its early depoliticization of economic policy. Drawn out over a longer period of time, its origins can be traced to much earlier reforms, notably those of US Economic advisor Lauchlin Currie's notion 'accelerated economic development' that was popularized in Colombian policy circles between the 1950s–1970s with an its emphasis on developing 'efficient' agri-businesses firms coupled with low tariffs and minimal social protection (Brittain, 2005, pp. 343–347). In fact, Colombian politics has been characterized by a strong consensus on the neoliberal economic policies advocated by Currie that channelled political disagreement into security questions – in part, how to deal with the country's guerilla movements, which have served to marginalize the country's Left from state power (Cannon, 2016, p. 77).

Technocrats within the Colombian state were established during the period of 'accelerated economic development', as part of a political pact to ensure the transition from authoritarian rule and to put an end *La Violencia*. During the period of the National Front (1958–1974), the Liberal and Conservative parties agreed to rotate forming government over four terms. It was recognized that a competent and relatively autonomous bureaucracy would be key to the transition, which led to the rise of the technocrats within the state and the growth in importance of economic agencies such as the Ministry of Finance and the National Planning Office (Dargent, 2014, p. 318). The rise of *los técnicos*, within the Colombian state, in many ways, preceded neoliberal transformations elsewhere.

The central economic ministries have generally maintained close ties with leading business organizations in consultation over major policy decisions. They, nevertheless, often adopted positions that ran counter to the interests of these organizations, such as the currency devaluation that took place in 1985 or the measures that were adopted to counter the financial crisis that took place at the end of the 1990s. This tendency was reinforced by the attempt to insulate monetary policy from business and public pressure through an independent board within the Central Bank (Dargent, 2014, pp. 323–324). Many of these reforms were put in place during the presidency of César Gaviria (1990–1994) and subsequent presidencies up to this day have continued with these neoliberal policies (Cannon, 2016, p. 62). The *apertura* period of liberalization, launched in February 1990, also saw the emergence of economic actors that supported the pursuit of free trade agreements, such as the Free Trade Area of the Americas (FTAA). However, support for trade liberalization has been uneven as new civil society organizations that oppose trade liberalization emerged during this period and rallied to older ones. (De Lombaerde et al., 2019, p. 87). This unevenness in support was expressed by Colombia's diverse business associations being resistant to a potential trade agreement, especially with China. This may have to do with the fact that the United States remains the primary export destination at 26.5% (2018), while China comes in a distant second with 9.4% (Observatory of Economic Complexity, 2018b). This has led to the seemingly contradictory position whereby: 'Business associations like ANDI and FENALCO oppose FTAs with Asia-Pacific countries but favor the PA … ' (De Lombaerde et al., 2019, p. 98). This can potentially be explained by their support for the potential domestic disciplinary dimension of the AP as opposed to its market access dimension.

Indeed, the persistent ability of the *técnicos* to maintain their hold on the economic policy of the Colombian state across different political administrations was facilitated by the fragmentation of the business community and their sectoral demands (Dargent, 2014, p. 84). Nevertheless, there have been signs that neoliberalism has some legitimacy via massive mobilisations that have taken place since 2019 against a package of neoliberal reforms introduced by current president Iván Duque (Hylton, 2020). As is the case in Chile and Peru, the forces behind the AP in Colombia are facing the greatest challenge to the authority within the state since they came to power.

Institutional structure of the Pacific Alliance

The AP's institutional framework replicates many of the institutional strategies and mechanisms that allow central economic agencies to maintain their authority over economic policy at the domestic level. It should be no surprise, therefore, that the AP's negotiation infrastructure is similar, in some ways, to the one that was put in place to negotiate the FTAA (see Nelson, 2015).[3] Importantly, the AP's negotiation infrastructure is designed to withstand political instability within the domestic contexts of each participating state. Notably, it is designed in a way that the consequences of electoral change and political instability are to be channeled to the the AP's outer institutional layer in order to permit its inner institutional layers to continue to drive the integration process forward.

Like the FTAA, the AP could thus be thought of as having an onion-like institutional framework with an important role accorded to its inner layers centered on the ministerial apparatuses of member countries beyond the role played by each respective president in the outer layer. To that end, although the presidents of each participating state represent the highest authority within the regional space, its Framework Agreement does not explicitly outline their role within the project (Tremolada Álvarez, 2014, pp. 739–740). While there have been several key interventions made by presidents during Presidential Summits to resolve certain political deadlocks (Tvevad, 2014, p. 8), what is essential is key roles outlined at the ministerial and sub-ministerial levels typically dominated by the *técnicos* of every state.

Beyond the outer layer of the Presidential Summits, we find the Council of Ministers (CM) made up of the members' foreign ministers and foreign trade ministers and it is the organ that has the most clearly delineated mandate by the Framework Agreement. In the absence of a permanent secretariat or administrative body, as well as ambiguous roles outlined for presidents, the CM constitutes a key body within the integration project because of its clearly outlined administrative responsibilities (Tremolada Álvarez, 2014, p. 741). Concretely, the CM is responsible for 'adopting the decisions to promote the goals and specific actions set out in the Framework Agreement and in the declarations from the presidential summits, monitoring that they are implemented correctly and evaluating the results achieved' (Tvevad, 2014, p. 7). This responsibility provides it with significant influence over the evolution of the project. The CM was entrusted with approving the programmes initiated by the AP, as well as defining its agenda. Furthermore, the CM was made responsible for defining the AP's relationship with third parties whether they are other states or regional projects as well as for convoking the High Level Group as well as the other working groups. And, lastly, it is responsible for adopting additional measures, if necessary, to ensure that the objectives of the AP are met (OAS, 2012). The centrality of the CM, accordingly, provides the AP project with a measure of insulation from the vagaries of electoral politics that mostly impact the role played by presidents.

Moving inward from the CM, the High Level Group (HLG) composed of the vice ministers adds another level of insulation between the integration process and the political concerns that might arise at the presidential level. The HLG is responsible for supervising progress in the working groups, investigating new areas of potential integration, and to prepare proposals for the extension of the relationship with the AP with other regional groupings. Finally, within the HLG there is the layer of the AP's 25 technical working groups that are responsible for generating the substance of the agreement (Alianzo del Pacifico [AP], n.d.).

Importantly, similar to the FTAA's Business Forum, the AP established a Business Council tasked with making direct proposals to the process. Made up of members from all four states, it has an advisory role and liaises with government agencies and business unions (Palacio Valencia, 2019, p. 10). Unsurprisingly, there is no civil society group or council representing the interests of groups that are not part of the private sector. It essentially replicates the relationship that domestic economic agencies have with their power bloc, in which business organizations are consulted on important issues while being kept at a distance from them (Dargent, 2011, p. 323).

Conclusion

The plurality of Latin America's regional landscape, and the seeming lack of coherence between them, is often framed as a problem from a governance perspective. Nevertheless, this reality is not simply the result of a political will or miscalculation, but a reflection of social forces within national state spaces. As such, the AP constitutes a regional project that emanates from the core national economic agencies dominated by technocrats. It is part of a broader multiscalar state project that lock-in neoliberal economic policies at that national level. The AP does so by seeking to judicialise its policies at the regional level and by having said policies embedded within the national institutional frameworks of member states. Indeed, the sheer scope of the AP, with its 25 technical working groups, represents an attempt to further extend the influence of these central economic agencies, and the *técnicos*, over other state institutions.

The continued evolution of the AP will depend, however, on the ability of *los técnicos* to maintain their grip on the economic policy-making process in view of potential political and economic instability. Though the AP process was designed to withstand instability, it remains an incomplete project and therefore vulnerable to political dynamics within each of its member states. The mass protests in three of its member states will test *los técnicos*' hold on their state apparatuses and, therefore, their ability to drive the integration project forward. Furthermore, the task of deepening and expanding the AP will be rendered even more difficult if it were to integrate additional core members, into its rank. Especially if the domestic institutional structures of new members are not under the same control of technocratic actors, which would open up the AP to alternative conceptions of economic development and integration.

Notes

1. According to David Collier technocrats can be defined as 'individuals with a high level of specialized academic training which serves as a principal criterion on the basis of which they are selected to occupy key decision-making or advisory roles in large, complex organizations—both public and private' (1979, p. 403). Technocrats in Latin America are also characterized by their education in particular elite universities domestically and overseas in the United States and the United Kingdom where they were imbued with a neoliberal outlook on the role of the state and the economy (Silva, 1996, p. 315).
2. The Washington Consensus can be defined by as a suite of policies developed by the Bretton Woods institutions located in Washington during the 1980s that promulgated economic liberalization in a bid to dismantle the welfare states that had been established during the postwar era. An important component of the Washington Consensus was to promote trade agreements, including regional ones, that would facilitate commercial exchange and insertion in the global economy (Ovando Aldana et al., 2017, p. 172).
3. Carlos Alberto Chaves García (2017), conversely, has noted that it is quite similar to Asian forms of regional cooperation and the Asia-Pacific Economic Cooperation (APEC) forum, specifically. He argues that what differentiates the AP from the integration projects associated with Open Regionalism is its emphasis on technical cooperation as well as on a structure based on ministerial meetings, technical working groups, and presidential summits (Chaves Garcia, 2017, p. 30). Characteristics, incidentally, that were also employed during the FTAA negotiations

Disclosure statement

No potential conflict of interest was reported by the author(s).

References

Alianzo del Pacifico (AP). (n.d.). *Sitio oficial*. https://alianzapacifico.net/en/#

Angeles Villareal, M. (2016). The Pacific Alliance: A trade integration initiative in Latin America. *Congressional Research Service Report*. https://fas.org/sgp/crs/row/R43748.pdf

Araujo, O. R. (2010). The emergence and entrenchment of a new political regime in Mexico. *Latin American Perspectives*, *37*(1), 35–61. https://doi.org/10.1177/0094582X09355428

Avilés, W., & Rosas, Y. R. (2017). Low-intensity democracy and Peru's neoliberal state: The case of the Humala administration. *Latin American Perspectives*, *44*(5), 162–182. https://doi.org/10.1177/0094582X17705867

Brand, U., Görg, C., & Wissen, M. (2011). Second-order condensations of societal power relations: Environmental politics and the internationalization of the state from a neo-poulantzian perspective. *Antipode*, *43*(1), 149–175. https://doi.org/10.1111/j.1467-8330.2010.00815.x

Briceño-Ruiz, J. (2019). The dynamics of institutionalized regionalism in the Pacific Rim. In J. Briceño-Ruiz & P. De Lombaerde (Eds.), *The political economy of new regionalisms in the Pacific Rim* (pp. 9–36). Routledge.

Brittain, J. J. (2005). A theory of accelerating rural violence: Lauchlin Currie's role in underdeveloping Colombia. *The Journal of Peasant Studies, 32*(2), 335–360. https://doi.org/10.1080/03066150500094535

Cannon, B. (2016). *The right in Latin America elite power, hegemony and the struggle for the state.* Routledge.

Carranza, M. E. (2006). Clinging together: Mercosur's ambitious external agenda, its internal crisis, and the future of regional economic integration in South America. *Review of International Political Economy, 13*(5), 802–829. https://doi.org/10.1080/09692290600950662

Chaves García, C. (2017). Aproximación teórica y conceptual para el análisis de la Alianza del Pacífico. *Desafíos, 30*(1), 21–45. https://doi.org/10.12804/revistas.urosario.edu.co/desafios/a.5775

Chodor, T. (2015). *Neoliberal hegemony and the Pink Tide in Latin America: Breaking up with TINA?* Palgrave Macmillan.

Ciupa, K. (2022). Shifting tides, regional reverberations: A class-relational analysis of the ALBA-TCP. *Globalizations, 19*(4), 587–603. https://doi.org/10.1080/14747731.2021.1991201

Clark, T. D. (2017). Rethinking Chile's 'Chicago Boys': Neoliberal technocrats or revolutionary vanguard? *Third World Quarterly, 38*(6), 1350–1365. https://doi.org/10.1080/01436597.2016.1268906

Collier, D. (1979). *The new authoritarianism in Latin America.* Princeton University Press.

Comisión Económica para América Latina y el Caribe (CEPAL). (2008). *El Arco del Pacífico Latinoamericano y su proyección a Asia-Pacífico.* https://www.cepal.org/es/publicaciones/2909-arco-pacifico-latinoamericano-su-proyeccion-asia-pacifico

Dargent, E. (2011). Agents or actors? Assessing the autonomy of economic technocrats in Colombia and Peru. *Comparative Politics, 43*(3), 313–332. https://doi.org/10.5129/001041511795274913

Dargent, E. (2014). *Technocracy and democracy in Latin America: The experts running government.* Cambridge University Press.

De Lombaerde, P., Jiménez-Peña, G., & Chen, L. (2019). The political economy of Colombia's integration in the Pacific Rim. In J. Briceño-Ruiz & P. De Lombaerde (Eds.), *The political economy of new regionalisms in the Pacific Rim* (pp. 85–107). Routledge.

Du, B., Serrano, A., & Vianna, A. (2018). Institutional development and foreign banks in Chile. *International Review of Financial Analysis, 58*, 166–178. https://doi.org/10.1016/j.irfa.2017.10.001

Duarte, D. (2020). The Latin American Integrated Market (MILA): A Misnomer? *Econ Americas.* https://econamericas.com/2020/08/latin-american-integrated-market-mila-misnomer/

Dubé, S. (2019). Chile: Asia-oriented globalization versus Latin America-oriented regionalism. In J. Briceño-Ruiz, & P. De Lombaerde (Eds.), *The political economy of new regionalisms in the Pacific Rim* (pp. 37–53). Routledge.

Fisse, H. R., & Thomas, C. S. (2014). The Chilean big business lobby: A long-standing and major influence on public policy. *Journal of Public Affairs, 14*(3-4), 310–330. https://doi.org/10.1002/pa.1520

Foster, K. (2020, March 29). The future of the Pacific Alliance. *Harvard International Review.* https://hir.harvard.edu/the-future-of-the-pacific-alliance/

Gill, S., & Cutler, A. C. (2014). *New constitutionalism and world order.* Cambridge University Press.

Gómez-Mera, L., & Barrett, B. (2012). The political economy of preferential trade agreements: Latin America and beyond. *Latin American Politics and Society, 54*(1), 181–196. https://doi.org/10.1111/j.1548-2456.2012.00147.x

Grugel, J., & Riggirozzi, P. (2012). Post-neoliberalism in Latin America: Rebuilding and reclaiming the state after crisis. *Development and Change, 43*(1), 1–21. https://doi.org/10.1111/j.1467-7660.2011.01746.x

Guevara, S. L. (2016). Integración automotriz en el Mercosur y sobreexplotación obrera: formas y contenido. *Cadernos CEMARX, 8*(8), 65–84. https://doi.org/10.20396/cemarx.v0i8.10899

Hogenboom, B. (2014). The changing politics of lobbying: Private sector organizations in Mexico. *Journal of Public Affairs, 14*(3-4), 296–309. https://doi.org/10.1002/pa.1456

Hylton, F. (2020, January). Algo está pasando en Colombia. *Nueva Sociedad.* https://www.nuso.org/articulo/algo-esta-pasando-en-colombia/

Jessop, B. (2004). Multi-level governance and multi-level meta-governance'. In I. Bache & M. Flinders (Eds.), *Multi-level governance* (pp. 49–74). OUP.

Jessop, B. (2007). *State power: A strategic-relational approach.* Polity.

Jessop, B. (2016). *The state: Past, present, future.* Polity Press.

Kleinberg, R. (1999). Strategic alliances: State-business relations in Mexico under neo-liberalism and crisis. *Bulletin of Latin American Research, 18*(1), 71–87. https://doi.org/10.1111/j.1470-9856.1999.tb00188.x

Leiva, F. (2019). Economic elites and new strategies for extractivism in Chile. *European Review of Latin American and Caribbean Studies, 0*(108), 131–152. https://doi.org/10.32992/erlacs.10511

León-Manríquez, J., & Alvarez León, L. F. (2019). The long shadow of NAFTA: An economic geography of Mexico's integration into the Pacific Rim. In J. Briceño-Ruiz & P. De Lombaerde (Eds.), *The Political Economy of New Regionalisms in the Pacific Rim* (pp. 120–144). Routledge.

Lubbock, R. (2020). The hidden edifice of (food) sovereignty: Rights, territory, and the struggle for agrarian reform in Venezuela. *Journal of Agrarian Change, 20*(2), 289–310. https://doi.org/10.1111/joac.12347

Lust, J. (2019). *Capitalism, class, and revolution in Peru 1980–2016.* Palgrave MacMillan.

Malamud, C. (2015). Regional integration and cooperation in Latin America: Diagnosis and proposals. *Global Journal of Emerging Market Economies, 7*(2), 92–120. https://doi.org/10.1177/0974910115574168

Marois, T. (2014). Historical precedents, contemporary manifestations: Crisis and the socialization of financial risk in neoliberal Mexico. *Review of Radical Political Economics, 46*(3), 308–330. https://doi.org/10.1177/0486613413506077

Martínez-Castillo, A. (2016). Alianza del pacífico y mercado común del sur: Dos enfoques de la integración económica regional. *Papel Político, 21*(2), 469–494. https://doi.org/10.11144/Javeriana.papo21-2.apmc

Morales Castillo, R., Maldonado, G., & Schiavon, A. (2016). Las bases sociales de la Alianza del Pacífico. *Revista Mexicana de Política Exterior, 106*, 133–164.

Muhr, T. (2011). Conceptualising the ALBA-TCP: Third generation regionalism and political economy. *International Journal of Cuban Studies, 3*(2/3), 98–115. http://www.jstor.org/stable/41945939

Nelson, M. (2015). *A history of the FTAA: From hegemony to fragmentation in the Americas.* Palgrave MacMillan.

Nestor Pastor, D. (2020, November 20). Peruvians reject politics as usual. *NACLA.* https://nacla.org/news/2020/12/09/peruvians-reject-politics-usual

Observatory of Economic Complexity. (2018a). *Chile.* https://oec.world/en/profile/country/chl

Observatory of Economic Complexity. (2018b). *Colombia.* https://oec.world/en/profile/country/col

Observatory of Economic Complexity. (2018c). *Mexico.* https://oec.world/en/profile/country/mex

Organization for American States (OAS). (2012). *Acuerdo marco de la Alianza Pacifico.* http://www.sice.oas.org/TPD/Pacific_Alliance/Agreements/Framework_Agreement_Pacific_Alliance_s.pdf

Organization for American States (OAS). (2018). *Pacific Alliance: Background and negotiations.* http://www.sice.oas.org/TPD/Pacific_Alliance/Pacific_Alliance_e.asp

Ovando Aldana, W., Canales García, R., & Munguía Vázquez, G. (2017). Comercio interregional de bienes manufacturados en los países de la Alianza del Pacífico desde la Teoría de Linder. *Desafíos, 29*(2), 169–197. https://doi.org/10.12804/revistas.urosario.edu.co/desafios/a.4876

Oyarzún Serrano, L. (2017). The Pacific Alliance and the construction of a new economic regime? In J. Briceño-Ruiz and Isidro Morales (Eds.), *Post-hegemonic regionalism in the Americas: Toward a Pacific-Atlantic divide?* (pp. 141–158). Routledge. https://doi.org/10.4324/9781315601663-8

Palacio Valencia, A. M. (2019). The Pacific Alliance: Building a pathway to the high-hanging fruits of deep integration. In P. Sauvé, R. Polanco Lazo, & J. Álvarez Zárate (Eds.), *The Pacific Alliance in a world of preferential trade agreements* (pp. 3–28). Springer.

Perry, A. (2016). *Financial integration in the Pacific Alliance.* Inter-American Development Bank. https://publications.iadb.org/publications/english/document/Financial-Integration-in-the-Pacific-Alliance.pdf

Poulantzas, N. (2014). *State, power, socialism.* Verso.

Quiliconi, C., & Salgado Espinoza, R. (2017). Latin American integration: Regionalism à la carte in a multipolar world? *Colombia Internacional, 92*(92), 15–41. https://doi.org/10.7440/colombiaint92.2017.01

Ramírez, G. L. A. (2014). Planteamiento teórico y evidencia del desplazamiento gradual del estado autoritario al estado pragmático en méxico: La transformación de las élites. *Revista Mexicana De Ciencias Políticas y Sociales, 59*(222), 1–33. https://doi.org/10.1016/s0185-1918(14)70220-x

Reinoso, A. F. (2019). Relations with Asia in Peru's trade agreements. In J. Briceño-Ruiz & P. De Lombaerde (Eds.), *The Political Economy of New Regionalisms in the Pacific Rim* (pp. 54–84). Routledge.

Ruiz, J. B. (2010). La iniciativa del arco del pacífico latinoamericano. *Nueva Sociedad, 228*, 44–59. https://nuso.org/articulo/la-iniciativa-del-arco-del-pacifico-latinoamericano-un-nuevo-actor-en-el-escenario-de-la-integracion-regional/

Santander. (n.d.). Chilean foreign trade in figures. https://santandertrade.com/en/portal/analyse-markets/chile/foreign-trade-in-figures

Sauvé, P., Polanco Lazo, R., & Álvarez Zárate, J. (2019). The Pacific Alliance in a world of preferential trade agreements: An introduction. In P. Sauvé, R. Polanco Lazo, & J. Álvarez Zárate (Eds.), *The Pacific Alliance in a world of preferential trade agreements* (pp. ix–xii). Springer.

Silva, E. (1996). From dictatorship to democracy: The business-state nexus in Chile's economic transformation, 1975–1994. *Comparative Politics, 28*(3), 299–320. https://doi.org/10.2307/422209

Solimano, A. (2012). *Chile and the neoliberal trap: The post-Pinochet era.* Cambridge University Press.

Stephens, H., & Navarro, J. (2018). *Canada and associate membership in the pacific alliance: An important part of a global trade strategy.* School of Public Policy Publications.

Tickell, A., & Peck, J. (2003). Making global rules: Globalization or neoliberalization. In J. Peck and H. Wai-chung Yeung (Eds.), *Remaking the global economy: Economic-geographical perspectives.* Sage Publications Ltd (pp. 3–26). https://www.doi.org/10.4135/9781446216767

Tremolada Álvarez, E. (2014). ¿La Alianza del Pacífico facilita la inserción de Colombia en la región Asia-Pacífico? *Papel Político, 19*(2), 721–752. https://doi.org/10.11144/Javeriana.PAPO19-2.apfi

Tvevad, J. (2014). The Pacific Alliance: Regional integration or fragmentation? http://www.europarl.europa.eu/RegData/etudes/briefing_note/join/2014/522318/EXPO-AFET_SP(2014)522318_EN.pdf

Vergara, A., & Encinas, D. (2016). Continuity by surprise: Explaining institutional stability in contemporary Peru. *Latin American Research Review, 51*(1), 159–180. https://doi.org/10.1353/lar.2016.0006

Vergara, A., & Wantanabe, A. (2016). Peru since Fujimori. *Journal of Democracy, 27*(3), 148–157. https://doi.org/10.1353/jod.2016.0054

World Bank. (2019). *Latin America & Caribbean export partner share to United States, in % 2005–2017.* Retrieved from https://wits.worldbank.org/CountryProfile/en/Country/LCN/StartYear/2005/EndYear/2017/TradeFlow/Export/Partner/USA/Indicator/XPRT-PRTNR-SHR

Shifting tides, regional reverberations: a class-relational analysis of the ALBA-TCP

Kristin Ciupa

ABSTRACT

The Bolivarian Alliance for the Peoples of Our America-Peoples Trade Treaty (ALBA-TCP) represents the most dramatic regional departure from neoliberalism under Latin America's pink tide, based on principles of anti-imperialism, mutual development, and barter exchange. Since 2015 however, trade and social programmes between member countries have deteriorated, while regional support for ALBA has declined. In order to account for the rise and relative fall of ALBA-TCP, this article mobilizes the theory of social property relations to trace the international, regional and national forces and structures that have shaped the development trajectory of the ALBA since its creation in 2004. It argues that ALBA's characteristics are principally constituted through concrete class formations, struggles and institutional resolutions that shape the pattern of ALBA's international relations. Ultimately, the contradictions of ALBA's social base with its uneven insertion into the broader international division of labour has created a series of tensions and roadblocks.

Introduction

Latin American regionalisms in the early twenty-first century have seen a number of reconfigurations. While the creation of the Union of South American Nations (UNASUR), the Community of Latin American and Caribbean States (CELAC), and even a reformulation of the Southern Common Market (MERCOSUR) to include provisions aimed at facilitating mutual development, all reflect the shifting tides of regionalism, it is the Bolivarian Alliance for the Peoples of Our America (ALBA) that has engendered the strongest regional reverberations. Based on principles of cooperation, complementarity, sovereignty and mutual development, the ALBA represents the most radical attempt to depart from the forms of 'open regionalism' or free trade agreements of the neoliberal era (see Briceño-Ruiz, 2017; ECLAC, 1994). ALBA was first conceptualized as an alternative to the US-led Free Trade Agreement of the Americas (FTAA) by Hugo Chávez and Fidel Castro in 2001 (Nelson, 2015). After its official inauguration in 2004, ALBA expanded its membership (11 members at its peak) and scope to become a substantial anti-imperial coalition, whose strength drew from an alliance between left-wing member governments supported by popular classes, as well as high commodity prices until 2014. However, the decline in primary commodity prices from 2015 onwards, the drop in Venezuelan oil production levels, and a resurgence of the right in Latin American civil society and electoral politics backed by an increasingly aggressive US stance in the region, have led to a decline in ALBA-based trading and social programmes, as well as a decline in ALBA membership.

Since its formation there has been an abundance of literature written on ALBA, which explores its potential as an alternative form of regional integration. Theoretical interventions on the ALBA have primarily situated the agreement as a counterweight to predominant global forces, focusing on ALBA states as cohesive entities and as the agents of economic and social change. Empirical studies have outlined the architecture of ALBA agreements, and analyse the successes and limitations of policy-making on, for example, trade, finance and education.[1] Few studies have explored the class relations that have shaped ALBA's formation and development as an anti-imperial and anti-neoliberal alliance: a factor that is crucial to understanding the uniqueness of ALBA, as well as the political economic context in which it operates.

In order to account for the rise and decline of the ALBA-TCP, this study aims to build upon approaches that analyse the class relations shaping the political space and foreign policy agendas of ALBA member countries (Lubbock, 2019; Muhr, 2012; Nelson, 2015, 2019), as well as those that situate the ALBA as a response to geopolitics and relations of power in the international sphere (Anderson, 2016; Briceño-Ruiz, 2017; Muhr, 2012a).[2] Employing the concept of social property relations, this article provides an overview of the local and international forces and relations of power that operate in tandem, and that have shaped the development trajectory of the ALBA since 2004. It does so via concrete examples that are illustrative, though not exhaustive, of the social forces that have shaped participation in ALBA over time. This methodological approach is the basis of social property relations, which mobilizes specific details of social conflict and 'social innovation' in order to theorize the broader significance of historical developments (Knafo & Teschke, 2020, pp. 19–21). The article thus explores how the ALBA developed as a result of particular class alliances that challenge unequal local and international structures, and the limitations of ALBA as a result of unevenness within and between states under global capitalism.

First, I outline a theoretical framework based on Political Marxism, in order to situate the ALBA as a form of regionalism that is constitutive of, and responds to, Latin America's role in the global political economy, regional relations of power, and social property relations in member countries. Second, I explore the ALBA's formation as an alternative to the FTAA in 2004 situating it within the neoliberal era and its contradictions. Third, the article outlines ALBA programmes, and relying on the social property relations approach, analyses how the balance of class forces in the pink tide era affected ALBA's spatialization strategies. Fourth, it explores how the changing balance of forces internationally and regionally since 2015 have led to a decline of ALBA programmes and membership.

Class struggle and the politics of property

The theory of social property relations provides an analytical framework for understanding how local class politics influence the creation, and composition, of regional political formations in response to unevenness and inequality in the international sphere. This approach has its origins in Political Marxism, principally the work of Robert Brenner and Ellen Meiksins Wood, which was later 'internationalised' by scholars such as Benno Teschke (2009) and Hannes Lacher (2006). Brenner links the possibility for changes in long-term economic development to the structure of class forces within a particular locale. Classes, he argues, are defined around the surplus extraction relationship (distinguishing between direct producers and the ruling class), as well as by the relations of direct producers to one another, and to the tools and land used in production (forces of production) (Brenner, 1995, p. 11). Classes are not static, and it is class relations, antagonisms and conflicts that are the principle of movement within a mode of production (Wood, 1995, p. 98), which either reaffirms or destroys existing property relations.

The theory of social property relations responds to the economic determinism of orthodox historical materialism, wherein relations of exploitation are considered to derive from 'the prior and external logic of productive forces', by instead focusing on class struggle as the source of historical movement (Lafrance, 2021, p. 9). Within this agency-centred approach, however, the primacy of structural 'rules of reproduction' in imposing pressures, incentives and patterns of action is a contested theme (cf. Knafo & Teschke, 2020; Lafrance, 2021; Post, 2021). Lafrance (2021, pp. 12–15) argues that what appear as autonomous economic laws of capitalism (rules of reproduction) that circumscribe human behaviour, are actually the result of alienated social relationships mediated by the market, historically specific class exploitation, and the need to compete under capitalism. Rules of reproduction thus do not preclude agency per se, but rather compel agents to follow roughly similar paths in order to ensure their survival (Post, 2021, pp. 3–4, 14). Once established, access to the means of production by economic actors shapes social reproduction, thereby determining the economic development of a given society (Allinson & Anievas, 2010, p. 199). Yet the structures that compel actors to follow certain reproductive rules also incentivize class struggles that challenge these rules as a result of periodic socio-economic crises (Lafrance, 2021, p. 18; Post, 2021, pp. 2–3). This perspective thus analyses the possibilities, and limitations, of class conflict in shaping long term economic development by altering conditions of surplus extraction and existing property relations.

Contemporary iterations of Political Marxism over the past decades have explored the mutually constitutive relationship between the multiplicity of social relations in different locales and global capitalist development. Teschke (2009, pp. 265–266) argues that differing capitalist social property relations between countries are the result of the way in which national capitalist expansion was mediated by pre-existing domestic class relationships, as well as by the timing of when countries were exposed to the competitive pressures of capitalism. Thus, the difference between national capitalisms, and their variations in institutions and state forms, can be attributed to internal conditions as well as to global market conditions when countries became capitalist (Post, 2021, p. 12). In the modern international system, these differences manifest as competition between states in the world market, as individual states or groups of states attempt to 'internationalize' their authority (Lacher, 2006, pp. 116–117). While the global system is politically managed by multilateral institutions in order to stave off crisis, the world economy is regulated by leading capitalist states (Teschke, 2009, p. 267), which produces and reinforces uneven relations of power and development between countries. Late developing countries are particularly prone to sociopolitical crises due to global unevenness, which gives way to class struggles that transform relations, space, and state forms, and thus can lead to new combinations of social property relations (Teschke, 2005, p. 21).

Embedded in these discussions is an analysis of how capitalist social relations constantly reshape strategies of territorialization and space (Dufour, 2007, p. 591; Lacher, 2006). Lacher (2006, p. 153) argues that states have played a crucial role in shaping the integration and fragmentation of global space. In so doing, states affect accumulation at different scales, shaping possibilities for firms and classes (Lacher, 2006, p. 155). In the context of regional agreements like the ALBA-TCP, states remain the primary actors shaping regional coordination and programming. Yet the constitution and identity of states as political units are primarily defined by relations between social classes, which shape the trajectory of state decision-making (Teschke, 2009, p. 7). Thus, international socio-political processes are mediated by socially situated actors that struggle to define the institutions and regulations that shape economic activity through innovative strategies (Knafo & Teschke, 2020; Teschke & Lacher, 2007). Yet the outcomes of this process often develop in unintended ways due to the complexities and multiple agencies involved in social struggles (Knafo & Teschke, 2020, pp. 15–16, 20).

Within such analyses of how capitalist social relations reshape spatialization strategies, we can situate the ALBA as an attempt to re-make global and regional geo-political space in ways that are representative of the balance of social forces within ALBA member countries, and that insulate member countries from the contradictions of global capitalism. The inequalities and unevenness within the global economy to which ALBA responds have their origins in the extractivist and export-oriented form of accumulation that predominates in Latin America, and its corresponding social property relations. Dating back to the late nineteenth and early twentieth centuries when Latin American extractive sectors expanded in response to European demand for raw materials, this form of accumulation relies heavily on foreign capital and is driven by external demand. These international ties, along with underdeveloped national industrial and agricultural sectors, make the region vulnerable to, and principally dependent upon, fluctuating conditions in global commodity markets. Burgeoning global demand for resources has also made the region one of strategic geopolitical importance, with direct and indirect (particularly US) intervention shaping the national and regional political economy.

Within countries, the development of export sectors transformed urban and rural spaces, by altering forms of production and social property relations as a result of broader global capitalist processes (Morton, 2011, p. 16). In the face of uneven development and technologically intensive extractive sectors, limited employment opportunities in increasingly urbanized settings have contributed to a large working poor population and high rates of social inequality and exclusion (Skidmore & Smith, 2005, pp. 46–51). When primary commodity prices decline, extractivist and export-oriented accumulation produces periodic crises, often giving way to sociopolitical struggles over access to resources. Earlier development models, like that of import substitution industrialization, responded to the interests of organized labour by incorporating a growing working class into capitalist production through employment opportunities in newly created industries, which had the effect of also integrating the working class into capitalist patterns of consumption (Ciupa, forthcoming). In contrast, the ALBA, and the pink tide in general, adopted an anti-neoliberal and in some cases anti-capitalist agenda, reflective in part of the diversity of pink tide states whose supporters were marginalized in the neoliberal period (Silva, 2009).

How, then, does Political Marxism conceive of popular struggles that seek to go beyond the confines of capitalist social property relations? Political Marxism has been far more focused on the transition(s) to capitalism (e.g. Lafrance & Post, 2019), than on potential transitions away from capitalism. However, as Ellen Wood once noted about the transition from capitalism to socialism, 'although the struggle between the exploiting and exploited classes has been a major force in every transformation of production-relations, no other social revolution has ever placed the exploited class of the old social order in command of the new one' (Wood, 2012, p. 305). Under capitalism, since the working class has a material interest in overturning its subordination within the labour process, its struggle will necessarily seek to bring strategic control of production back towards the direct producers. Yet emancipatory struggles will always go beyond the boundaries of narrow 'class politics', necessarily creating coalitions around alternative axes of 'peace, gender, environment, and culture' (Wood, 2012, p. 306). These coalitions, however, must be grounded in the interests of the 'collective labourer', insofar as the breaking of capitalist class power will necessarily concentrate itself within the transformation of social property relations that determine the collective production of society as a whole (Wood, 2012, pp. 306–307). It was precisely these strategic considerations that animated the Bolivarian process in particular, and the ALBA regional space in general, as popular classes including formal and informal workers, women, peasants and indigenous people formed alliances to challenge capitalist social property relations (Ciccariello-Maher, 2013).

ALBA as an anti-imperialist and anti-neoliberal alternative

While ALBA was officially launched on 14 December 2004, Cuban medical assistance to Venezuela during a flood in Caracas in 1999, and a subsequent Integral Cooperation Agreement between the two countries signed on 30 October 2000, provided the foundation for ALBA's first bilateral agreement. This agreement saw approximately 20,000 Cuban doctors sent to Venezuela in exchange for heavily subsidized Venezuelan oil, in addition to the elimination of tariff barriers between the two countries (McCarthy-Jones, 2016, p. 54). In Venezuela, new popular class alliances centred around support for Chávez, and rising oil prices, supported Chávez's goal to promote a 'multi-polar' world order that would redistribute global relations of power via regional integration (McCarthy-Jones, 2016). For Cuba, which had been providing material assistance and political solidarity to the Bolivarian process from the outset, the ALBA represented a continuation of its cooperative foreign policy dating back to the 'Special Period' initiated in 1991 (Yaffe, 2011, p. 132). Bolivia joined ALBA in April 2006, shortly after Morales took office following a period of massive left-indigenous mobilization against the previous neoliberal regime. ALBA's literacy, education, and healthcare programmes aligned with goals contained in Bolivia's 2006–2011 National Development Plan (Artaraz, 2011), and at Bolivia's request, the three member countries entered into a People's Trade Agreement (*Tratado de Comercio de los Pueblos* – TCP) based on principles of fair trade in May 2006 (see Pearce, 2013). The following countries subsequently joined the ALBA: Nicaragua, Dominica, Honduras, Ecuador, Saint Vincent and the Grenadines, Antigua and Barbuda, St. Lucia, Grenada, and St Kitts and Nevis.

The ALBA-TCP's principles reflected mass mobilizations across the region that began in the 1980s against the negative socio-economic effects of austerity and free trade, and continued into the 2000s in response to the proposed FTAA. In response to conditional debt restructuring and open regionalism during the neoliberal era that restored capital profitability and protected the economic interests of advanced capitalist states, the ALBA was an attempt to reduce social inequality and to reconfigure international relations of power and space to improve the standing of member states in the international sphere. It did so through socio-economic programmes that promoted flexible and reciprocal integration, increased regional autonomy via development strategies free from external intervention, promoted 'cooperative advantage' rather than 'comparative advantage' between members; and built institutions promoting direct democracy (ALBA-TCP, 2008; Muhr, 2010).

In contrast to the austerity measures that characterized neoliberal governments, the ALBA prioritized delivering social services within and between national spaces. Direct investment and energy agreements between Nicaragua and Venezuela were used to finance water, health, and sanitation programmes; housing infrastructure projects; transportation subsidies; and credit at concessionary rates (Carrión, 2018, pp. 95–99). In Venezuela, exchanging oil for goods and services from other member countries helped to support the government's social missions that for example, provided healthcare clinics in local neighbourhoods staffed by Cuban doctors (*Misión Barrio Adentro*), and free eye operations (*Misión Milagro*). In Bolivia, a literacy campaign launched with the help of Cuban advisors (*Yo Sí Puedo!*) saw more than 800,000 illiterate adults meet the programme's objectives between 2006 and 2008, and UNESCO declared the country free of illiteracy (Artaraz, 2018, p. 62). Cuba's medical presence has also helped to establish clinics in Bolivian rural communities (Artaraz, 2011, p. 97).

Participation was not limited to pink tide governments, however, and one of the unique features of ALBA programmes was that in countries still under neoliberal leadership, municipal governments and associations, political parties and civil society groups coordinated ALBA programmes at subnational scales (Muhr, 2012, p. 773). For example, Nicaragua's participation in ALBA began in 2004 at the municipal level with the assistance of the national opposition party Sandinista National Liberation Front (FSLN), until Daniel Ortega of the FSLN was subsequently elected as President in 2007, and Nicaragua joined ALBA as a full member in January 2007 (Muhr, 2012). The FSLN was key in signing a Hydrocarbon Agreement with Petrocaribe in 2006 that created a jointly-owned enterprise, ALBA Petroleos de Nicaragua (ALBANIC), between Petrocaribe and the Association of Nicaraguan Town Councils (a not-for-profit civil association formed by 153 FSLN municipalities) (Muhr, 2012, p. 774). In the context of an energy crisis, this led to a reduction in bus fares and an alleviation of routine power cuts. *Misión Milagro* and *Yo Sí Puedo!* were also launched at the municipal levels in Nicaragua, offering medical assistance and literacy programmes, with the help of local organizations, grassroots actors and community members (Muhr, 2012, p. 775).

In place of conditional lending from the international financial institutions (IFIs) – which limited state autonomy to respond to increasing social inequality – ALBA countries took on multilateral agreements with regional lending institutions and bilateral agreements with other nations. Having paid off its debt to the IFIs in 2007, Venezuela also assisted Argentina in paying its $9.81 billion debt to the IMF by buying $1.5 billion in Argentine bonds. This was part of Chávez's initiatives to build an anti-imperial bloc in Latin America, and to move towards the creation of the proposed 'Bank of the South' (the future UNASUR institution), which he envisioned would displace the IMF and offer loans free from conditionalities (van Schaick, 2007).

An additional institution aimed at increasing regional economic independence, the Bank of ALBA, was founded in 2008 in response to the effects of the global economic crisis in Latin America. Further, a regional trading currency, the SUCRE, was created for intra-ALBA exchanges. The SUCRE system allowed countries to pay and receive funds in their national currencies. This shielded them from international currency fluctuations and high transaction costs, thereby reducing the region's vulnerability and dependence on the US dollar and foreign capital. The SUCRE provided the opportunity for small, medium and cooperative enterprises to participate in regional trade, which also offered the chance to diversify the export baskets of countries typically dependent upon primary commodities (Pearce, 2018, pp. 73–75). Barter exchange promoted flexible integration and cooperative development by allowing countries to pay for goods and services in kind. This avoided extra transaction costs and eased the financial burden of importing goods and services. For example, through the ALBANISA holding company, half of Nicaragua's oil quota from Venezuela can be repaid with agricultural exports, including sugar, beef, beans, coffee and dairy products (Carrión, 2018, pp. 96–97). This not only created a cushion against the 2008 global financial crisis in Nicaragua, but also provided a source of food imports to Venezuela. Coupled with the social economy, barter exchange of social services under the ALBA served to reduce social inequality and achieve important socio-economic improvements until about 2014.

From 2008, ALBA sought to further regionalize socio-economic development through the creation of Grandnational enterprises, comprised of both state-owned and private sector companies organized on a regional basis through state-led development strategies (Aponte-García, 2014). Promoting territorial specialization, and the participation of communal, indigenous, rural, cooperative, and small and medium-sized productive units, grandnationals aimed to facilitate shared development processes among member countries, diversify production, and promote participation in, and access to, local productive economies and services (ALBA-TCP, 2008). Grandnational enterprises were envisaged as vehicles for enhancing productive capacity, socializing the means of production, and providing goods and services to satisfy basic human needs (ALBA-TCP, 2012).

ALBA programmes can thus be understood as multiple strategies in response to crises of neoliberalism and extractivist export-oriented accumulation, aimed at reshaping space and the interconnections of global capitalism, and constituted by the balance of class forces within and between ALBA countries (cf. Lubbock, 2019; Muhr, 2011). They were made possible by class struggles developing out of the neoliberal period, represented by predominantly pink tide governments in member countries. By including the participation of organizations and actors at the local, national, international and transnational scales, the ALBA reconfigures neoliberal social relations of power by creating new spaces for participation and social inclusion (Muhr, 2012, pp. 770–771). The ALBA reconfigures regional space by creating a new economic area (ALBA-TCP, 2012) focused on strengthening and diversifying production via alternative networks of trade and productive cooperation. ALBA's socio-economic strategy thus aimed to alter global relations of power that characterize world market competition, as well as the unevenness of international production and trade, which places ALBA countries at a disadvantage. This strategy moves away from models like the US-centric FTAA, and towards a mode of spatialization that 'attempts to transcend the nation-state grid … in the spirit of global governance, but from the angle of internationalism' (Van der Pijl, 2014, p. 187). These regional initiatives were assisted by a changing international balance of power wherein direct US influence in Latin America declined, while emerging economies including China, Russia, Brazil and Argentina became sources of investment and trade, all of which supported the ALBA agenda to create a multipolar world order (ALBA-TCP, 2010; Strange, 2014).

Nevertheless, despite the relative wane of US influence in the region, the challenges of ALBA's spatialization strategies to US dominance did not go uncontested. The experience of Honduras is demonstrative of the role of class conflict and imperialist geopolitics in shaping state participation within ALBA. Honduras' membership was short lived (2008–2009) after a 2009 coup supported by conservative forces within the country including the military, resource sectors, and the majority of Congress, as well as the US State Department. The coup ousted President Manuel Zelaya, who in addition to implementing a number of moderately progressive social and economic reforms, had joined ALBA in 2008 to facilitate trade and economic growth in the context of the 2008 global crisis and economic downturn (Gordon & Webber, 2016, p. 364). The Honduran experience is indicative of the counter forces that affected spatialization strategies under the ALBA, even during its peak. In the following section, I will analyze how social relations of power under the pink tide affected ALBA initiatives at various scales.

Evaluating the ALBA-TCP

Until 2014, high commodity prices as well as strong support for left-wing governments in ALBA member countries marked the relative political, economic, and social stability of the pink tide and its policy initiatives, leading to an expansion of ALBA programmes. Since that time, the sustained decline in primary commodity prices (particularly Venezuelan oil), a resurgence of the right in Latin American civil society and electoral politics, a more aggressive US stance in the region, growing external debt, and economic and sociopolitical crisis in Venezuela, have led to a decline in ALBA-based trading and social programmes, as well as a decline in ALBA membership.

National developments

Left governments sought to alter primary commodity export-oriented forms of accumulation via state-directed programmes that distributed revenues to productive operations and vulnerable sectors of the population. They thereby attempted to channel market participation to benefit the popular classes through institutional and policy reforms that aimed to increase national and regional independence from international capital, to lessen national sectoral unevenness, and to integrate the popular sectors into local and transnational forms of socialized production. Despite these initiatives, however, resource dependency generally grew in the context of the 2000s primary commodity boom. In Bolivia, for example, the hydrocarbons and minerals sectors increased as a percentage of GDP from 10.1 percent in 1999 to 13.7 percent in 2012, while the share of industrial products in total exports fell under the Morales government from 47.4 percent in 2001 to 26.3 percent in 2010 (Webber, 2017a, p. 172). In Venezuela, oil's share of total export value rose from 68.7 percent in 1998 to 96 percent in 2014. Industry's contribution to GDP shrank from 17 percent in 2000 to 13 percent in 2013 (Lander, 2014, p. 2).

This precipitated a shifting balance of class forces in ALBA member countries, in which pink tide governments began to support the interests of national and international capital, and bureaucratic sectors, in order to reproduce extractive capitalism as the years progressed (North & Clark, 2018). In Nicaragua, for example, while social movements, cooperatives and mayoral offices played a crucial role in implementing ALBA in 2006 via a private-public company called ALBANIC, by 2008 such organizations had been excluded in favour of the state oil company, PETRONIC, which began overseeing all ALBA transactions (Carrión, 2018, p. 104). While cooperatives were initially encouraged to form alternative production chains, exporting black beans, sesame, corn, beef, beans and rice to Venezuela with preferential market access, in 2008 the state centralized the ALBA transaction process under ALBANISA, which along with its network of private enterprises, has emerged as a powerful new economic group with strong ties to the FSLN and the Ortega family.[3] The exclusion of cooperatives, peasant movements and mayoral offices was part of a purposive strategy to maintain control of social actors linked to the FSLN ruling party (La Botz, 2016). By 2008, the government began to establish a closer nexus with business that was seen as more effective for state development and national modernization than social movements (Carrión, 2018, p. 103). In this way, bureaucratic elements within the Nicaraguan state began to limit new forms of participatory democracy associated with the ALBA, and began working more closely with national business interests. This reproduced pre-existing institutions and social property relations that maintained the power of Nicaragua's agro-extractive elite (Martí i Puig & Baumeister, 2017).

In both Bolivia and Venezuela, policy-making also began to favour the interests of capital with linkages to the state. In Bolivia, development policy under the Morales government served to maintain the interests of foreign capital in the extractive sector, as well as old and newly emergent smaller domestic capitalists, with both sectors benefiting from the exploitation of labouring classes (Webber, 2017a, p. 175). While cash transfer programmes and public infrastructure spending helped to reduce poverty between 2002 and 2011 (Webber, 2017a, p. 172), during Morales' first administration (2006–2009) popular demands were largely incorporated into the existing power matrix (Webber, 2017b, p. 336), without changing the underlying structure of the Bolivian economy and its corresponding social property relations. Emergent petty capitalists (largely drawn from Bolivia's indigenous population into cooperative mining, commercial trading and contraband), allied with older dominant Bolivian sectors (agro-industrialists, mining capital, and foreign oil corporations). These sectors sought to have their interests articulated through the government when those interests were threatened by indigenous workers and peasants who sought to socialize wealth, natural resources, land and production (Webber, 2017a, pp. 176–177); and a new state alliance with agro-industrial capital was solidified beginning in 2010 after a period of class struggle between indigenous-peasant movements and agro-industrialists in the eastern lowlands (Webber, 2017b, p. 331). These class alliances and the changing composition of the state meant that demands from petty capitalists and small-scale producers on the state to improve their competitiveness vis-à-vis large-scale capitalist enterprises in the extractive industries were resolved at the expense of waged labour, peasants and indigenous people. This was achieved through policies that increased profit margins via depression of salaries, precaritization of work, flexibilization of indigenous territorial rights, and relaxation of environmental standards (Webber, 2017a, p. 173).

In Venezuela, the Bolivarian government's economic policy served to enrich financial and importing sectors of the capitalist class, along with new bureaucratic sectors associated with the Bolivarian state, including the military (Sutherland, 2018). Until the mid-2010s, workers and movements benefited from government distribution schemes that promoted the social economy, public spending and participatory democracy (Azzellini, 2017). At the same time, however, the government's strategy continued to empower private capital. The Chávez government favoured small- and medium-sized businesses (as opposed to the traditional business sectors) to import and carry out industrial and public-works projects (Ellner, 2017, pp. 41–42). As well as amassing significant wealth, small-scale capitalists often proved to be unreliable allies, and the government eventually re-established working relations with traditional Venezuelan capitalists (Ellner, 2017). Further, the government's multi-tiered exchange rate system enabled importers and state officials to illegally benefit from discrepancies between official and black-market rates. As demand for manufactured goods increased, this preferential currency transfer from the state to importers grew exponentially with only a fraction of the benefits being passed on to consumers (Sutherland, 2018). A precipitous decline in oil prices in 2014 saw significant reductions in government spending on education, healthcare and infrastructure, and greater concessions to national and international capital. This led to increased precarious work, and severely reduced imports and food subsidies; all of which disproportionately affected popular classes (Babroff, 2019).

Ultimately, the social economy functioned alongside and subservient to the rentier economy in Venezuela, with bureaucratic factions of the state seeking to undermine more radical transformations within the national economy. Class struggles around the question of production have often focused on the material transformation of the productive forces, with more radical elements seeking substantial investments into national industries. For example, Lubbock (2018, p. 181) notes that in the case of ALCASA, a state-owned aluminum producer, it was bureaucratic factions within the Venezuelan state that remained unconcerned with technical upgrading of production. By failing to upgrade the technical capacity for production, such enterprises did not operate at a scale necessary to recover the costs of production independently (Purcell, 2013, p. 156), and thus remained dependent on state transfers of oil rent. Other state-run industries, including several ALBA-created firms (PescALBA, ALBA-Leguminosas) have been subject to struggles between the workforce and bureaucratic management, with officials blocking workers' attempts to control production (Lubbock, 2019, p. 11). This, alongside other economic distortions caused by currency manipulations, contributed to profitability issues for cooperative production and the need for continual rent transfers. For example, for grandnational company ALBA-Arroz, inflationary pressures due to currency manipulations as well as government price caps imposed on subsidized rice meant that the Venezuelan government's attempts at wealth redistribution made production unsustainable (Lubbock, 2019, p. 13). Despite a month-long worker occupation of the ALBA-Arroz factories, the state returned to company to its original form of management and cost-structure, leading to the eventual liquidation of the firm (Aporrea, 2017). By 2012, private interests controlled 75 percent of the financial sector, 92 percent of the manufacturing sector, and 70 percent of the media (Yaffe, 2018, p. 147), evidence that as Brenner (1995) argues, pre-existing class relations tend to reproduce patterns of economic development if class struggles are not sufficiently strong and organized to produce an alternative.

Across ALBA countries, since the structure of social property relations under extractivist accumulation remained unchanged, conflicting demands on the state were often resolved in ways that reinforced extractive capitalism, favouring old sectors of national capital, and new ones that had been enriched under pink tide distribution models. In the context of declining export revenues, continued dependence on global markets meant that capital investment and competitiveness was prioritized over new socially-oriented policies and production models. Claudio Katz (2015, p. 39) describes this 'duality' that exists between progressive political transformation and continued primary export specialization as the result of both the limitations of government policy-making to modify a dependent economic model, and as the result of popular uprisings that were unable to assume a hegemonic position within the state. When commodity prices declined and spending across all social sectors could not be maintained, state power and national and international capital were consolidated at the expense of workers, peasants, social movements and indigenous groups.

Regional reverberations

At the regional level, spatialization strategies under the ALBA are influenced by shifting economic and political conditions within and between member countries. Productive conflicts that were resolved in favour of the state and capital, have contributed to the limited scope of public and cooperative participation in SUCRE transactions. With SUCRE states maintaining capitalist economies despite their proposed 'movement towards socialism', the vast majority of SUCRE users have been large private sector businesses that have benefited from transaction cost savings and access to new markets (Pearce, 2018, pp. 80–81). In 2011, 72.3 percent of transactions were with private companies, while ALBA's grandnational enterprises accounted for only 0.01 percent; and by 2013, use by the private sector had increased to account for 97 percent of transactions (Pearce, 2018, p. 77). In total, during the first five years of transactions, 90.2 percent were private, 7.3 percent public, and 2.5 percent with mixed enterprises (Pearce, 2018, p. 77).

An additional limitation of the SUCRE was the centrality of Venezuela within ALBA's trade network. For example, in 2010, the first year of SUCRE trade, 60.7 percent of transactions were between Ecuador and Venezuela trading food for oil; and by 2013, these had reached a peak of 96 percent (Pearce, 2018, p. 78). In 2014, only 4.26 percent of trade interactions (between Cuba and Ecuador) did not involve Venezuela (Pearce, 2018, p. 78). The decline in Venezuelan oil production, coupled with low oil prices, and growing political instability and polarization, have therefore resulted in a decline in ALBA trading. In January 2015, the price of oil declined to $50 per barrel, before recovering slightly and hitting its lowest point in January 2016 at $36 per barrel. From this time onward, the Maduro government could no longer meet its spending commitments, with Victor Álvarez, Venezuelan economist and previous Minister of Mining and Industry, estimating that the price of oil needed to be at about $120 per barrel for the government to do so (Álvarez, 2015).

These national developments were reflected in the fate of ALBA's programmes. In 2014, the overall value of SUCRE transactions halved to $497 million, and fell by a further third in 2015 to $345 million, mostly due to a decline in total trade between Venezuela and Ecuador (Pearce, 2018, p. 78). By 2017, conditions had sufficiently worsened so that exports to Venezuela only constituted 0.26 percent of Ecuador's total exports, while imports from Venezuela made up 0.087 percent of Ecuador's total imports, reducing the two countries' trade relationship to numbers far below pre-ALBA levels (Simoes & Hidalgo, 2019). Venezuela had no notable exports to Bolivia, while Bolivian exports made up only 0.0095 percent of Venezuela's imports with a value of $865 thousand (Simoes & Hidalgo, 2019). Lastly, by June of 2018, Venezuela announced it would indefinitely suspend oil deliveries to over half of the nineteen Petrocaribe members. Petrocaribe was negatively affected by the dramatic decline in oil revenue, and subsequent decline in Venezuelan oil production; as well as by President Maduro's increasingly limited ability to navigate foreign policy objectives in the context of the domestic opposition, a resurgent regional right, and the Trump administration in the United States (Cederlöf & Kingsbury, 2019, p. 124).

In the context of national governments attempting to 'walk the tightrope' between progressive policies and reproduction of capitalist class power (Nelson, 2019), ALBA states increasingly turned away from their social base, grounded in popular movements and cooperative sectors, and instead favoured class factions that maintained established economic sectors. This meant that the ALBA remained limited in its goal to transform social property relations to those favouring popular participation in economic management, inclusive development and cooperative organization. Exacerbating this balance of class power was the relative disorganization of ALBA institutional initiatives, particularly ALBA's grandnationals, which remained highly underdeveloped, and materialized as a string of national firms producing for the Venezuelan market (Lubbock, 2019). The end result was, contrary to ALBA's spatialization strategy, merely an 'aggregation of individual countries', rather than a coherent regional bloc (ALBA-TCP, 2012; Cusack, 2019).

Changing regional and international relations of power

While left-wing parties were victorious in most elections until 2015, their political momentum has begun to wane, with a resurgence of the right in certain countries. The ALBA, and the regional context in which it operates, have been negatively affected by recent discontent with the limitations of the elected left, growing social polarization in Latin America, and the growing influence of the US in the region once again. This regional shift to the right represents a reformulation of the class alliances that made ALBA possible. In Venezuela, increasingly top-down governmental decision-making and concessions to national and foreign capital, rampant inflation, and the unwillingness of the government to acknowledge, let alone address, the scope of economic crisis meant that certain far-left organizations have broken ties with the government beginning in 2014 (Romero, 2016). In the political arena, Chavismo experienced its first electoral defeat in the National Assembly elections of 2015. The shifting balance of power between the government and opposition in Venezuela, worsening economic conditions in Venezuela, and the transformation of the US state under Donald Trump have facilitated a series of US sanctions beginning in August 2017 contributing to already deteriorating humanitarian conditions, and to a decline in oil production (Weisbrot & Sachs, 2019).

Other countries in the Americas have come together to form the Lima Group, which seeks regime change in Venezuela, but that differentiates itself from the US approach in its calls for democratic elections without foreign intervention. St. Lucia, which is a full member of ALBA, joined the Lima Group in January 2018, an indication that the regional solidarity once afforded to Venezuela as a result of Petrocaribe is waning. The US, Lima Group and other Western nations have recognized Juan Guaidó as the self-declared interim President, and have given their support to the opposition. Within the region, any meaningful involvement in ALBA from members besides Cuba has essentially ended, while non-member interaction is 'almost uniformly hostile' (Cusack, 2019, p. 194). In March 2019, governments in Argentina, Brazil, Colombia, Chile, Ecuador, Guyana, Paraguay and Peru came together to form Prosur, an agreement that all South American countries were invited to sign except Venezuela. Analysts have noted that Prosur's founding declaration states that the 'full exercise of democracy' is a pre-requisite for membership, arguing that this agreement may represent a regional complement to the Lima Group (Nunes, 2019).

In Ecuador, participation in ALBA had been reduced to discursive support by the time Correa's presidential term ended in 2017 (Cusack, 2019). When Correa's successor, Lenin Moreno, was elected, former Correa advisor Decio Machado stated that due to increasing divisions between social struggles and government policy, 'the political left in Ecuador no longer exists' (Machado, 2017). What was not known at the time was that Moreno would undo the progressive policies of the Correa administration, effectively signalling a shift to the right. In the context of increased polarization and crisis of the left, Ecuador withdrew from ALBA in August of 2018, and took a $4.2 billion loan with the IMF in March 2019 to be distributed over the three years (Weisbrot & Arauz, 2019). The official reason for leaving ALBA was the failure of the Venezuelan government to address the humanitarian crisis (La Republica, 2018), which had resulted in over 1.5 million displaced Venezuelans by the end of 2017 (UNHRC, 2018). However, Ecuador's exit from ALBA points toward the establishment of a new power bloc under Moreno and the transformation of the Ecuadorian state.

For Bolivia, a year-long hiatus ended when the country re-joined ALBA in December 2020 (ALBA-TCP, 2020) after MAS presidential candidate Luis Arce was elected in the wake of a right-wing coup and interim presidency that ousted Evo Morales from power in late 2019. While evidence of the continued symbolic importance of ALBA membership for the left, the year-long gap in ALBA membership is also indicative of the ease with which a national and regional shift to the right has the potential to undo international cooperation under ALBA. Though ALBA meetings continue, the organization has largely become a discursive counter-weight to US intervention in the region, denouncing the US resuscitation of the Monroe Doctrine and the threat of military intervention in Venezuela, the rise of right-wing governments and their allegiances with the US, negative portrayals of the Latin American left in Western media, and interventionist actions by organizations like the Lima Group and the Organization of American States (ALBA-TCP, 2018).

Conclusion

The class alliances that led to the election of pink tide leaders, and to the creation of ALBA, appear to be shifting. This movement is occurring both within ALBA countries, as well as within non-member countries that were once sympathetic to the principles of social development and anti-imperialism. Understanding state forms as constituted by relations between social classes (Teschke, 2009), the shifting balance of power within pink tide countries has resulted in policy-making that resolves the contradictions of capitalist accumulation in the current period in favour of certain factions of national and international capital rather than pink tide supporters. As Knafo and Teschke

(2020) argue, the outcomes of class struggle are never fully controlled, and instead develop in unintended ways; in this case, growing divisions between bureaucratic and popular sectors meant that the latter were ultimately unable to consolidate their interests through institutions and policy that would transcend capitalist social property relations.

These political developments, occurring in tandem with low primary commodity prices and crises of accumulation in the region, are producing a regional shift. This shift has enabled international actors that have long opposed the principles of ALBA and pink tide countries to intervene, promoting open regionalism and neoliberal regimes. Grassroots movements and anti-neoliberal sentiment remain strong, however, evidenced for example by widespread protests in Quito, Ecuador in October 2019 against the Moreno government ending fuel subsidies as part of its agreement with the IMF. Despite this, the growing divisions between bureaucratic and grassroots factions of the left (evidence of, and a factor contributing to, the changing balance of class forces in the region) are apparent in state policies that seek the financial benefits of extractive expansion while underplaying their social, political and environmental costs. A series of concessions to foreign and national capital by ALBA countries served to maintain, and in some cases enrich, certain capitalist sectors while distancing state officials from their support base. For a regional organization like ALBA, which seeks to remake geopolitical space by altering the fundamental nature of politico-economic power, and thus to alter Latin America's place in the global capitalist system, having an active and engaged social base is crucial to challenging predominant relations of power. Moving forward, the possibilities for reinvigorating ALBA programmes will depend upon engaging with extra-parliamentary anti-neoliberal organizing and sentiment that persists separately from the electoral arena. It will also depend on reviving a policy agenda that recognizes and seeks to address the root causes of unevenness in commodity export within and between ALBA countries.

Notes

1. For a comprehensive overview on literature on the ALBA from 2004 to 2016, see Absell (2018).
2. This approach follows previous work that analyzes how relations of power shape regional integration in Latin America, including: Gamble and Payne 1996; Fernández Jilberto and Mommen 1998; Niemann 2000; Hadjimichalis 2005; as well analyses of relations of power that shape ALBA in particular: Muhr 2011; Emerson 2013; Lubbock 2019.
3. See Carrión (2018, p. 105) for a list of companies bought by ALBANISA and their relationship to the Ortega family.

Acknowledgements

I would like to thank Jeffery Webber for feedback on the initial draft of this paper, as well as the special issue editors for their comments and suggestions.

Disclosure statement

No potential conflict of interest was reported by the author(s).

References

Absell, C. D. (2018). Self-awareness and critique: An overview of ALBA research. In A. K. Cusack (Ed.), *Understanding ALBA: progress, problems, and prospects of alternative regionalism in Latin America and the Caribbean* (pp. 13–37). Institute of Latin American Studies, School of Advanced Study, University of London.

ALBA-TCP. (2008, January 26). Conceptualización de Proyecto y Empresa Grannacional en el Marco del ALBA. VI Summit, Caracas, Venezuela. https://www.albatcp.org/acta/conceptualizacion-de-proyecto-y-empresa-grannacional-en-el-marco-del-alba/

ALBA-TCP. (2010). Construyendo un Mundo Pluripolar. Cumbres 2004–2010. https://www.civilisac.org/civilis/wp-content/uploads/cumbres-del-alba-1.pdf

ALBA-TCP. (2012, February 3). Acuerdo para la Constitución del Espacio Económico del ALBA-TCP ECOALBA-TCP. XI Summit, Caracas, Venezuela. https://www.portalalba.org/index.php/alba/documentos/1305-2012-02-04-y-05-xi-cumbre-caracas-venezuela-acuerdo-para-la-constitucion-del-espacio-economico-del-alba-tcp-ecoalba-tcp

ALBA-TCP. (2018, December 14). Declaración Íntegra de los Jefes de Estado y de Gobierno de los Países Miembros de la ALBA-TCP, XVI Cumbre "En La Defensa de América Latina y el Caribe Como Zona de Paz", La Habana, Cuba. https://www.portalalba.org/index.php/alba/documentos/18999-2018-01-12-declaracion-la-habana-cuba-declaracion-integra-de-los-jefes-de-estado-y-de-gobierno-de-los-paises-miembros-de-la-alba-tcp-en-la-xvi-cumbre

ALBA-TCP. (2020, December 14). Declaración Final de la Cumbre Virtual de Jefes de Estado y de Gobierno del ALBA-TCP, XVIII Cumbre. https://portalalba.org/documentos-alba/declaracion-cumbre-virtual-jefes-de-estado-y-de-gobierno/

Allinson, J. C., & Anievas, A. (2010). Approaching 'the international': Beyond political marxism. In A. Anievas (Ed.), *Marxism and world politics: Contesting global capitalism* (pp. 197–214). Routledge.

Anderson, T. (2016). Chávez and American integration. In L. F. Angosto-Ferrández (Ed.), *Democracy, revolution, and geopolitics in Latin America: Venezuela and the international politics of discontent* (pp. 13–46). Routledge.

Aponte-García, M. (2014). La Teorización del Nuevo Regionalismo Estratégico en el ALBA-TCP. In M. A. García y G. A. Puntiel (Ed.), *El ALBA-TCP: Origen y Fruto del Nuevo Regionalismo Latinoamericano y Caribeno* (pp. 25–68). CLACSO.

Aporrea. (2017, December 21). Decretan 'supresión y liquidación' de cuatro empresas estatales de alimentos. https://www.aporrea.org/economia/n318783.html

Artaraz, K. (2011). New Latin American networks of solidarity? ALBA's contribution to Bolivia's national development plan (2006–10). *Global Social Policy, 11*(1), 88–105. https://doi.org/10.1177/1468018110392194.

Artaraz, K. (2018). A very Latin American social policy: ALBA, counterhegemonic regionalism, and 'living well'. In A. K. Cusack (Ed.), *Understanding ALBA: Progress, problems, and prospects of alternative regionalism in Latin America and the Caribbean* (pp. 53–72). Institute of Latin American Studies, School of Advanced Study, University of London.

Azzellini, D. (2017). *Communes and workers' control in Venezuela*. Haymarket Books.

Álvarez, V. (2015, May 5). Victor Alvarez: 'Venezuela's currency controls are no longer justified, and are only used as a means of political domination'. Interview by Mario Villegas. Vezenuelanalysis.com. https://venezuelanalysis.com/analysis/11371

Babroff, C. (2019, May 22). Problemas reales para la negociación. *Viento Sur*.

Brenner, R. (1995). Agrarian class structure and economic development in pre-industrial Europe. In T. H. Aston & C. H. E. Philpin (Eds.), *The Brenner debate: Agrarian class structure and economic development in pre-industrial Europe* (pp. 10–63). Cambridge University Press.

Briceño-Ruiz, J. (2017). Latin America beyond the continental divide: Open regionalism and post-hegemonic regionalism co-existence in a changing region. In J. Briceño-Ruiz & I. Morales (Eds.), *Post-hegemonic regionalism in the Americas: Toward a Pacific-Atlantic divide?* (pp. 73–98). Routledge.

Carrión, G. (2018). ALBA in Nicaragua: Political, economic and development implications. In A. K. Cusack (Ed.), *Understanding ALBA: Progress, problems, and prospects of alternative regionalism in Latin America and the Caribbean* (pp. 93–114). Institute of Latin American Studies, School of Advanced Study, University of London.

Cederlöf, G., & Kingsbury, D. V. (2019). On PetroCaribe: Petropolitics, energopower, and post-neoliberal development in the Caribbean energy region. *Political Geography, 72*, 124–133. https://doi.org/10.1016/j.polgeo.2019.04.006

Ciccariello-Maher, G. (2013). *We created Chávez: A people's history of the Venezuelan revolution*. Duke University Press.

Ciupa, K. (forthcoming). *The political economy of oil in Venezuela: Class conflict, the state, and the world market*. Brill.

Cusack, A. K. (2019). *Venezuela, ALBA, and the limits of postneoliberal regionalism in Latin America and the Caribbean, Studies of the Americas*. Palgrave Macmillan.

Dufour, F. G. (2007). Social-property regimes and the uneven and combined development of nationalist practices. *European Journal of International Relations, 13*(4), 583–604. https://doi.org/10.1177/1354066107083148

ECLAC. (1994, March). *Open regionalism in Latin America and the Caribbean. Economic integration as a contribution to changing production patterns with social equity* (LC/L.808(CEG.19/3)). Santiago, Chile.

Ellner, S. (2017). Implications of Marxist state theory and how they play out in Venezuela. *Historical Materialism, 25*(2), 29–62. https://doi.org/10.1163/1569206X-12301419

Emerson, R. G. (2013). Institutionalising a radical region? The Bolivarian alliance for the peoples of our America. *Journal of Iberian and Latin American Research, 19*(2), 194–210. https://doi.org/10.1080/13260219.2013.853352

Fernández Jilberto, A. E., & Mommen, A. (1998). *Regionalization and globalization in the modern world economy: Perspectives on the third world and transitional economies*. Routledge.

Gamble, A., & Payne, A. (1996). *Regionalism and world order*. Macmillan.

Gordon, T., & Webber, J. R. (2016). *Blood of extraction: Canadian imperialism in Latin America*. Fernwood Publishing.

Hadjimichalis, C. (2005). *Uneven development and regionalism. State, territory and class in Southern Europe*. Croom Helm.

Katz, C. (2015). Dualities of Latin America. *Latin American Perspectives, 42*(4), 10–42. https://doi.org/10.1177/0094582X15574714

Knafo, S., & Teschke, B. (2020). Political Marxism and the rules of reproduction of capitalism: A historicist critique. *Historical Materialism, 29*(3), 54–83. https://doi.org/10.1163/1569206X-00001441

La Botz, D. (2016). *What went wrong? The Nicaraguan revolution: A Marxist analysis*. Brill.

La Republica. (2018). Ecuador anuncia salida de la ALBA por crisis Venezolana. Dated August 23. https://www.larepublica.ec/blog/politica/2018/08/23/ecuador-anuncia-salida-de-la-alba-en-respuesta-a-crisis-venezolana/

Lacher, H. (2006). *Beyond globalization: Capitalism, territoriality and the international relations of modernity*. Routledge.

Lafrance, X. (2021). The vacuity of structurelessness: Situating agency and structure in exploitative and alienated social relations. *Historical Materialism, 29*(3), 84–106. https://doi.org/10.1163/1569206X-12342047

Lafrance, X., & Post, C. (Eds.). (2019). *Case studies in the origins of capitalism*. Palgrave Macmillan.

Lander, E. (2014). *Venezuela: Terminal crisis of the rentier petro-state model?* Transnational Institute. https://www.tni.org/files/download/venezuela_terminal_crisis_of_the_rentier_petro-state_model._with_very_minor_chaanges_0.pdf

Lubbock, R. (2018). From magical state to magical region? Ecology, labour and socialism in ALBA. In A. K. Cusack (Ed.), *Understanding ALBA: progress, problems, and prospects of alternative regionalism in Latin America and the Caribbean* (pp. 195–210). Institute of Latin American Studies. School of Advanced Study, University of London.

Lubbock, R. (2019). The social contradictions of regional development in the ALBA-TCP: The case of food production. *New Political Economy, 25*(2), 213–230. https://doi.org/10.1080/13563467.2019.1586863

Machado, D. (2017, April 4). Decio Machado: 'Después del domingo ya no existe izquierda política en Ecuador'. Interview by Felipe Pineda Ruiz. Democracia en la Red. https://www.democraciaenlared.com/2017/04/decio-machado-despues-del-domingo-ya-no.html

Martí i Puig, S., & Baumeister, E. (2017). Agrarian policies in Nicaragua: From revolution to the revival of agro-exports, 1979–2015. *Journal of Agrarian Change, 17*(2), 381–396. https://doi.org/10.1111/joac.12214

McCarthy-Jones, A. (2016). 'Ploughing the sea' in a world of regions: Venezuela's role in reviving Latin American regionalism for the twenty-first century. In L. F. Angosto-Ferrández (Ed.), *Democracy, revolution, and geopolitics in Latin America: Venezuela and the international politics of discontent* (pp. 47–66). Routledge.

Morton, A. D. (2011). *Revolution and state in modern Mexico: The political economy of uneven development*. Rowman & Littlefield Publishers.

Muhr, T. (2010). Nicaragua: Constructing the Bolivarian alliance for the peoples of our America (ALBA). In U. Schuerkens (Ed.), *Globalization and transformations of social inequality* (pp. 115–134). Routledge.

Muhr, T. (2011). *Venezuela and the ALBA: Counter-hegemony, geographies of integration and development, and higher education for all*. VDM Verlag.

Muhr, T. (2012). The politics of space in the ALBA–TCP: Transnationalism, the organized society, and counter-hegemonic governance. *Globalizations*, *9*(6), 767–782. https://doi.org/10.1080/14747731.2012.739339

Muhr, T. (2012a). Bolivarian globalization? The new left's struggle in Latin America and the Caribbean to negotiate a revolutionary approach to humanitarian militarism and international intervention. *Globalizations*, *9*(1), 145–159. https://doi.org/10.1080/14747731.2012.627725

Nelson, M. (2015). *A history of the FTAA: From hegemony to fragmentation in the Americas*. Palgrave Macmillan.

Nelson, M. (2019). Walking the tightrope of socialist governance: A strategic-relational analysis of twenty-first-century socialism. *Latin American Perspectives*, *46*(1), 46–65. https://doi.org/10.1177/0094582X18798795

Niemann, M. (2000). *A spatial approach to regionalism in the global economy*. Palgrave.

North, L. L., & Clark, T. D. (Eds.). (2018). *Dominant elites in Latin America. From neo-liberalism to the 'pink tide'*. Palgrave.

Nunes, F. (2019, April 3). *Explainer: What is Prosur?* Americas Society / Council of the Americas. https://www.as-coa.org/articles/explainer-what-prosur

Pearce, S. (2013). *Twenty-first century countertrade: The case of Venezuela 2004–2011* [PhD Thesis]. Queen Mary University of London.

Pearce, S. (2018). The first five years of the SUCRE: Success and limitations of ALBA's regional virtual currency. In A. K. Cusack (Ed.), *Understanding ALBA: Progress, problems, and prospects of alternative regionalism in Latin America and the Caribbean* (pp. 73–90). Institute of Latin American Studies, School of Advanced Study, University of London.

Post, C. (2021). Structure and agency in historical materialism: A response to Knafo and Teschke. *Historical Materialism*, *29*(3), 107–124. https://doi.org/10.1163/1569206X-12342040

Purcell, T. (2013). The political economy of social production companies. *Latin American Perspectives*, *40*(3), 146–168. https://doi.org/10.1177/0094582X13476007

Romero, C. (2016, October 4). Chavismo from below. Interview by Eva Maria, Jacobin. https://www.jacobinmag.com/2016/04/chavez-maduro-venezuela-mud-psuv

Silva, E. (2009). *Challenging neoliberalism in Latin America*. Cambridge University Press.

Simoes, A. J., & Hidalgo, C. A. (2019). The economic complexity observatory: An analytical tool for understanding the dynamics of economic development. https://oec.world/en/

Skidmore, T. E., & Smith, P. H. (2005). *Modern Latin America* (6th ed.). Oxford University Press.

Strange, G. (2014). *Towards a new political economy of development: States and regions in the postneoliberal world*. Palgrave Macmillan.

Sutherland, M. (2018). La ruina de Venezuela no se debe al 'Socialismo' ni a la 'Revolución', NUSO N 274, Marzo-Abril.

Teschke, B. (2005). Bourgeois revolution, state formation and the absence of the international. *Historical Materialism*, *13*(2), 3–26. https://doi.org/10.1163/1569206054127273

Teschke, B. (2009). *The myth of 1648: Class, geopolitics and the making of modern international relations*. Verso.

Teschke, B., & Lacher, H. (2007). The changing 'logics' of capitalist competition. *Cambridge Review of International Affairs*, *20*(4), 565–580. https://doi.org/10.1080/09557570701680514

UNHCR 'United Nations Human Rights Council'. (2018). *Venezuela situation: Responding to the needs of people displaced from Venezuela*. United Nations Human Rights Council. https://www.unhcr.org/

partners/donors/5ab8e1a17/unhcr-2018-venezuela-situation-supplementary-appeal-january-december-2018.html?query=venezuela%202018%20situation
Van der Pijl, K. (2014). *The discipline of Western supremacy*. Pluto Press.
van Schaick, A. (2007, September 25). *Argentina. Government pays back IMF debt*. NACLA. https://nacla.org/article/argentina-government-pays-back-imf-debt
Webber, J. R. (2017a). *The last day of oppression and the first day of the same: The politics and economics of the new Latin American left*. Haymarket Books.
Webber, J. R. (2017b). Evo Morales, *transformismo*, and the consolidation of agrarian capitalism in Bolivia. *Journal of Agrarian Change*, *17*(2), 330–347. https://doi.org/10.1111/joac.12209
Weisbrot, M., & Arauz, A. (2019). *'Headwinds to growth': The IMF program in Ecuador*. Center for Economic and Policy Research. https://cepr.net/images/stories/reports/ecuador-imf-2019.pdf
Weisbrot, M., & Sachs, J. (2019). *Economic sanctions as collective punishment: The case of Venezuela*. Center for Economic and Policy Research. https://cepr.net/images/stories/reports/venezuela-sanctions-2019-04.pdf
Wood, E. M. (1995). *Democracy against capitalism: Renewing historical materialism*. Cambridge University Press.
Wood, E. M. (2012). *The Ellen Meiksins Wood reader* (L. Patriquin (ed.)). Brill.
Yaffe, H. (2011). The Bolivarian alliance for the Americas: An alternative development strategy. *International Journal of Cuban Studies*, *3*(2/3), 128–144, Special Issue: A New Dawn? ALBA and the Future of Caribbean and Latin American Integration (Summer/Autumn).
Yaffe, H. (2018). Venezuela, ALBA, and the communal economic system. In A. K. Cusack (Ed.), *Understanding ALBA: Progress, problems, and prospects of alternative regionalism in Latin America and the Caribbean* (pp. 143–166). Institute of Latin American Studies, School of Advanced Study, University of London.

OPEN ACCESS

The credibility of regional policymaking: insights from South America

Pia Riggirozzi and Matt Ryan

ABSTRACT

Regional responses to international threats and opportunities have become prevalent. Yet significant lacunae persist in our recognition of some impacts of regional policies. Where measuring impact of regional policy does exist, this tends to focus on economic impact, heavily influenced by the EU model, or focuses on impacts that we have come to expect from national level policymaking. In this paper we show that important effects of regional policymaking in South American regionalism are being overlooked. Specifically, we argue that failure to recognize the creation of normative frameworks, dynamics of regional diplomacy, and social policy outcomes from regional policymaking has negatively affected the credibility of regional organizations. Lack of understanding of the impact of regional policy risks trivializing progress in regional policy and, critically, affects the legitimacy and credibility of regional governance. We make this case by focusing on regional health and migration policies in South America.

1. Introduction: regional policymaking misjudged

The study of 'regionalism' as a process of policy formation and implementation, and 'region' as the grounding of that policy have been an ever-increasing phenomenon in an era of globalization. The creation of regional organizations to manage supra-national and inter-governmental relations in geographic, politico-strategic and ideational senses has been a critical manifestation of that trend (Acharya, 2017; Buzan, 2003; Fawcett & Hurrell, 1995). Beyond its conceptual value the regional political space offers an important venue for deliberation, where state and non-state actors can work out modalities of cooperation, coordination and governance. Making policies at the regional level not only offers a mechanism for cross-border exchange and cooperation, but also makes sense because some social problems, such as those related to migration, health, and the environment, for example, are exacerbated or facilitated by regional developments and exchanges (Deacon et al., 2010; Riggirozzi, 2014). Regional organizations can create an authoritative set of institutions and policy regulations for individual member states to 'lock-in' national legislation (Pevehouse, 2005), to respond to economic and political challenges (Riggirozzi & Tussie, 2012), and to improve collective action in the international arena (Gehring et al., 2013).

The last half decade has seen the political compass in Latin America moving to the Right in a large part of the region, including Brazil, Chile, Ecuador and sporadically in Argentina. This change has produced a significant constraint for what became known as 'post-hegemonic regionalism' to refer to those organizations that emerged in the early 2000s to contest or at least to compensate for the commercial impetus that had defined national and regional policies since the 1990s (Riggirozzi & Tussie, 2012). Looking back to these developments, particularly the last two decades, we can claim that failures in regional politics are not always a zero-sum game. The articulation of political and regional commitments is always possible, even in the most testing circumstances. Also, certain elements of regionalism survive in a broader way, not only as distinct short-term political projects associated with a limited time mandate, but as long-term developments that fit into a grander dialectical narrative in the development of cross-national policymaking.

In Latin America, and more recently in Europe, regional institutions have become a more salient focus of political and social contention. It has become increasingly clear as domestic politics become more tightly coupled with regional policy outcomes, that normative arguments about regional institutions are starting to represent more distinct political ideologies and cleavages. National referendums in EU member states, and financial and migration policies in particular, have highlighted frustration and lack of credibility of the public in the EU as a regulatory instrument (Bulmer & Quaglia, 2018; Rose, 2019). In Latin America, underwhelming economic performance and political and administrative stagnation due to political and ideological divisions led to the discrediting of regional organizations (Malamud, 2013; Quiliconi & Rivera, 2019). But rather than seeing regionalism in South America as a series of highly disappointing failures we propose unpacking further what regional policy making may mean for social and wellbeing agendas even in contexts of weak institutionalization. Here we consider how such regional organizations demonstrate value and provide recognizable and believable consequences of regional political interactions. How do we analyse regional governance in the absence of supranational institutions, and what forms of legitimacy underpins such regionalism?

We explore these questions in relation to regional governance in South America. This is relevant because little effort has been made to systematically assess the significance (if any) that regional organizations in Latin America have played in addressing social development, poverty and welfare. More fundamentally, the perceived effects of regional policy have important implications for public trust, legitimacy and credibility of regional organizations. Credibility of regionalism requires better recognizing alternative outputs of regionalism to those that are foregrounded by existing theories. Understanding of regional organizations' impacts needs to move beyond classifications of ideal types of weak or strong institutionalization to providing more nuanced accounts of the impact of regional organizations. There *may* be a causal relationship between institutionalization and the credibility of regional politics as legitimate policymaking – but they are not the same thing. We recognize legitimacy of regionalism in South America in activities that are overlooked or underplayed by general theories of regional policy legitimacy. We agree with Tallberg and Zürn (2019, p. 584) that legitimacy 'lies with the beliefs and perceptions of audiences, not the normative goodness of an institution'. One of the challenges assessing legitimacy in South American regional governance is precisely that *the audience*' is difficult to identify. While regional organizations are recognized focal arenas for states' efforts to coordinate policies and solve problems, one defining feature of South American regionalism is a clear lack of 'public' in regional policy making. Regionalism in South America is another venue for intergovernmental policy making. Furthermore, in the absence of recognizably integrated *demoi*, the democratic authority of institutions derives from the member state's governments. In this context in contrast to analyses that go looking for input legitimacy through an assessment of the institutional texture, we propose that because of the lack of demos, regional legitimacy is likely to come 'back-to -front'. That is outputs can be instrumental in guiding perception of legitimacy based not only on what policies and programmes regional organizations adopt and implement but also socialization of norms and expectations amongst groups of networked actors (see Mace & Lockhart, 2019). Building on this discussion, we identify three important lacunae in current conceptualizations of output of regional policy and explain the consequences of their neglect for the credibility of regional organizations.

First, assessments of regional policy outputs that focus on strong institutionalization as the output itself (or outputs implied by institutionalization) trivializes what semi-institutionalized regions do achieve and what they can possibly achieve. We show that in spite of, or perhaps aided by, less rigid institutional architectures of regionalism in South America, regional policy actors have focused on regional agenda-setting and creation of normative frameworks through networks of institutions. We also show that the significance of those frameworks is that they create new opportunities for tangible policy outputs in areas of social protection, health and education, and migration.

Second, rather than equate institutional attrition and upheaval with loss of leadership and returns to minimalist regional agendas, an expanded understanding of regional politics reveals how regionalism can overcome abeyances of regional leadership. Here we point to how regional framing of issues continues to operate in a coordinated manner by enabling new dynamics of representation and diplomacy.

Third, investment in regionalism is resilient to changes in institutions. We show that in the context of more fluid and semi-organic institutionalization of regional organizations, transnational networks of epistemic and diplomatic communities can work hard to maintain agendas and find new opportunities for financial, technical and public support.

Our argument supports the claim that like all projects of governance, any form of regional organization requires legitimacy, understood as a process of validation of action taken by political and social actors (Reus-Smit, 2007, p. 158). Legitimacy, in other words, validates and supports the credibility of an organization and its activities – and is a *sine qua non* to mobilize resources and acquire necessary support from constituents to survive. Organizations will enhance their legitimacy if they are credible and validated as a project of governance. Lack of credibility affects an organization's legitimacy. Without this credibility, regional governance will remain fragile and dysfunctional (Ribeiro Hoffmann & van der Vleuten, 2007). In acknowledging that legitimacy of regional organizations decreases if they lose credibility, we echo a concern raised by Tallberg and Zürn (2019) regarding the way in which perceptions of legitimacy of organizations are affected by public opinion, while perception of practices can boost or undermine the legitimacy of these organizations. We are concerned that the prevailing perspectives assessing legitimacy of regional organization privilege a focus on institutional and constitutional procedures, and economic outcomes, while neglecting other ways of assessing and identifying regional policymaking in South America, and results in negative feedback rather than positive reinforcement of credibility of regional governance.

In what follows we first address the issue of legitimacy vis-à-vis outputs across regional organizations. We focus on outputs as distinct from inputs and outcomes, though claim that outputs may extend into impactful outcomes, reinforcing both credibility and legitimacy of regional organizations. We then outline the social promise of South American regionalism in the twenty-first century to provide a more coherent delineation of the expectations of regional outputs and the problem of credibility. We conclude with a discussion of how to capture the bond between regional policy and the people in support of credible social roles for regional organizations in South America.

2. How to understand legitimacy and policymaking in regional governance in South America

Regionalism is not just another aspect of national or international politics but a distinct and important space for formulation and implementation of coordinated policies above states. International threats increasingly affect territories and cultures shared across states, bringing to centre stage the role of regional organizations in providing solutions and supporting states and non-state actors to pursue credible and achievable policy to achieve public goods. Regional policy can imply rules that bind state behaviour, or it can involve framing (new) ideas and norms that can guide and structure practice and agency across multiple levels of governance. An overt focus on regional governance in terms of regional economic frameworks (Acharya & Johnston, 2007; Fawcett & Hurrell, 1995; Gomez Mera, 2008) or security complexes (Adler & Barnett, 1998; Buzan, 2003), supranationality and sovereignty (Malamud, 2013; Mattli, 1999) has meant that research and practice has been somewhat blind to the 'social role' of regional organizations and regional policy in Latin America. This has not been entirely a matter of academic neglect, but rather the case of clear lack of 'public' in regional policy making, except for that delegated to governmental agencies. For this reason, regionalism in South America has been associated with high presidentialism (Malamud, 2013).

Furthermore, in the absence of recognizably integrated *demoi,* there is no clear democratic authority appearing in the form of institutionalized inputs and direct participation of social actors in decision making. In fact, there is a problematic relationship between legitimacy of institutions and their acceptance that is directly related to their responsiveness to the public interest; and accountability of intergovernmental governance. In this context, assertions on the credibility and legitimacy of regional organizations have shaped perspectives, reinforcing accounts of democratic deficits based on the (absence of) the legal and procedural aspects of representation, accountability and democratic allocation of political authority (Dingwerth et al., 2020; Rittberger & Schroeder, 2016).

That view, highly influenced by EU studies, assumes a bond between regional policy and policy making based on versions of a regional demos understood as public discourse, social recognition, delegated authority and fair participation in institutionalized electoral practices (Moravcsik, 2008, p. 173). But the theory of the public in these accounts of intergovernmental regional governance as agent and beneficiary of regional policy can be problematic. For instance, it fails to account for important elements of politics that define regional integration in South America and its sources of legitimacy. Member states often created particular institutions at the regional level to enhance authority and management of economic and political relations in reaction to specific actions and pressures external to the region (Riggirozzi & Tussie, 2012). In this context while both participation of citizens and performance of the political authority in support of social goals remain necessary conditions for obtaining legitimacy, the understanding that citizens or nation-states transfer their authority to a single regional political entity that performs as a site for all regional politics does not. Multiple regional initiatives that secure not only trade, investment, and security but increasingly tackle issues of social policy, such as health, education and migration policy pursue distinctive strategies in their concerted action, and reimagine the terms of legitimacy of regional governance in Latin America.

This leads us to a corollary critique; that is, any discussion about legitimacy in regional organizations will always be deficient without observations and measures of outputs that are sensitive to the varieties of forms that regional politics take. This article builds upon a contention largely developed in the study of regionalism that highlights the centrality of policy outputs of multilateral organizations to understanding their capacity to deal with societal problems as wider legitimation processes (see Duina & Lenz, 2017; Mace, 2020; Mace & Lockhart, 2019; Tallberg & Zürn, 2019). This literature has made significant inroads into innovative accounts of legitimacy in regional and multilateral organizations beyond measures of input legitimacy that privilege issues of representation, decision making procedures and law-based norms (Clark, 2005; Reus-Smit, 2007, p. 158; Steffek, 2014). This is not to deny the centrality of technocratic procedures and performance, or the normative appropriateness of democratic authority and their representatives in regional organizations. These considerations are undoubtedly important for the reproduction of democratic global governance in practice and of internationally shared conceptions of good governance (Dingwerth et al., 2020; Zürn, 2018). But while those aspects of regional legitimacy have captured scholarly attention, we still know very little about the possibilities for regional organizations to affect and lead social policy, and the importance of scrutinizing output of the organizations in those areas.

A focus on South American regionalism allows attention to forms of regional performance and interventions in pursuit of social goals through regional policy. A focus on the 'social' also allows us to understand how regionalism acts and enables acting upon different areas of social policy. By exploring these dynamics in South American regionalism, we contribute with a perspective that places modalities of regional actions as central to the understanding of output legitimacy, where these outputs are recognized by whether and how regional governance (i) creates coherent normative or conceptual frameworks structuring inter-governmental and expert network models of regional governance; (ii) facilitates the re-allocation of material and knowledge resources in support of public policy and policy implementation; and (iii) enables new dynamics of representation and diplomacy (Riggirozzi, 2014, p. 451; also Riggirozzi & Yeates, 2015; Yeates, 2014).

The first assessment requires that we can identify effects of framing debates and getting issues on to the political agenda: regional organizations can highlight issues, bringing otherwise underappreciated discourses to the fore and in some cases creating new norms. They can take specific actions that make modalities of governance more favourable in an issue area. For example, by promoting and instantiating the requirements of international treaties or declarations, regional organizations can influence the opportunity space for policymaking at the national level. They can effectively work to constrict options through setting discursive norms. At a more concrete level they can choose which 'problems' to define and provide policy guidance on. Creating normative frameworks is also an important mechanism for policy diffusion, drawing attention to issues and affecting the awareness, attitudes or perceptions of key stakeholders within regional states and their societies, promoting, for example, recognition of specific groups or endorsements of international declarations. Regional organizations can provide normative and institutional resources for the harmonization of international and national policies and definition of regional strategies. This is not a minor output, as who frames what and why depends on how the actors, including government officials, non-governmental organizations, multilateral institutions, and public-private partnerships, define their goals and objectives, and exercise political action, including power relations. That regional organizations can affect how policy is thought about and practiced adds nuance to conventional analysis, particularly within comparative regionalism, that has centred almost exclusively on scrutinizing 'tangibles' as a measure of meaningful and effective regionalism (Börzel, 2011; De Lombaerde et al., 2010). Little attention has been paid to how regional organizations contribute to creating what Acharya identifies as 'normative congruence' (2011) or the capacity of regional organizations to 'translate' international norms into local settings, sometimes amalgamating and compromising with already rooted systems of beliefs and prevailing norms in the region and in domestic arenas. We thus argue that more attention needs to be paid to how regions set agendas in spite of any perceived lack of institutionalization.

Second, regional organizations can facilitate re-allocation of resources through the mobilization of human, financial and knowledge resources in support of social policy delivery. The key idea underpinning regionalism in this sense is that it provides a space above the state not only for debate, knowledge-sharing and the promotion of norms and methods of regional policy formation and practice, but also that it can provide governments with some technical knowledge and/or financial support mechanisms to which actors can turn when faced with internal and external pressures. One measure of regional organizations' functionality, therefore, is whether and how much they can deliver expertise to support national-level policy-making, working directly with governments or other key actors improving the institutional framework surrounding policy and claim making. Another is that regional organizations can effectively bridge regional and national policies and sustain the cross-border policy networks required to ensure efficient policy outcomes for citizens. In some cases, where institutionalization is weak and organizations overlap one or two regional level political organizations can act as lightning rods for disagreement, which allows other regional actors in governing networks to venue shop, reallocate resource and get on with the work of policy-making where consensus does exist.

Finally, regional organizations can open up political opportunities for advocacy and collective action. They can effectively bridge the gap between more localized campaigns on more immediate issues facing publics, and the global goals of international communities. In turn the output of regional brokering can increase activism and pressure on national governments to produce outcomes that respond to global problems in ways that would be difficult for national governments to achieve. In this sense the semi-organic development of regionalism in places like South America where regional organizations have waxed and waned in their authority, shifted their jurisdiction, or dissolved and revived elsewhere, allows for agile responsiveness to emerging movements.

What this categorization suggests is that there are different articulations of values and strategies that characterize regional governance and those bear different relevance for the outputs of regional policy in practice. This conceptualization is also important not only because it sets grounds for describing and comparing the role of regional governance in different issue areas but also because it offers grounds to assess output legitimacy and credibility as the outcome of such effective and sustained processes and performance. Table 1 summarizes these forms of output legitimacy that can be recognized in regional organizations.

In the next section we elucidate how these roles and outputs are recognized in the case of South American regionalism. We look at Mercosur and UNASUR, providing an assessment of how they

Table 1. Roles of regional organizations that lend output legitimacy.

Roles of regional organizations	Recognized outputs
Creation of Normative Frameworks	Changing issue salience and/or discourse use
	Specific actions taken linked to RO
	RO/regional network constricts agenda
	RO/regional network defines problems
	Specific policy guidance at regional level
	Strategically act as lightening rod /locking-in national policy
Reallocation of Resources	Supporting specialist policy networks
	Sharing expertise
	Reallocate support regionally (technologies/finance/administrative resources)
Establishment of Dynamics of representation	Represent local concerns not addressed by national governments at international level.

act in specific areas such as health and migration, and identifying outputs derived from the role of regional organizations.

3. The social agenda in South American regionalism

In *The Customs Union* (1950) Jacob Viner was concerned with the effects of regional integration on welfare. Viner asked whether regional trade agreements were beneficial to welfare, concluding that not all trade agreements lead to higher economic welfare when some tariffs and preferential trade agreements deviate rather than create trade amongst nations. Trade was in effect the driver of regional integration at the time of his writing and became the anchor to assess effectiveness of regional integration. In this context, expectations of what the role of regionalism was about were defined by intra-regional trade in goods and services, and movement of people and capital, in the understanding that this trend would allow pathways to growth and poverty reduction through effects on prices, jobs, investment, and economic output (Viner, 1950; see also Te Velde et al., 2006). To a large extent market governance rationality shaped region building in South America, often tied to US leadership in Inter-American relations (Fawcett & Hurrell, 1995). Specifically, this was the case of the Southern Common Market (MERCOSUR) in 1991, grouping Brazil, Argentina, Uruguay and Paraguay; the North American Free Trade Agreement (NAFTA) signed by the United States, Canada and Mexico in 1994; and the renewed impetus from previous projects like the Andean Community created in 1969. In these cases, it was expected that by loosening the restrictions on finance and trade, new market projects could enhance the capacity of states to manage the pressures of globalization through regionalization and growth opportunities (Phillips, 2003).

In the first instance regional organizations across South America have opened agendas (and later restricted them to tangible goals), while offering specific policy guidance at regional levels. It is difficult to imagine how these outputs could have been achieved without a regional dimension. Despite the emphasis on trade, both the Andean Community and MERCOSUR made significant inroads into shaping a regional social agenda. For instance, cross-border projects on health, education and labour regulations were supported within the structure of both the Andean Community and MERCOSUR (Riesco, 2010; Hoffman & Bianculli, 2016). In the Andean Community, two managing bodies, the Hipólito Unanúe Agreement and the Andres Bello Convention, were established to deal with common challenges in the areas of health and education, respectively (SELA, 2010). In the case of MERCOSUR, the social agenda was introduced through cooperation in health, particularly in the area of transborder disease control and epidemiological surveillance in the triple border shared by Brazil, Argentina and Paraguay. This led to the creation of the Health Minister Assembly and the Health Working Group (GTS11), established in 1996 at a ministerial level for the discussion of health policy and strategies of surveillance (MERCOSUR Decision CMC No 03/1995). Regulations on pharmaceuticals for trade and joint health and safety inspections were also introduced in the work of the GTS11 (MERCOSUR Decision CMC No 03/1995, see also Riggirozzi, 2014). Likewise, a general strategy to make the education systems across member nations compatible was established with two aims; to obtain the recognition of studies and the homologation of degrees in order to facilitate the mobility of students and professionals in the region, and to harmonize a system of accreditation and quality assurance (Perrotta, 2014). These goals were institutionalized in a MERCOSUR education system (Sistema Educativo del Mercosur, SEM) which represents a regional space to foster the integration of educational sectors of member countries.[1]

Moreover, we witness regionalists in South America exploit opportunities to reallocate or grow resources at the regional level and represent concerns at the international level. At the turn of the last century however a combination of economic difficulties, financial constraints and low levels of co-ordination for implementation and compliance affected the depth and pace of progress on regional social policy (Riesco, 2010). In the end, neoliberal reform and the governance arrangements associated with it, including regional governance, unravelled, leading to a new spectrum of policy responses by widespread election of new Leftist governments (Riggirozzi & Grugel, 2015). The new Left took office across the region – in Venezuela (1998), Brazil (2002), Argentina (2003), Uruguay (2004), Bolivia (2005), Ecuador (2006), Paraguay (2008) and Peru (2011) – promising mixed economies and a generally pragmatic combination of welfare and populist policies which reasserted equity and sovereignty as distinctive national and regional identities in South America (Sanahuja, 2012). This shift in context paved the way for a new space for rebuilding the contours and the purpose of regional governance in Latin America, and with it agendas developing beyond primarily market-oriented, free-trade goals. The move to the Left across Latin America must not be simply seen simply as a political ideological swing but a recognition of political opportunity for new leaders to synchronize governmental policies. Broad political change resulted in moves to greater incorporation in multi-scalar regional projects while creating greater collective autonomy *vis-a-vis* external actors. Regional formations such as the Bolivarian Alliance for the Peoples of Our America (ALBA) in 2004, the Union of South American Nations (UNASUR) in 2008, the Community of Latin American and Caribbean States (CELAC) in 2011 are well documented (e.g. Riggirozzi & Tussie, 2012; Sanahuja, 2012). These formations provided a novel analytical perspective on modes of 'post-hegemonic governance' in Latin America (Riggirozzi & Tussie, 2012). Although embryonic, new consensuses set regional boundaries beyond the economic, market-led rationale that has historically defined regional governance (and its kudos). In effect, new spaces for state and non-state actors' actions meant that a new rhetoric about how regionalism could re-engage with the social question took centrality.

Although embryonic, these consensuses set new regional boundaries moving beyond the historical hub and spoke regionalism where the United States and the market formed a sole pillar into which South American regionalism had to reach. From this perspective, not only the notion of region is re-signified to reflect new spaces for state action; more fundamentally, this is leading to a new rhetoric about what regionalism *is* and *is for*. Engaging with this emerging debate, Riggirozzi (2014) proposes that regional governance is about setting normative parameters as much as creating spaces of co-operation for the design and implementation of policies at different levels of authority. Riggirozzi and Grugel (2015) analyse how Latin-American regionalism is shoring up rights, democracy, and managing the regional social deficit. In effect, new modes of mobilization and coordination pushed the states of South America to redefine the nation state with inter-state coordination functioning to create a sub- regional political identity in terms of peace, security, social justice and development. New spaces and actions created a distance from the US in key issue areas (Riggirozzi & Tussie, 2012) and brought a primarily social agenda back into the ambit of democratic government where social regional policy had been almost completely dependent on market needs. In South America for instance, MERCOSUR and UNASUR assumed new obligations in the area of health, education, and migration that are of particular interest for the study of the 'social turn' in regional governance and its legacy beyond trade.

These developments in scope mean that regional actors could also define problems, issue policy guidance, shape discourses, and increase the salience of issues. Two key illustrative areas of this social agenda have been health and migration. In the case of health, states subscribed to the Buenos

Aires Charter on Social Commitment in MERCOSUR, Bolivia and Chile (2000); a framework that sets obligations towards the achievement of access to comprehensive health services This regional normative framework also stipulates the obligation of member states to improve the quality of life of their populations, with particular attention to the most vulnerable sectors in attainment of the right to health for all.

In addition, MERCOSUR's Strategic Social Action Plan (PEAS) 2010 established the obligation to ensure access to and comprehensive quality of humanized health services, as a basic right. It develops coordinated strategies for the universalization of access to public health services; and scientific guidance and education on sexual and reproductive health, with a focus on reducing female morbidity and mortality. We can further trace how regional organizations represented local concerns at the international level. Of key relevance here is the obligation to promote and harmonize specific policies for indigenous populations and public health policies for women and early childhood care, articulating policies and promoting regional agreements that guarantee access to public health in border areas. Decision CMC 13/2014 promotes guidelines on gender equality policy. Other regional frameworks have been set to regulate organ donation and transplantation (DONASUR System – MERCOSUR Donation and Transplants Registry) and regional policies for epidemiological control to respond to spread of Dengue, Zika and Chikungunya (IPPDH, 2016).

UNASUR has also committed itself to supporting effective social policy in member states since it was established in 2004 in Cuzco, Peru, based on three principal goals. Two were fairly standard: the promise to reinvigorate intra-regional relations and the commitment to the creation of physical infrastructure (roads, energy and communications) to support better regional development. But alongside these was a promise of greater political cooperation in poverty eradication. Here we identify how regionalism in South America produced opportunities for shared expertise that were maintained in special policy networks of time. Within this agenda, health became an issue-area carefully linked to the idea of socially and democratically responsive regionalism (UNASUR, 2009, 2011). In order to advance the agenda, UNASUR framed a Five Year Plan (*Plan Quinquenal*) in 2009 which outlined actions on five priority areas: (1) surveillance, prevention and control of diseases; (2) development of Universal Health Systems for South American countries; (3) information for implementation and monitoring health policies; (4) strategies to increase access to medicines and foster production and commercialization of generic drugs; and (5) capacity building directed at health practitioners and policy makers for the formulation, management and negotiation of health policies at domestic and international levels (UNASUR, 2009). It also institutionalized a regional health think tank, the South American Institute of Health Governance (Instituto Sudamericano de Gobierno en Salud, ISAGS) under the auspices of the Health Council and reporting directly to it. ISAGS tasks are to provide policy-oriented and informative research, training and capacity building for member states 'supporting decision-making process and advocacy' and 'the formulation of UNASUR's common external policies to back up negotiations in global and international agendas' (Herrero & Tussie, 2015).[2] Despite political change diplomacy has been resilient in pressing regional agendas in some of these areas. In its institutional architecture UNASUR was conducive to a productive policy nexus between national policy arenas and expert engagement. ISAGS' thematic networks and working groups have a been critical for implementing various projects combating HIV/AIDS; for training human resources for health; for supporting national health policies, and for the production of new technologies across the region. The Network of National Institutions of Cancer (RINC), coordinating cooperation amongst national public institutions across UNASUR member countries, developed cancer control policies and programmes and research in South America (Agostinis, 2019; Riggirozzi, 2014).

Both MERCOSUR and UNASUR contributed to a new way of conducting diplomacy that, perhaps because of a market-focus, created spaces for international competitive advantages for negotiating internationally access to medicines. For instance, MERCOSUR coordinated with UNASUR and PAHO mechanisms of joint purchase of medicines, as a (regional) buyer cartel, to reduce the prices of high-cost medications through either joint negotiations, pooled procurement, or both, reducing prices of high cost medicines such as antivirals, oncological and Hepatitis C (O'Keefe, 2019; PAHO, 2015). UNASUR developed a shared bank of prices in support of negotiations with international pharmaceuticals while securing representation in the World Health Organization to present coordinated positions in the Annual Assembly between 2010 and 2015. This included successful discussions on the role of the WHO in combating counterfeit medical products in partnership with the International Medical Products Anti-Counterfeiting Taskforce (IMPACT), an agency led by Big Pharma and the International Criminal Police Organization (Interpol) and funded by developed countries engaged in intellectual property rights enforcement (Riggirozzi, 2015, 2017).

In the area of migration, responses to mobility and residence regimes led to new developments (Geddes et al., 2019). For its part, the Action Plan for the Statute of Citizenship MERCOSUR (2010) set objectives for the implementation of policies in support of free movement of people in the region, equality of rights and civil, social, /cultural and economic freedoms for the MERCOSUR states. In this context, member states adopted regional norms that called for the right to free movement, the right to migrate, the non-criminalization of migrants, and equal treatment of foreigners and nationals. The regime has allowed for the regularization of almost three million South Americans residing in the region (Geddes et al., 2019). The signing of a Residence Agreement as regional legislation adopted by the Common Market Council back in 2002 facilitated this process and acted as a fundamental instrument in the regulation of territorial mobility, covering the movement of workers, as one of the pillars of the common market (Mondelli, 2018). The MERCOSUR Residence Agreement has been recognized as pioneering new regional policies in support of mobility in South America (Acosta & Brumat, 2020). The Residence Agreement has also been recognized as a successful normative framework enhancing access to rights of migrants in the region which proved to have institutional 'lock-in' effects in national legislation and policies. The Agreement established that any citizen of a member state or associate member state may reside and work, as well as access other rights, for a period of 2 years in a host state. By 2017, just under 3 million residence permits had been granted under the agreement (Acosta & Brumat, 2020).

What all this suggests is that the value of economic integration or even institutional convergence is not the sole yardstick to assess the value of regionalism. The potential for regulation, contestation, cooperation and reworking of social policy dynamics and the impact of regional policy on societies in areas like health, migration and education need further recognition.

In general, critiques of South American regionalism have pointed to national-based interest and sovereignty trumping institutionalized commitments, and the absence of economic complementarity as a brake on the creation of an effective supranational integration. The result has been much scepticism and a quasi-campaign highlighting what Riggirozzi and Grugel (2015) identified as a 'credibility gap' explained by a proliferation of weak and sector-based regional agendas, and often overlapping regional organizations, that only supported erratic implementation of regional policies across Latin America (Gardini, 2010; Malamud, 2013). They blame this erraticism the absence of supranational binding mechanisms of policy enforcement, and of indications of policy impact (Malamud, 2013; Phillips, 2003).

Certainly, in Latin America regional organizations coexist with ideological frictions and situations where the same actors that give authority to regional organizations, that is governments of member states, also periodically and in reaction to ideological stands, may retrieve authority to regional organizations (Quiliconi, 2017). This seeming paradox of legitimacy feeds the credibility gap of regional organizations in Latin America. This gap grew further since 2015 when a swing to the right in the Southern Cone meant that governments increasingly distanced themselves from, and halted operations of UNASUR.

It is indeed difficult in this more variable context for social scientists to differentiate the regional from the national, and fundamentally how social effects of regional policies could be identified. Any pronouncement on the credibility of regional policymaking is in fact weakened by the lack of institutional continuity identified by the paradox of legitimacy. But the point we emphasize here is that measuring success or failure in terms of institutional formation or legislative prerogatives can misguide any analysis of regional governance performance even in times of crisis. In fact, failures in regional governance are not always zero-sum; cross-border dynamics may find ways to advance policy and specific regional commitments, particularly in crisis situations. This became evident as Latin America is transitioning through great health, and socio-economic crises as a consequence of the spread of Covid-19. Mercosur members have agreed as early as March 2020 to share information and statistics on the evolution of the coronavirus, as part of a common strategy to combat the pandemic, as well as to eliminate obstacles that could hinder or impede the transit and transportation of supplies and essential elements, such as food, hygiene and health care products. Soon after the Mercosur Structural Convergence Fund (FOCEM), committed funds for 'Research, Education and Biotechnologies applied to Health' while US$6 million was made available to strengthen the virus's diagnostic capacity, purchase of supplies and protection materials. Meanwhile, the UNASUR Network of National Cancer Institutes and Institutions (RINC), founded in 2011 as a regional hub in the fight against cancer was re-founded as Network of National Cancer Institutions of Latin America and the Caribbean (RINC-ALC) in October 2019 despite UNASUR being paralysed (Buonaguro, 2019), emphasizing the resilience of some networks of diplomacy we have alluded to.

Enhancing access to medicines, healthcare, education, rights of migrants and security are areas where concrete examples of modalities of regional policy making and implementation can be observed. Recognizing these is a first step to developing a monitoring and evaluation system for these initiatives to disaggregate regional policy and to understand its nuance and significance in different contexts. We require this better organizing framework that is inclusive beyond institutional relativism to identify when and how regional policymaking is used – and to what effect.

4. Conclusion: redressing the credibility gap and understanding the consequences of South American regionalism

Regional policymaking faces challenges of implementation that cannot be interpreted in the same way as measures of national policymaking can. The South American case evidences delays linked to differences between national legislations and ratification of agreement, meaning that efforts to develop a social dimension in regional agreements were often incomplete or unevenly implemented across the region, with variable effects in and across societies. Nonetheless, regional organizations are increasingly developing a broad remit to make political decisions over an inter-state space and shared normative affinity. Regional policymaking can be assessed by the extent to which it moves regions from a baseline of uneven social policymaking in the direction of upholding recognizable social standards and rights.

Policy, at any level of decision making, requires acceptance of a problem in society, and thus politically visibility in order for responses to become legitimized as part of the public agenda (Kingdon, 1984). Of course, not all individuals, groups or communities have the same ability to problematize an issue and to push it onto the public agenda. Individuals, groups, or communities may have very different goals and aspirations, or simply unequal access to resources, including information and political systems. Policy scholarship is not immune itself to those forces. The effects of prioritizing certain kinds of policy at the expense of others needs to also be recognized in the measures we use to investigate policymaking at the regional level. In the past two decades the European Union captured the scholarly attention that focused on policy effectiveness, impact and implementation of programmes, as well as expectations regarding EU cohesion policy and aid guidelines (Polverari et al., 2016). And while many scholars have studied the implementation of decisions made by the EU (e.g. Duina & Lenz, 2017; Tallberg, 2016; Thomann & Sager, 2017) less attention has been placed to formulation and implementation of decisions made by other regional organizations, except for impacts of trade and economic activity (see De Lombaerde et al., 2010; Sbragia, 2008). Intergovernmental regional organizations' achievements in specific areas of policy remain overlooked, and so is the potential for regional policy development, all of which widens the credibility gap.

Much of the literature in regional policymaking has focused on problems related to input legitimacy and integration. More recently valuable work has helped better understand through empirical analysis the construction of legitimation strategies through networks of actors in international and regional organization (Gronau & Schmidtke, 2016), particularly non-state actors (Mace, 2020). Still, very little has been said about whether and how to understand and compare the results of regional policymaking with a more expanded understanding of legitimate outputs as we propose above. Future research will be required to scrutinize and measure the gaps between policy formulated at the regional level and policy implemented on the ground. But, crucially, regional policymaking has other objectives in the form of convening and enabling opportunities for information sharing, training, and mutual learning that need to be measured in tandem with other goals. Increased awareness and evidence about an issue among regional networks can spark and support regional policy and the credibility of regional governance. The recognition and evaluation of regional policy impact will demand a shift in focus from what regional governance enables (actors and actions) to include the impact of actions and means to their outcomes in terms of people's well-being. That will require developing indicators that can measure progress and that can contribute to policy effectiveness and shape agendas for further decisions, such that citizens can recognize where regional policymaking contributes to improved well-being.

The post-hegemonic regional formations associated with left governments have not sustained as the South American region shifted to the right. The left turn shared a regionally expressed political framework based on social progress, employment and distribution, hand in hand with the distancing of trade and free trade rules. Today that agenda has lost its vigour as a new cycle of ideological and political splits between South American presidents deepens and with it the credibility gap of the regional organizations. The change in the political cycle revived differences and detachment among countries such as Argentina and Brazil while the social dimension of regional cooperation lost momentum to new economic priorities and alliances. But even if integrationist ambitions and dynamics face challenges it is possible that new regional opportunities find ways to advance debates and practices in specific areas. A decade ago, UNASUR and Mercosur allowed coordination and cooperation in the face of the health crisis, as well as a joint strategy for the purchase of medicines. Today, in the race for the production and acquisition of the Covid-19 vaccine, the imperative of social, humanitarian, environmental and resource crises demand more not less regional governance. It is possible that different configurations of regional formations may (re)emerge, even with overlapping agreements (Garzón & Nolte, 2018) as we have shown, especially given the impact of the probable recession that will hit developing countries post-pandemic. That is why we argue that regional policymaking should be assessed through a plurality of political logics, not easily reducible to a single rule or expression of economic integration.

In this paper we took a critical approach to show that a 'credibility gap' based on input legitimacy disproportionately overlooks some merits and achievements of more fluid forms of regionalism that have taken hold in recent decades. We make this case by focusing on regional social policies in inter-governmental organizations in South America and argue that any understanding and measurement of policy impact will require a suite of policy indicators that make sense not only for different types and levels of institutionalization, but across varying domains of regional policy. We argued in particular that in assessing regional legitimacy observers need to look for the capacity for agenda setting and the creation of normative frameworks; the allocation of resources (technical and financial) in order to create/sustain public support; and the enabling of new dynamics of representation and diplomacy. We suggest that it is possible that these kinds of impacts of regional organizations can serve the purpose of comparing regional formations across the globe, for which more empirical work is needed in future research. Otherwise, lack of understanding of the impact of regional policy risks trivializing whatever progress in regional policy might be made and, critically, affects the legitimacy and credibility of regional governance.

Notes

1. MERCOSUR/CMC/DEC. N° 07/92: PLAN TRIENAL PARA EL SECTOR EDUCACION EN EL PROCESO DE INTEGRACION DEL MERCOSUR. Available at http://www.sice.oas.org/trade/mrcsrs/decisions/DEC792.asp. For follow up see MERCOSUR/CMC/DEC. N° 15/08.
2. See also UNASUR Declaration CSS 05/2009.

Disclosure statement

No potential conflict of interest was reported by the author(s).

Funding

Part of this work builds from research carried out with support from the Economic and Social Research Council (ESRC) and UK Research and Innovation (UKRI) [Grant Ref. ES/L005336/1 and Grant Ref. MR/S032711/1].

ORCID

Pia Riggirozzi http://orcid.org/0000-0001-5809-890X
Matt Ryan http://orcid.org/0000-0002-8693-5063

References

Acharya, A. (2011). Norm subsidiarity and regional orders: Sovereignty, regionalism, and rule-making in the third world. *International Studies Quarterly*, *55*(1), 95–123. https://doi.org/10.1111/j.1468-2478.2010.00637.x

Acharya, A. (2017). After liberal hegemony: The advent of a multiplex world order. *Ethics & International Affairs*, *31*(3), 271–285. https://doi.org/10.1017/S089267941700020X

Acharya, A., & Johnston, A. (Eds.). (2007). *Crafting cooperation. Regional international institutions in comparative perspective*. Cambridge University Press.

Acosta, D., & Brumat, L. (2020). Political and legal responses to human mobility in South America in the context of the covid-19 crisis. More fuel for the fire? *Frontiers in Human Dynamics*. https://doi.org/10.3389/fhumd.2020.592196

Adler, E., & Barnett, M. (1998). *Security communities*. Cambridge University Press.

Agostinis, G. (2019). Regional intergovernmental organizations as catalysts for transnational policy diffusion: The case of UNASUR health. *JCMS: Journal of Common Market Studies*, *57*(5), 1111–1129. https://doi.org/10.1111/jcms.12875

Börzel, T. (2011). *Comparative regionalism: A new research agenda* (KFG Working Paper). Freie Universität Berlin. http://userpage.fu-berlin.de/kfgeu/kfgwp/wpseries/WorkingPaperKFG_28.pdf

Bulmer, S., & Quaglia, L. (2018). The politics and economics of brexit. *Journal of European Public Policy*, *25*(8), 1089–1098. https://doi.org/10.1080/13501763.2018.1467957

Buonaguro, F. (2019). *Red de Institutos Nacionales de Cancer de Latinoamérica RINC-ALC*. https://blogs.biomedcentral.com/on-biology/2019/06/26/red-de-institutos-nacionales-de-cancer-de-latinoamerica-rinc-alc/

Buzan, B. (2003). Security architecture in Asia: The interplay of regional and global levels. *Pacific Review*, *16*(2), 143–173. https://doi.org/10.1080/0951274032000069660

Clark, I. (2005). *Legitimacy in international society*. Oxford University Press.

De Lombaerde, P., Söderbaum, F., Van Langenhove, L., & Baert, F. (2010). The problem of comparison in comparative regionalism. *Review of International Studies*, *36*(3), 731–753. https://doi.org/10.1017/S0260210510000707

Deacon, B., Macovei, M. C., Van Langenhove, L., & Yeates, N. (Eds.). (2010). *World-regional social policy and global governance: New research and policy agendas in Africa, Asia, Europe and Latin America*. Routledge.

Dingwerth, K., Schmidtke, H., & Weise, T. (2020). The rise of democratic legitimation: Why international organizations speak the language of democracy. *European Journal of International Relations*, *26*(3), 714–741. https://doi.org/10.1177/1354066119882488

Duina, F., & Lenz, T. (2017). Democratic legitimacy in regional economic organizations: The European Union in comparative perspective. *Economy and Society*, *46*(3), 398–431. https://doi.org/10.1080/03085147.2017.1377946

Fawcett, L., & Hurrell, A. (1995). *Regionalism in world politics: Regional organization and international order*. Oxford University Press.

Gardini, G. L. (2010). *The origins of Mercosur democratization and regionalism in South America*. Palgrave Macmillan.

Garzón, J., & Nolte, D. (2018). The new minilateralism in regional economic governance: Crossregionalism and the Pacific alliance. In P. Riggirozzi & C. Wylde (Eds.), *Routledge handbook of South American governance* (pp. 173–189). Routledge.

Geddes, A., Espinoza, M. V., Abdou, L. H., & Brumat, L. (2019). *The dynamics of regional migration governance*. Edward Elgar Publishing.

Gehring, T., Oberthür, S., & Mühleck, M. (2013). EU actorness in international institutions. *JCMS: Journal of Common Market Studies, 51*(5), 849–865. https://doi.org/10.1111/jcms.12030

Gomez Mera, L. (2008). How 'new' is the 'new regionalism" in the Americas? The case of MERCOSUR. *Journal of International Relations and Development, 11*(2), 279–308. https://doi.org/10.1057/jird.2008.14

Gronau, J., & Schmidtke, H. (2016). The quest for legitimacy in world politics – international institutions' legitimation strategies. *Review of International Studies, 42*(3), 535–557. https://doi.org/10.1017/S0260210515000492

Herrero, B., & Tussie, D. (2015). UNSAUR health: A quiet revolution in health diplomacy in South America. *Global Social Policy, 15*(3), 261–277. https://doi.org/10.1177/1468018115599818

Hoffman, A., & Bianculli, A. (Eds.). (2016). *Regional organizations and social policy in Europe and Latin America: A space for social citizenship?* Palgrave Macmillan.

Instituto de Politicas Publicas y Derechos Humanos. (2016). Institucionalidad Pública en Derechos Humanos del Mercosur. http://www.ippdh.mercosur.int/wp-content/uploads/2018/08/Resumen-IPPDH.2016-color.pdf

Kingdon, J. W. (1984). *Agendas, alternatives and public policies*. Little, Brown.

Mace, G. (2020). Dynamics of legitimation in regional organisations: The OAS and non state actors. *Global Society, 34*(4), 507–527. https://doi.org/10.1080/13600826.2020.1756230

Mace, G., & Lockhart, N. (2019). Legislators and regional organizations: The issue of legitimacy. *Latin American Policy, 10*(1), 6–28. https://doi.org/10.1111/lamp.12162

Malamud, A. (2013). *Overlapping regionalism, no integration: Conceptual issues and the Latin American experiences* (EUI Working Paper, RSCAS 2013/20). European University Institute.

Mattli, W. (1999). *The logic of regional integration: Europe and beyond*. Cambridge University Press.

Mondelli, M. (2018). Scaling up citizenship: The case of the statute of MERCOSUR citizenship. In P. Riggirozzi & C. Wylde (Eds.), *Handbook of South American governance* (pp. 426–441). Routledge.

Moravcsik, A. (2008). The European constitutional settlement. *World Economy, 31*(1), 158–183. https://doi.org/10.1111/j.1467-9701.2007.01086.x

O'Keefe, T. (2019). Latin America takes on Big Pharma. *AULA Blog*. https://aulablog.net/2019/02/19/latin-america-takes-on-big-pharma/

Pan-American Health Organisation. (2015). *Países del Mercosur y Estados Asociados concretaron mecanismo de compra de medicamentos de alto costo con el apoyo de la OPS*. https://www.paho.org/uru/index.php?option=com_content&view=article&id=1000:paises-del-mercosur-y-estados-asociados-concretaron-mecanismo-de-compra-de-medicamentos-de-alto-costo-con-el-apoyo-de-la-ops&Itemid=451

Perrotta, D. (2014). La educación superior en el MERCOSUR: la acomodación entre las políticas domésticas y la política regional. *Revista Perspectivas de Políticas Públicas, 3*(6), 177–206. https://doi.org/10.18294/rppp.2014.658

Pevehouse, J. (2005). *Democracy from above: Regional organizations and democratization*. Cambridge University Press.

Phillips, N. (2003). Hemispheric integration and subregionalism in the Americas. *International Affairs, 79*(2), 327–349. https://doi.org/10.1111/1468-2346.00311

Polverari, L., Bachtler, J., & van der Zwet, A. (2016). *Evaluating the effectiveness of regional policy* (European Policies Research Paper No 91). www.eprc-strath.eu/uploads/eprc/documents/PDF_files/EPRP_91.pdf

Quiliconi, C. (2017). From open regionalism to neo-extractivism: A new geography of trade in Latin America? In J. Briceño Ruíz & I. Morales (Eds.), *Post-hegemonic regionalism in the Americas. Toward a Pacific-Atlantic divide?* (pp. 57–72). Routledge.

Quiliconi, C., & Rivera, R. (2019). Ideology and leadership in regional cooperation: The cases of defense and the world against drugs councils in Unasur. *Revista Uruguaya de Ciencia Política, 28*(1), 219–248. https://doi.org/10.26851/RUCP.28.1.8

Reus-Smit, C. (2007). International crises of legitimacy. *International Politics, 44*(2–3), 157–174. https://doi.org/10.1057/palgrave.ip.8800182

Ribeiro Hoffmann, A., & van der Vleuten, A. (Eds.). (2007). *Closing or widening the gap? Legitimacy and democracy in regional integration organizations*. Ashgate.

Riesco, M. (2010). Binding material for a young giant? Regional policies in Latin America. In B. Deacon, M. Macovei, L. Van Langenhove, & N. Yeates (Eds.), *World-regional social policy and global governance: New research and policy agendas in Africa, Asia, Europe and Latin America* (pp. 108–139). Routledge.
Riggirozzi, P. (2014). Regionalism through social policy: Collective action and health diplomacy in South America. *Economy and Society, 43*(2), 432–454. https://doi.org/10.1080/03085147.2014.881598
Riggirozzi, P. (2015). Regionalism, activism, and rights: New opportunities for health diplomacy in South America. *Review of International Studies, 41*(2), 407–428. https://doi.org/10.1017/S026021051400028X
Riggirozzi, P. (2017). Regional integration and welfare: Framing and advocating pro-poor norms through southern regionalisms. *New Political Economy, 22*(6), 661–675. https://doi.org/10.1080/13563467.2017.1311847
Riggirozzi, P., & Grugel, J. (2015). Regional governance and legitimacy in South America: The meaning of UNASUR. *International Affairs, 91*(4), 781–797. https://doi.org/10.1111/1468-2346.12340
Riggirozzi, P., & Tussie, D. (Eds.). (2012). *The rise of post-hegemonic regionalism: The case of Latin America.* Springer.
Riggirozzi, P., & Yeates, N. (2015). Locating regional health policy: Institutions, politics, and practices. *Global Social Policy, 15*(3), 212–228. https://doi.org/10.1177/1468018115599819
Rittberger, B., & Schroeder, P. (2016). The legitimacy of regional institutions. In T. Borzel & T. Risse (Eds.), *The Oxford handbook of comparative regionalism* (pp. 579–599). Oxford University Press.
Rose, R. (2019). Referendum challenges to the EU's policy legitimacy – and how the EU responds. *Journal of European Public Policy, 26*(2), 207–225. https://doi.org/10.1080/13501763.2018.1426034
Sanahuja, J. A. (2012). *Post-liberal regionalism in South America: The case of UNASUR* (Working Paper RSCAS 2012/05). European University Institute.
Sbragia, A. (2008). Review article: Comparative regionalism: What might it be? *Journal of Common Market Studies, 46*(1), 29–49. https://doi.org/10.1111/j.1468-5965.2008.00809.x
SELA. (2010). *Cooperation experiences in the health sector in Latin America and the Caribbean: Critical assessment and proposals for actions with a regional scope.* Permanent Secretariat of SELA.
Steffek, J. (2014). *The democratic output legitimacy of international organizations* (Discussion Paper, SP IV 2014-101). Social Science Research Center, Technische Universität Darmstadt.
Tallberg, J. (2016). Transparency and openness. In J. Katz Cogan, I. Hurt, & I. Johnstone (Eds.), *Oxford handbook of international organizations* (pp. 1170–1192). Oxford University Press.
Tallberg, J., & Zürn, M. (2019). The legitimacy and legitimation of international organizations: Introduction and framework. *The Review of International Organizations, 14*(4), 581–606. https://doi.org/10.1007/s11558-018-9330-7
Te Velde, D., Page, S., & Morrissey, O. (2006). *Regional integration and poverty.* Ashgate.
Thomann, E., & Sager, F. (2017). Toward a better understanding of implementation performance in the EU multi-level system. *Journal of European Public Policy.* https://doi.org/10.1080/13501763.2017.1314542. https://ore.exeter.ac.uk/repository/bitstream/handle/10871/29498/Thomann_Sager%202017_JEPP_conclusion_%20accepted.pdf?sequence=1&isAllowed=y
UNASUR. (2009). *Plan Quinquenal, 2010–2015.* http://www.ins.gob.pe/repositorioaps/0/0/jer/rins_documentosunasur/PQ%20UNASUR%20Salud.pdf
UNASUR. (2011). *Report of the Pro Tempore Secretariat, 2011.* http://isags-unasul.org/site/wp-content/uploads/2011/12/Informe-2011.pdf
Viner, J. (1950). *The customs union issue, Carnegie endowment for international peace.* Stevens & Sons.
Yeates, N. (2014). The socialization of regionalism and the regionalization of social policy: Contexts, imperatives, and challenges. In A. Kaasch & P. Stubbs (Eds.), *Transformations in global and regional social policies* (pp. 17–43). Palgrave Macmillan.
Zürn, M. (2018). *A theory of global governance: Authority, legitimacy and contestation.* Oxford University Press.

Indigenous regionalism in the Andes*

Roberta Rice

ABSTRACT

Top-down processes of regional integration among the Andean countries of South America are occurring alongside bottom-up processes of Indigenous regionalism in Bolivia and Ecuador that weave together Indigenous peoples' territories across local administrative units and even national borders. In light of this dynamic, the study asks: What explains the new Indigenous regionalism in the Andes? And, what are its implications for formal processes of regional integration? The study examines the cases of the Coordinator of Indigenous Organizations of the Amazon River Basin (COICA) and the National Council of Ayllus and Markas of Qullasuyo (CONAMAQ) as examples of Indigenous regionalism in relation to the institutional innovations of the Andean Community of Nations (CAN) to incorporate Indigenous organizations into its structure and agenda. The article argues that the intersections of regional integration, the enactment of the plurinational state, and Indigenous autonomies have provided the necessary institutional space for expressions of Indigenous regionalism to flourish.

The Andean countries of South America are undergoing a dual process of regionalism. Top-down processes of integration within the Andean Pact (1969) and later the Andean Community of Nations (1996) are occurring alongside bottom-up processes of Indigenous regionalism that amalgamate traditional and adapted governance structures which cut across local administrative units and even national borders. Regional integration has softened national borders by facilitating trans-border policy coordination on a variety of issues at the same time that the constitutional reconfiguration of the state along plurinational lines in Bolivia (2009) and Ecuador (2008) has hardened internal borders between Indigenous peoples and the state through the establishment of a bilateral, government-to-government relationship (Schilling Vacaflor and Kuppe 2012; Walsh 2009). New forms of regionalism have produced a complex, multi-scalar arena where social movement forces, national governments, and regional powers pursue competing political projects (Tussie 2009). In response to this dynamic, the paper addresses the following questions: What explains the new Indigenous regionalism in the Andes? And, what are its implications for formal processes of regional integration? The new Indigenous regionalism is understood in this study to mean the process of amalgamation of Indigenous autonomies within and/or between countries that has taken place over the past thirty years (González, Burguete Cal y Mayor and Ortiz-T 2010). The cases of Bolivia

*Fieldwork for this article was carried out by the author in La Paz, Bolivia in August 2014 and Quito, Ecuador in August 2012 under the auspices of a standard research grant by the Social Sciences and Humanities Research Council of Canada (SSHRC). I also draw on previous research in the region carried out between July 2003 and May 2004. Out of respect for Indigenous peoples as subjects of international law, I capitalize the "I" in Indigenous throughout the article.

and Ecuador are highlighted in the paper as the two countries in the region that have advanced Indigenous agendas the furthest, both in legislation and in practice, by affirming distinct legal and political orders within the state, thereby opening up avenues through which the new Indigenous regionalism has emerged.

Based on a comparative analysis of the organizational histories of the Coordinator of Indigenous Organizations of the Amazon River Basin (COICA), a transnational Indigenous rights organization, and the National Council of Ayllus and Markas of Qullasuyu (CONAMAQ), a confederation of traditional governing bodies, this paper argues that the reconfiguration of regional integration, the enactment of the plurinational state, and the expansion of Indigenous autonomies have provided the necessary institutional space for the growth of Indigenous regionalism to occur. The principal characteristics of Indigenous regionalism are found to be: (a) based on the recovery and reconstitution of pre-colonial governance structures that were torn apart by colonial borders and logics; (b) rooted in collective rights to land and natural resources; and (c) pursued by Indigenous actors seeking to achieve political and economic self-determination. Instead of assuming that governing authority must be centralized, bounded and unitary, Indigenous regionalism is based on the possibility of a coalition of sovereignties or of nested or embedded sovereignties that exist within interdependent scales of governance (Preciado and Uc 2010; Simpson 2014; Smith 2005). The paper makes a contribution to the 'practice turn' in international relations scholarship (see Hopf 2018) by revealing the myriad ways in which the daily practices of Indigenous communities in the Andes that are aimed at resisting prevailing social structures ultimately pave the way for observable changes in those structures over time.

The paper is divided into three sections. The first section of the paper examines the phenomenon of Indigenous regionalism in historic and theoretical perspectives. This section explores constructivist understandings of national borders and their implications for Indigenous organizing. The second section of the paper begins with an overview of the history of formal processes of integration in the Andes and the recent institutional innovations of the Andean Community of Nations (CAN) to incorporate Indigenous movement organizations into its organizational structure and agenda, including COICA and the Andean Coordinator of Indigenous Organizations (CAOI), of which CONAMAQ is a member. The section then examines the case of COICA and its efforts at *inter*regional integration in the Amazonian lowlands. COICA is part of a web of transnational networks and movements in the Amazon that includes Indigenous representatives, non-governmental organizations, multinational resource companies and international development agencies (Martin 2014). The case of CONAMAQ and its *intra*regional integration efforts in the Bolivian highlands is then explored. CONAMAQ seeks to restore collective rights to land and redefine administrative units through the practice of self-determination by Indigenous communities (Schilling-Vacaflor 2008). Finally, the paper concludes with a brief discussion on the implications of the dynamic of Indigenous regionalism for the future of regional integration in the Andes as well as for advancing the Indigenous rights agenda.

Indigenous regionalism: historic and theoretical considerations

Global processes of colonization and settler state formation have resulted in the geographical fragmentation of whole peoples or nations across regions and national borders. By way of a few examples, the San of southern Africa now live in Botswana, South Africa, Namibia, Angola, Zambia and Zimbabwe (Sylvain 2002); the Mohawk people straddle the Canada-U.S. border (Simpson 2014); contemporary Inuit communities are found in the United States, Canada, Greenland and

Russia (Samson and Gigoux 2017); and the Saami are located in present-day Norway, Finland, Sweden and Russia (Broderstad 2001). Colonial borders generate Indigenous minorities. In this way, the project of Indigenous regionalism, which involves the recovery and reconstitution of traditional lands and governance structures across colonially imposed borders, can be understood as being part of the larger project of decolonization pursued by Indigenous peoples worldwide. One of the first colonial borders of the early modern era was established by the Spanish in the Americas (Graziano 2018, p. 75). In the process of territorial conquest and division, the Maya were separated by several borders in Central America; the Quechua were divided among Colombia, Ecuador, Bolivia and Peru; the Aymara were fragmented across Peru, Bolivia and Chile; the Mapuche were partitioned between Chile and Argentina; and so on, all with little regard for the territorial integrity of the region's Indigenous peoples (Albó et al., 1996; Graziano 2018). From the moment of their independence from colonial rule, Latin American states followed the blueprints for their national borders that had been drawn up by the European colonizers. Strong notions of territorial sovereignty that underpinned nation-building projects in Latin America continue to inform state reactions to Indigenous demands for territorial autonomy (Schulz 2018).

How can we grasp the meaning of these modern borders? The constructivist school of international relations theory provides a powerful analytical toolkit to address this question. The core constructivist framework consists of three main elements (Copeland 2006). First, constructivists focus on the role of shared ideas, norms, and values, or ideational structures, which shape and constrain state behaviour. From this perspective, global politics is guided by the shared ideas held by actors. Second, ideational structures have a constitutive effect on actors. In other words, constructivists consider how ideational structures shape the way actors define themselves, including their identities, goals and the roles they are supposed to play (Onuf 1989; Wendt 1999). In contrast to rationalist theories, such as realism and liberalism, which hold interests and identities constant, constructivism suggests that the ideational structure leads actors to redefine their interests and identities through their interactions with other actors (Guzzini 2013, p. 190). Finally, constructivists hold that ideational structures and actors co-constitute and co-determine one another. While ideational structures may constitute actors in terms of their interests and identities, actors may also produce, reproduce and alter these structures through their reciprocal interactions. In short, the constructivist approach to international relations suggests that an actor's reality is the product of historical social practices, which, in theory, can be changed by instantiating new social practices (Guzzini and Leander 2006; Onuf 2013).

Borders are a political tool – a means, rather than an end – which take on a specific meaning at one moment in time and then a different or even opposite meaning in the next depending on historically constructed and contingent circumstances (Graziano 2018). For example, borders between colonial powers tend to be formally recognized and respected. States only violate the terms of treaties or other written conventions that they have signed in exceptional situations or if the penalties for such violation seem very small (Goldstein and Pevehouse 2009, p. 86). In Latin America, the Madrid Agreement of 1750 established the borders between the Spanish and Portuguese empires in South America, ceding much of what is today the country of Brazil to Portugal as a means to end conflict in the region (Graziano 2018, p. 75). More than a century earlier, the Parliament of Quilín of 1641 between Spain and the Mapuche people of present-day Chile recognized the border of the Biobío River and the independence of Mapuche territory to its south (Bengoa 2000, p. 37). Yet, Chilean independence from Spain in 1810 led to the military defeat of the Mapuche by the Chilean army in 1881 that saw the decimation of the Mapuche population, the expropriation of their lands, and their forced relocation onto dispersed *reducciones* or reserves surrounded by

Chilean settlements (Saavedra 2002; Schulz 2018). As a result of independence and the imposition of a new national border, the Mapuche became an ethnic minority within Chilean society, while Brazil became the political and economic powerhouse of South America.

In the contemporary period, borders can also take on new meanings. The rise of Indigenous peoples as important new social and political actors is a positive trend in Latin American democracies. Indigenous peoples' interests have long been excluded from national political agendas, that is, until the 1990s when Indigenous peoples began to mobilize on a variety of fronts in defense of their rights. The emergence of autonomous forms of organizing and mobilizing on the part of Indigenous groups has challenged existing models of citizenship, democracy and the state in Latin America (Van Cott 2005; Yashar 2005). The current bid for Indigenous incorporation into the polity in Bolivia and Ecuador was prompted by the massive tide of protest against neoliberalism that managed to topple successive national governments in the late 1990s and early 2000s (Silva 2009). In Bolivia and Ecuador, Indigenous movements have artfully linked Indigenous peoples' demands to issues of political and economic inclusion for the masses to produce powerful movements that not only seek to reconfigure the character of the state, but to challenge the boundaries and borders between Indigenous groups and the state (Rice 2012; Uc 2019). A constructivist approach aids in our understanding of what such borders mean and how their character can change over time. However, just as the complexity of Latin American regionalism tends to elude capture by any singular theoretical approach or framework, so does Indigenous regionalism.

Regional integration and indigenous movements in the Andes

The Andean Pact (now the Andean Community) is one of the oldest regional integration movements in existence today. The strong sense of regionalism that pervades the Andean countries dates back to the unionist project of Venezuelan independence leader Simón Bolívar and the process of nineteenth century nation-building. The breakup of Gran Colombia and the emergence of New Grenada (present-day Colombia), Venezuela and Ecuador following Bolívar's death in 1830 also attests to the tenuousness of many nation-states and the artificiality of borders in the region (Barton 1997; Langer 2008). Regionalism can be understood as 'a form of trans-border coordination across and between different policy areas and actors' (Riggirozzi and Tussie 2018, p. 159). Drawing on the work of Vivares and Dolcetti-Marcolini (2016), I understand regionalism to include formal and informal dynamics (or visible and invisible aspects) in the bottom-up formation of regions, both material and ideational. To add to their framework of analysis, I suggest that non-formal dynamics must also be incorporated into the study of regionalism. Non-formal institutions are neither informal institutions nor formally recognized by the state. They include Indigenous peoples' customary laws and practices and traditional authority and governance structures (Eversole 2010; Retolaza Eguren 2008). Such institutions play an important, albeit underappreciated, role in regional integration efforts. In the contemporary era, regionalism is viewed as a means to overcome economic and political vulnerability at the domestic and international levels (Gómez-Mera 2018). The Andean Pact of 1969 represented an innovative integrationist project in that it sought to promote a more balanced form of development through the equitable distribution of benefits among member countries (Hojman 1981; Mytelka 1979).

Over the course of almost five decades, the Andean Pact has undergone considerable alteration, not only in the configuration of its membership, but also in its original vision for integration along developmentalist lines. The roots of the Andean Pact, as well other older or classic integrationist projects of the 1960s, can be found in the dependency school of thought and the development ideas put forward by the United Nations Economic Commission for Latin America (ECLA). Researchers at ECLA argued that economic relations between the core, industrialized countries and those of the periphery tended to generate conditions of underdevelopment (Puyana de Palacios 1982). In response, many Latin American nations looked to self-reliance on a regional basis as the way forward. The signing of the Agreement on Andean Subregional Integration (known as the Cartagena Agreement) in May 1969 by the governments of Bolivia, Chile, Colombia, Ecuador and Peru, officially gave rise to the Andean Pact. Venezuela gained full member status in February 1973 (Gómez-Mera 2018). What distinguished the Andean Pact from other regional integration efforts of this time period was its more ambitious target of creating an economic union, in which there would be a degree of harmonization of national economic policies, and its operational principal of solidarity (Morawetz 1974). The Andean Pact sought to eliminate or decrease dependency on the industrialized nations, particularly the United States, to limit the power of multinational corporations and to accommodate the less developed members, Bolivia and Ecuador, with special concessions (Atkins 1995). Andean leaders set out to reconceptualize both national development policies and the role of integration in the development process.

The Andean Pact found itself in crisis by the mid-1970s when Chile and Colombia began to liberalize their economies and came into conflict with the economic model followed by the other member countries. The crisis reached its peak in 1976 when Chile withdrew from the Pact (Puyana de Palacios 1982). By the 1980s, classic regionalism in Latin America collapsed under the weight of the radical change in development thinking that occurred in response to the international debt crisis. Many countries in the region adopted policies of structural adjustment that fundamentally transformed their development strategies. Traditional protectionism was replaced by trade liberalization policies as the central focus moved from the domestic to the global marketplace. These new directions in economic policy had a decisive impact on regional integration schemes. The old view that trade liberalization was incompatible with regional integration no longer held (Rodríguez 1998). Countries began to reevaluate how they could organize themselves within an international economic system in which trade and foreign direct investment assumed primacy. By the 1990s, the new approach to regionalism emphasized North–South relations and allied regional economic integration with the neoliberal economic policies of the Washington Consensus. In 1996, Andean leaders signed the Trujillo Protocol and formerly relaunched the Andean Pact as the Andean Community of Nations as part of this new wave of open or liberal regionalism (Gómez-Mera 2018).

The Andean Community of Nations has yet to achieve its objective of promoting economic and political integration. In 2006, Venezuela withdrew from the CAN in protest over the signing of free trade agreements with the United States by Colombia and Peru (Tussie 2009). The CAN currently counts on just four member countries: Bolivia, Colombia, Ecuador and Peru. With the exception of Colombia, Indigenous peoples are a marginalized majority (Bolivia) or a significant minority (Ecuador and Peru) within these member countries. In an attempt to bolster the legitimacy of its organizational agenda, the CAN has increasingly reached out to Indigenous movements. Decision 674 of September 2007 established the Consultative Council of Indigenous Peoples of the Andean Community (CCPI-CAN), marking the beginning of a series of actions to promote the active participation of Indigenous peoples in matters related to regional integration (CAN, 'Pueblos Indígenas').[1] The CCPI-CAN seeks to promote dialogue on and cooperation for integration among Indigenous peoples, entities of the state, international human rights organizations and civil society groups within the member countries. The Council consists of one Indigenous delegate from each of the four member countries as well as one representative from regional Indigenous organizations who serve in the capacity of observers (CAN, 'Derechos de los Pueblos Indígenas en la Comunidad Andina').[2] The regional associations of the CCPI-CAN include: the Fund for the Development of the Indigenous Peoples of Latin America and the Caribbean (FONDO INDÍGENA), the Coordinator of Indigenous Organizations of the Amazon River Basin (COICA), the Andean Coordinator of Indigenous Organizations (CAOI), and the Continental Network of Indigenous Women of South America. While the Consultative Council of Indigenous Peoples is touted by the CAN as an important political actor within the organization, it serves merely in an advisory capacity as its decisions are non-binding on the organization's main administrative bodies (CAN, 'Consejo Consultativo de Pueblos Indígenas').[3]

Regionalism in Latin America has been viewed as an opportunity for diverse forms of governmental engagement and activism that occur 'beyond and above states' (Riggirozzi and Tussie 2018, p. 159). Perhaps the most compelling and largely untold story, however, lies within the interdependent scales of governance inside the state. Whereas government centralizes power in the state, governance disperses political authority amongst governmental and nongovernmental actors as well as Indigenous communities in potentially democratizing ways (Krahmann 2003; Swyngedouw 2005). The concept of plurinationality – many nations within the nation-state – represents the potential to reset Indigenous-state relations in Latin America on more equal footing in part by respecting Indigenous autonomies and the weaving together of territories through the process of Indigenous regionalism (see Figure 1). Indigenous peoples of the Andean region have historically maintained relations with diverse Indigenous nations across the formal boundaries established by colonial and republican states. Contemporary expressions of Indigenous regionalism can be seen in the everyday workings of traditional and adapted governance structures and socio-economic systems that extend across official borders as well as in the establishment of regional organizations and forms of representation by Indigenous peoples over the last thirty years (Smith 2005). In the words of Ecuadorian Indigenous leader Blanca Chancoso (cited in Plaza 2008, p. 11):

> With regard to so-called integration, it would be necessary to clarify what we are talking about because the pretext of integration has always been to impose on and make others disappear; this has always been a violent integration constructed from above.

In contrast, Indigenous regionalism – or regionalism from below – recognizes that the process of integration should be the expression of communities and not just of governments and that it must respect Indigenous territorial autonomy and the right of self-determination. As the case studies that

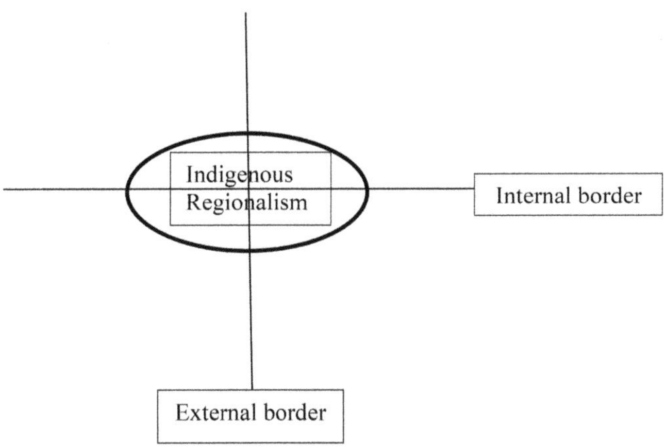

Figure 1. Plurinationality and Indigenous Regionalism. Source: Author's own elaboration.

follow will indicate, Indigenous peoples continue to construct their own agenda for regional integration.

COICA and interregional integration in the lowlands

The Coordinator of Indigenous Organizations of the Amazon River Basin (COICA) is a transnational social movement organization whose members are exclusively South American Indigenous peoples. Founded in 1984, COICA coordinates the activities of nine Amazonian or lowland confederations from Brazil, Bolivia, Colombia, Ecuador, French Guyana, Guyana, Peru, Surinam and Venezuela. It claims to represent the interests of over four hundred Indigenous communities in the Amazon basin (Martin 2014, p. 94). In 1993, COICA's headquarters were permanently established in Quito, Ecuador. COICA's organizational objectives include: the promotion and development of mechanisms that encourage the interaction of Indigenous peoples with the member organizations; the defense of the right to self-determination of Indigenous peoples; the coordination of the actions of its member organizations at the international level; and the cultivation and strengthening of collaboration among the Indigenous communities of the region. Its principal administrative bodies are: the Congress, which meets every four years and counts on the participation of ten representatives from each member organization with equal voting rights; the Coordination Council, which consists of the presidents of each of the member organizations; and the Coordinating Board of Directors comprised of the General Coordinator, the Vice-Coordinator and the various project coordinators (Mejías 2006). The organization's highest priority area is to guarantee the control, use and management of Indigenous peoples' traditional territories (COICA, 'Agenda Indígena Amazónica: Territorios y Recursos Naturales').[4]

Indigenous organizing in the Amazonian region can be traced back to the 1960s as a response to state-sanctioned colonization and oil-exploration programmes that threatened local lands and livelihoods (Yashar 2005). During this time period, transnational networks began to form between Indigenous communities and anthropologists, missionaries and environmental activists concerned with developments in the Amazon. The catalyst for COICA's formation came from an international conference of Amazonian countries held in Lima, Peru in 1984 that was sponsored by the United Nations Working Group on Indigenous Populations (Escárcega 2010). The purpose of this important international meeting was to construct a common identity and establish a common agenda in defense of the Amazon. The common identity became that of Indigenous peoples, and the master frame that COICA would come to utilize was that of the environment. The Amazon has been home to a diverse array of Indigenous peoples, including the Shuar, Achuar, Ashaninka, Cofan, Shipibo and Huarani among numerous others, organized into small and relatively isolated hunting and gathering societies. According to Martin (2014, p. 96), 'The idea behind this decision was their common understanding that all indigenous peoples of the Amazon were one whole community bound by the commitment to defend their collective lands and rights'. Up until 2000, COICA's focus was on four thematic areas: the environment; territorial rights; autonomous economic development; and human rights (Mejías 2006). Today, COICA's six-point Amazonian Indigenous agenda includes: (1) Sustainability; (2) Territories and Natural Resources; (3) Traditional Justice; (4) Ancestral Knowledge; (5) Economy and Development; and (6) Technology and Communications Systems (COICA, 'Agenda Indígena Amazónica: Ejes Organizadores').[5] From its inception, regionalism has been viewed by COICA as a strategy to protect Indigenous interests from external pressures.

Amazonian Indigenous communities have developed a system of collective action that operates both within and outside of their state borders. COICA itself does not manage local level development projects but rather is focused on the overall Amazonian region, creating forums, networks and linkages that unite their member organizations behind a common agenda (Martin 2014). This multi-scalar organizational approach has proven effective at allowing Indigenous peoples in the Amazon, who were once invisible to national and international audiences, to amplify their political voice while simultaneously consolidating local communities across the region (Perreault 2003). Amazonian Indigenous groups have pursued a strategy of engagement with domestic and international actors. At the international level, Indigenous representatives from the Amazon have been active participants in the UN Working Group on Indigenous Populations, where they have advanced international protections for Indigenous peoples, learned new strategies and tactics and formed stronger bonds among themselves (Escárcega 2013) At the regional level, Amazonian Indigenous representatives have worked within the Consultative Council of Indigenous Peoples of the Andean Community of Nations to influence the agenda for regional integration (Mejías 2006). And at the national level, Indigenous movements in the Amazon have been at the forefront of the push for the creation of new political parties and public policies to better reflect Indigenous and Amazonian interests within the formal political system (Rice 2012).

Ecuador's Amazonian Indigenous movement, in particular, has been a key driving force for change with important implications for the country's political institutions and policies. The Confederation of Indigenous Peoples of the Ecuadorian Amazon (CONFENIAE), along with the highland Indigenous organization Ecuador Runacunapac Riccharimui (ECUARUNARI) and the Coordinator of Indigenous Organizations of the Coast of Ecuador (COICE), make up the three legs of the country's powerful national-level umbrella organization – the Confederation of Indigenous Nationalities of Ecuador (CONAIE). CONAIE, which initially rejected the option of participating in electoral politics for Indigenous peoples, was pressured into reversing its stance when Amazonian leaders formed their own electoral vehicle, the Pachakutik Movement, to compete in the 1996 elections (Andolina 1999; Van Cott 2005). In response, CONAIE officially launched the nationally successful Pachakutik Movement for Plurinational Unity-New Country (MUPP-NP) party. While a complex set of factors led to the decline of the MUPP-NP by the mid-2000s – including its participation in a military-supported coup, ill-fated electoral alliances, and its perceived shift to a more radical, ethnicist stance – its central objective of creating a plurinational state was subsequently taken up and implemented by left-leaning President Rafael Correa (2007-2017) as part of the constitutional reform process. Ecuador's 2008 Constitution recognized the plurinational nature of the state, the historic goal of the Indigenous movement.[6] Plurinationality challenges previous governmental attempts to divide Indigenous peoples, to categorize them in ways that obscure their ethnicity, to discount them from national policy debates, and to denigrate them as obstacles to development. A plurinational state recognizes the plurality of cultural, legal, and political systems that exist within a territory and places them on an equal footing (Becker 2011; Walsh 2009). It seeks to end the unidirectional system of domination and replace it with relations of mutual respect and consideration.

Indigenous regionalism in the Amazon has a lengthy history. Contestation over Indigenous spaces is a sign of colonialism's ongoing existence as well its failure to erase Indigenous peoples from the landscape. Latin America came into political existence by way of Indigenous dispossession. However, as the concept of plurinationality suggests, Indigenous sovereignty co-exists with state sovereignty despite the tension in which they stand (Simpson 2014). Changing identities, norms and ideas that shape, and are shaped by, autonomous Indigenous organizing and mobilizing in the contemporary period are serving to undo colonially-imposed borders in practice. To more fully understand regional integration processes in the Andean countries, greater analytical attention should be paid to the expressions of regionalism from below found in the interregional representational forms and activities of Indigenous communities in the Amazon as well as in the intraregional integration efforts of Indigenous movements in the highlands.

CONAMAQ and intraregional integration in the highlands

The *ayllu* is a fundamental part of Indigenous peoples lives in the Bolivian highlands. In Ecuador, this traditional Indigenous associational form is known as the *comuna* (Macas 2001). It is the basic organizational unit of pre-colonial Andean society based largely on kinship groups and stretched out over vast territories and multiple ecosystems in archipelago-like fashion (Choque and Mamani 2003; Lucero 2006). In Bolivia, large groupings of *ayllus*, known as a *marka*, were governed by traditional authorities known as *mallkus*. In turn, confederations of *ayllus* and *markas*, known as a *suyu*, were integrated into *Tawantinsuyu* as part of the four-united *suyus* or regions of the Inca Empire. In the past, the *ayllu* served an important socio-economic role, ensuring the basic needs of its inhabitants through its diversity of soils, climates and altitudes while maintaining the social fabric of their existence. Today, the *ayllu* serves as a de facto space of autonomy from the state. According to Fernández Osco (2010, p. 29), 'Far from being destroyed or deactivated, the ayllu has kept functioning vigorously because at no point has it been incorporated into colonial hegemony'. Colonial administrators fragmented many of the larger *ayllus* and *markas* into smaller, more manageable units. For instance, the *suyu* Pakajaqi of Qullasuyu (present day Bolivia) is estimated to have had a territorial extension of 10,584 km^2, with a population of some 43,359 inhabitants (Choque and Mamani 2003, p. 155). Under colonial rule, Pakajaqi was divided into three provinces: Sicasica, Omasuyus and Pacajes (which carries the name of the original *suyu*). Contemporary processes of Indigenous regionalism in the highlands are driven by a desire to return to community – to the *ayllu* or *comuna* – as the nucleus of modern-day Indigenous society and the safeguard for traditional values and practices.

The movement to recover and reconstitute Bolivia's *ayllus* is led by the National Council of Ayllus and Markas of Qullasuyu (CONAMAQ). Since its formation in 1997, CONAMAQ has played an increasingly important political role at both the national and regional levels (Rice 2012; Uc 2019). CONAMAQ played a key role in the constituent assembly process that led to the drafting of Bolivia's 2009 Constitution as well as in the formation of the Andean Coordinator of Indigenous Organizations (CAOI), which is an active participant in the Consultative Council of Indigenous Peoples of the Andean Community of Nations (CCPI-CAN).[7] During the 1980s, in the initial phase of the modern *ayllu* movement, grassroots activists worked closely with Indigenous communities in areas where *ayllu* traditions were the strongest – in the departments of Oruro and Potosí (Lucero 2006). Under the guidance of the Andean Oral History Workshop (THOA), Indigenous communities in these departments returned to organizing themselves in self-governing *ayllus* as a means of expressing their autonomy and self-determination (Choque and Mamani 2003). By the end of the 1980s, a number of provincial *ayllu* federations had formed, including the Federation of Ayllus South of Oruro (FASOR) and the Federation of Indigenous Ayllus of North Potosí (FAOINP). Today, CONAMAQ seeks to change Bolivia's internal administrative-political borders to accommodate the growing number of *ayllus* (Schilling-Vacaflor 2008). CONAMAQ's central objective is to advance the recovery and reconstitution of *ayllus* and *markas* in the highlands to the point that they extend into the Amazonian lowlands and aggregate all of Bolivia's Indigenous peoples into a regional governance structure (CONAMAQ 2008, p. 75).

CONAMAQ is a social movement organization that maintains its independence from political parties, including the governing Movement toward Socialism (MAS) party founded by Bolivia's first Indigenous head of state, President Evo Morales (2006-2019).[8] It rejects the existing political system and avoids relations with peasant unions in the highlands. Instead, CONAMAQ has sought to establish alliances with Indigenous organizations in the lowlands, such as the Confederation of Indigenous Peoples of Bolivia (CIDOB), which are perceived as having a more Indigenous as opposed to class-based orientation (Schilling-Vacaflor 2008). However, in an effort to promote its agenda and influence the direction of the new constitution, CONAMAQ came together with the country's main Indigenous and peasant organizations as part of the so-called Unity Pact to draft their own proposal (Zegada et al., 2011; Tapia 2011). The document put forward by the Unity Pact introduced the concepts of communitarian democracy, decolonization, plurinationality and Indigenous autonomy subsequently taken up by the MAS and incorporated into the constitutional text, albeit in reduced form (Hilborn 2014).[9] Bolivia's new constitution recognizes the heterogeneity of the country's Indigenous population through its explicit recognition of a new political subject: First Peoples Indigenous Peasants (*naciones y pueblos indígenas originario campesinos*). This hybrid term is inclusive of the First Peoples (*originarios*) of the highland plateau, the Indigenous peasants (*campesinos*) of the highland valley region, and the Indigenous peoples (*indígenas*) of the Bolivian lowlands (Rice 2012).

The new constitution also provides for multiple pathways to self-government for Indigenous communities. The 2010 Framework Law of Autonomy and Decentralization regulates the new territorial organization of the state as defined in the 2009 Constitution. In addition to the recognition of the three hierarchical levels of government in Bolivia (e.g. departmental, regional, and municipal), the constitution also identified First Peoples Indigenous Peasant autonomies (*autonomía indígena originario campesina* or AIOC) as a separate and distinct order of government, one that is not directly subordinate to the other levels (CIPCA 2009). Under current provisions, existing Indigenous territories as well as municipalities and regions with a substantial Indigenous presence may convert themselves into self-governing entities based on cultural norms, customs, institutions, and authorities in keeping with the rights and guarantees in the new constitution (Faguet 2013). Currently, two municipalities (Charagua Iyambae and Uru Chipaya) and one territory (Raqaypampa) have completed the requirements to establish themselves as AIOCs (Postero and Tockman 2020).

The Andean Coordinator of Indigenous Organizations (CAOI) provides regional support for CONAMAQ's domestic agenda, as well as that of the main highland Indigenous organizations in Colombia, Ecuador and Peru and its affiliates in Argentina and Chile. It is intended to serve as an instrument of inter-national (e.g. between Indigenous nations) diplomacy for Andean Indigenous nations within the Andean Community of Nations (CAN). The CAOI, which was formed in July 2006, is a network comprised of four main organizations: the National Council of Ayllus and Markas of Qullasuyu (CONAMAQ); the National Indigenous Organization of Colombia (ONIC); Ecuador Runacunapac Riccharimui (ECUARUNARI); and the National Coordinator of Communities Affected by Mining (CONACAMI) of Peru (CAOI, 'Organizaciones Integrantes').[10] Its central mission is to work towards the territorial, political, economic and cultural reconstitution of Indigenous nations in the Andean highlands. The CAOI's specific strategic objectives include: (1) defense of land and territories in unity with Mother Earth; (2) construction of plurinational states and intercultural societies; (3) implementation of the collective rights of Indigenous peoples;

(4) reconstitution of Indigenous nations and the international representation of their interests; (5) international political advocacy on behalf of Indigenous movements; (6) de-criminalization of Indigenous protest activities and the de-militarization of Indigenous territories; (7) promotion of the Andean Indigenous principle of 'Living Well' as a means to confront the climate crisis; and (8) to strengthen and legitimize the participation of Indigenous women in national and international organizations and arenas (CAOI, 'Objetivos Estratégicos').[11] In sum, the CAOI works in concert with social movements to transform the Andean region's mono-cultural, exclusionary states into genuine plurinational states.

Repairing and rebuilding Indigenous-state relations on a more just and equal footing requires recognition of and respect for Indigenous regionalism and other forms of Indigenous governance. The practice of Indigenous regionalism means redefining sovereign boundaries to allow for overlapping or multiple forms of sovereignty. The new constitutional texts of Bolivia (2009) and Ecuador (2008) provide an important step in this direction through the reconfiguration of their respective states along plurinational lines. Both constitutions were heavily influenced by the United Nations Declaration on the Rights of the Indigenous Peoples (2007) – which was itself shaped by the active participation of Indigenous groups worldwide (Charters and Stavenhagen 2009). Bolivia became the first country in the world to incorporate UNDRIP into domestic law, yet important contradictions remain between legislation and practice, particularly in the implementation of the principle of free, prior, and informed consent (FPIC) in natural resource governance in Indigenous territories (Albó 2010; Schilling-Vacaflor and Kuppe 2012). As constructivist scholars suggest, international organizations, such as the United Nations, can influence the policies and practices of countries of the Global South through the diffusion of new ideas and norms about appropriate, or inappropriate, state behaviour (Goldstein and Pevehouse 2009). It is through the interaction of global, regional and local processes that Indigenous peoples in Latin America can exercise their rights as equal, yet different citizens.

Conclusion

This paper set out to explain the new Indigenous regionalism in Latin America and its implications for regional integration efforts. In the process, I was able to shed light on the new experiments in Indigenous regionalism that are occurring at the intersections of regional integration, the plurinational state, and Indigenous autonomies in the Andes. There is no one grand design for what Indigenous regionalism should look like, but rather particular forms of regional practice based on local norms, needs and priorities. In the highlands, Indigenous regionalism looks like a regionalized structure of local *ayllus* or *comunas* within the nation-state. In the lowlands, it looks like a transnationalized network of Indigenous communities that cuts across multiple nation-states. A comparative analysis of the organizational trajectories of COICA and CONAMAQ revealed the central characteristics of Indigenous regionalism to include the reconstitution of pre-colonial governance structures, the implementation of collective land rights and the practice of self-determination. These features are not unique to the Andean region, but rather are being pursued by a multitude of Indigenous actors throughout the Americas (Simpson 2014). The constructivist framework employed by this study illuminated how the project of Indigenous regionalism is guided by the shared ideas, norms and values held by local Indigenous actors as well as by global players such as the United Nations.

Indigenous regionalism poses both challenges and opportunities for the study and practice of regional integration in the Andes. In terms of policy relevance, the findings of this paper suggest that in order to maintain its organizational relevance and legitimacy, the Andean Community of Nations must recognize and respect the plurinational nature of the states they seek to integrate. This critical task can be accomplished by granting meaningful decision-making powers to the Consultative Council of Indigenous Peoples of the Andean Community. To do so would not only create a powerful arena for sharing experiences and expectations of regional integration, but would also bridge the dual process of regionalism underway in the Andean region and ensure that it is contributing to the region's integration and harmony rather than its fracture and distancing (Vivares and Dolcetti-Marcolini 2016). The examination of Indigenous regionalism both challenges and enriches the conventional literature on regional integration that looks to regional organizations as a space above, rather than within or below, the state for the articulation and promotion of norms, methods and strategies of policy coordination (Riggirozzi and Tussie 2018). Regionalism in the Andes is not only presently being constructed from the top down by states and regional associations, but also from the bottom up by Indigenous communities (Legler 2013). Finally, the study of Indigenous regionalism reminds us that Indigenous self-determination and self-government can also be advanced through various forms of regional representative arrangements and organizations such as COICA and CONAMAQ (Smith 2005). Greater attention is warranted to the multi-scalar organizational efforts of Indigenous movements in Latin America in the ongoing struggle for identity, territory and autonomy.

Notes

1. "Pueblos Indígenas." *Comunidad Andina.* 2010. Retrieved February 21, 2019. http://www.comunidadandina.org/Seccion.aspx?id=78&tipo=TE&title=pueblos-indigenas.
2. "Derechos de los Pueblos Indígenas en la Comunidad Andina." *Comunidad Andina.* 2013. Retrieved February 10, 2019. http://www.comunidadandina.org/StaticFiles/2013819121949indigenasJUL2013.pdf.
3. "Consejo Consultivo de Pueblos Indígenas." *Comunidad Andina.* 2010. Retrieved February 24, 2019. http://www.comunidadandina.org/Seccion.aspx?id=45&tipo=SA..
4. "Agenda Indígena Amazónica: Territorios y Recursos Naturales." *COICA*. 2018. Retrieved February 13, 2019. http://coica.org.ec/agenda-indigena-amazonica/.
5. "Agenda Indígena Amazónica: Ejes Organizadores." *COICA*. 2018. Retrieved February 13, 2019. http://coica.org.ec/agenda-indigena-amazonica/.
6. The 2008 Ecuadorian Constitution can be downloaded at. Retrieved February 7, 2019. http://pdba.georgetown.edu/Constitutions/Ecuador/english08.html.
7. The 2009 Bolivian Constitution can be downloaded at. Retrieved February 9, 2019. http://pdba.georgetown.edu/constitutions/bolivia/bolivia.html.
8. Víctor Condori Molle, director of communications, CONAMAQ. Author interview, La Paz, Bolivia, March 10, 2004.
9. The Unity Pact proposal is available for download at: www.cebem.org/cmsfiles/archivos/propuesta-organizaciones-indigenas.pdf
10. "Organizaciones Integrantes." *CAOI.* 2014. Retrieved February 15, 2019. http://www.coordinadoracaoi.org/web/nuestra-organizacion/nuestras-organizaciones-integrantes/.
11. "Objetivos Estratégicos." *CAOI.* 2014. http://www.coordinadoracaoi.org/web/nuestra-organizacion/objetivos-estrategicos/.

Disclosure statement

No potential conflict of interest was reported by the author(s).

Funding

This work was supported by Social Sciences and Humanities Research Council of Canada: [grant number Standard Research Grant (2011-2014)].

References

Albó, X. (2010). Las Flamantes Autonomías Indígenas en Bolivia. In M. González, A. B. Cal, & P. Ortiz-T (Eds.), *La Autonomía a Debate: Autogobierno Indígena y Estado Plurinacional en América Latina* (pp. 355–387). FLACSO.

Albó, X., Arratia, M. I., Hidalgo, J., Núñez, L., Llagostera, A., Remy, M. I., & Revesz, B. (1996). *La Integración surandina Cinco Siglos Después*. Centro de Estudios Regionales Andinos "Bartolomé de las Casas.

Andolina, R. J. (1999). "Colonial Legacies and Plurinational Imaginaries: Indigenous Movement Politics in Ecuador and Bolivia." PhD Dissertation, University of Minnesota, Minneapolis.

Atkins, P. G. (1995). *Latin America in the international political system*. Westview Press.

Barton, J. R. (1997). *A Political Geography of Latin America*. Routledge.

Becker, M. (2011). *Pachakutik: Indigenous movements and electoral politics in Ecuador*. Rowman & Littlefield.

Bengoa, J. (2000). *Historia del Pueblo Mapuche: Siglo XIX y XX*. Editorial LOM.

Broderstad, E. G. (2001). Political autonomy and integration of authority: The understanding of Saami self-determination. *International Journal on Minority and Group Rights*, *8*(2), 151–175. https://doi.org/10.1163/15718110120908385

Centro de Investigación y Promoción del Campesinado. (2009). *Posibles Caminos Hacia las Autonomías Indígena Originario Campesinas*. CIPCA.

Charters, C., & Stavenhagen, R. (Eds.). (2009). *Making the declaration work: The United Nations declaration on the rights of indigenous peoples*. IWGIA.

Choque, M. E., & Mamani, C. (2003). Reconstitución del Ayllu y Derechos de los Pueblos Indígenas: El Movimiento Indio en los Andes de Bolivia. In E. T. Alejo (Ed.), *Los Andes desde Los Andes* (pp. 147–170). Ediciones Yachaywasi.

Consejo Nacional de Ayllus y Markas del Qullasuyu. (2008). *Plan Estratégico 2008-2013*. CONAMAQ.

Copeland, D. C. (2006). The constructivist challenge to structural realism: A review essay. In S. Guzzini, & A. Leander (Eds.), *Constructivism and international relations: Alexander Wendt and his critics* (pp. 1–20). Routledge.

Escárcega, S. (2010). Authenticating Strategic essentialisms: The politics of indigenousness at the United nations. *Cultural Dynamics*, *22*(1), 3–28. https://doi.org/10.1177/0921374010366780

Escárcega, S. (2013). The global indigenous movements and paradigm wars: International activism, network building, and transformative politics. In J. S. Juris, & A. Khasnabish (Eds.), *Insurgent encounters: Transnational activism, ethnography, and the political* (pp. 129–140). Duke University Press.

Eversole, R. (2010). Empowering institutions: Indigenous lessons and policy perils. *Development*, *53*(1), 77–82. https://doi.org/10.1057/dev.2009.81

Faguet, J.-P. (2013). Can subnational autonomy strengthen democracy in Bolivia? *Publius: The Journal of Federalism*, *41*(1), 1–31. https://doi.org/10.1093/publius/pjt020

Fernández Osco, M. (2010). Ayllu: Decolonial critical thinking and (an)other autonomy. In M. Blaser, R. d. Costa, D. McGregor, & W. P. Coleman (Eds.), *Indigenous peoples and autonomy: Insights for a global age* (pp. 27–45). UBC Press.
Goldstein, J. S., & Pevehouse, J. C. (2009). *Principles of international relations*. Pearson Longman.
González, Miguel, Araceli Burguete Cal y Pablo Ortiz-T. (Eds.). 2010. *La Autonomía a Debate: Autogobierno Indígena y Estado Plurinacional en América Latina*. Quito: FLACSO.
Gómez-Mera, L. (2018). Governance as regional integration: ALADI, CAN and MERCOSUR. In P. Riggirozzi, & C. Wylde (Eds.), *Handbook of South American governance* (pp. 147–158). Routledge.
Graziano, M. (2018). *What is a border?* Stanford University Press Briefs.
Guzzini, S. (2013). *Power, realism and constructivism*. Routledge.
Guzzini, S., & Leander, A. (2006). *Constructivism and International Relations: Alexander Wendt and his critics*. Routledge.
Hilborn, P. J. (2014). Can a state decolonize itself? A Critical Analysis of Bolivia's State-Led Decolonization Press. Master's Thesis, Dalhousie University, Canada.
Hojman, D. E. (1981). The Andean pact: Failure of a model of economic integration? *JCMS: Journal of Common Market Studies*, *20*(2), 139–160. https://doi.org/10.1111/j.1468-5965.1981.tb00255.x
Hopf, T. (2018). Change in international practices. *European Journal of International Relations*, *24*(3), 687–711. https://doi.org/10.177/1354066117718041
Krahmann, E. (2003). National, regional, and global governance: One phenomenon or many? *Global Governance: A Review of Multilateralism and International Organizations*, *9*(3), 323–346. https://doi.org/10.1163/19426720-00903006
Langer, E. (2008). Regionalism. In J. Kinsbruner, & E. D. Langer (Eds.), *Encyclopedia of Latin American history and culture* (pp. 512–514). Charles Scribner's Sons.
Legler, T. (2013). Post-hegemonic regionalism and sovereignty in Latin America: Optimists, skeptics, and an emerging research agenda. *Contexto Internacional*, *35*(2), 325–352. https://doi.org/10.1590/S0102-85292013000200001
Lucero, J. A. (2006). Representing 'Real Indians': The challenges of indigenous authenticity and strategic constructivism in Ecuador and Bolivia. *Latin American Research Review*, *41*(2), 31–56. https://doi.org/10.1353/lar.2006.0026
Macas, L. (2001). Instituciones Indígenas: La Comuna Como Eje Histórico. In P. Dávalos (Ed.), *Yuyarinakuy: Digamos lo que Somos, Antes que Otros Nos Den Diciendo lo que no Somos* (pp. 92–93). Ediciones Abya Yala.
Martin, P. (2014). *The globalization of contentious politics: The Amazonian indigenous rights movement*. Routledge.
Mejías, C. (2006). Las Organizaciones Sociales y el Nuevo Multilateralismo: Una Aproximación a Partir del Estudio de Caso COICA. *Politeia*, *29*(36), 129–143.
Morawetz, D. (1974). *The Andean group: A case study in economic integration among developing countries*. MIT Press.
Mytelka, L. K. (1979). *Regional development in a global economy: The multinational corporation, technology, and Andean integration*. Yale University Press.
Onuf, N. G. (1989). *World of our making: Rules and rule in social theory and international relations*. University of South Caroline Press.
Onuf, N. G. (2013). *Making sense, making worlds: Constructivism in social theory and international relations*. Routledge.
Perreault, T. (2003). Changing places: Transnational networks, ethnic politics, and community development in the Ecuadorian Amazon. *Political Geography*, *22*(1), 61–88. https://doi.org/10.1016/S0962-6298(02)00058-6
Plaza, A. (2008). Integración con Participación Decisoria de los Pueblos Indígenas. In A. Alvarado (Ed.), *Los Pueblos Indígenas y La Integración Andina: Primer Foro de Intelectuales e Investigadores Indígenas* (pp. 11–14). Secretaria General de la Comunidad Andina.
Postero, N., & Tockman, J. (2020). Self-Governance in Bolivia's first indigenous autonomy: Charagua. *Latin American Research Review*, *55*(1), 1–15. doi:https://doi.org/10.25222/larr.213
Preciado, J., & Uc, P. (2010). La(s) Autonomías en América Latina: Una Expresión Socio-Espacial del *Estado Novísimo* y Sus Efectos en el Proceso de Integración Regional. *L'Ordinaire des Amériques*, *214*(214), 199–220. https://doi.org/10.4000/orda.747

Puyana de Palacios, A. (1982). *Economic integration among unequal partners: The case of the Andean group*. Pergamon Press.
Retolaza Eguren, I. (2008). Moving up and down the ladder: Community-based participation in public dialogue and deliberation in Bolivia and Guatemala. *Community Development Journal*, *43*(3), 312–328. https://doi.org/10.1093/cdj/bsn016
Rice, R. (2012). *The new politics of protest: Indigenous mobilization in Latin America's neoliberal era*. The University of Arizona Press.
Riggirozzi, P., & Tussie, D. (2018). Regional governance in South America: Supporting states, dealing with markets and reworking hegemonies. In P. Riggirozzi, & C. Wylde (Eds.), *Handbook of South American governance* (pp. 159–172). Routledge.
Rodríguez, M. (1998). Regional integration and convergence of legal systems. In E. Jarquín, & F. C. Flórez (Eds.), *Justice delayed: Judicial reform in Latin America* (pp. 111–115). Inter-American Development Bank.
Saavedra, A. P. (2002). *Los Mapuche en la Sociedad Chilena Actual*. LOM Ediciones.
Samson, C., & Gigoux, C. (2017). *Indigenous peoples and colonialism: Global perspectives*. Polity Press.
Schilling-Vacaflor, A. (2008). Identidades Indígenas y Demandas Político-Jurídicas de la CSUTCB y el CONAMAQ en la Constituyente Boliviana. *T'inkazos*, *11*(23–24), 1–17.
Schilling-Vacaflor, A., & Kuppe, R. (2012). Plurinational constitutionalism: A New Era of indigenous-state relations? In D. Nolte, & A. Schilling-Vacaflor (Eds.), *New constitutionalism in Latin America: Promises and practices* (pp. 347–370). Ashgate.
Schulz, C.-A. (2018). Territorial sovereignty and the end of inter-cultural diplomacy along the 'southern frontier. *European Journal of International Relations*, *25*(3), 878–903. https://doi.org/10.1177/1354066118814890
Silva, E. (2009). *Challenging neoliberalism in Latin America*. Cambridge University Press.
Simpson, A. (2014). *Mohawk interruptus: Political life across the borders of settler states*. Duke University Press.
Smith, D. (2005). Regionalism for indigenous governance: emerging models and policy challenges. Report from the Indigenous Community Governance Project, Centre for Aboriginal Economic Policy Research, Australian National University.
Swyngedouw, E. (2005). Governance innovation and the citizen: The janus face of governance-beyond-the-state. *Urban Studies*, *42*(11), 1991–2006. https://doi.org/10.1080/00420980500279869
Sylvain, R. (2002). Land, water, and truth: San identity and global indigenism. *American Anthropologist*, *104*(4), 1074–1085. https://doi.org/10.1525/aa.2002.104.4.1074
Tapia, L. (2011). Consideraciones Sobre el Estado Plurinacional. G. Gosálvez, & J. Dulon (Eds.), In *Descolonización en Bolivia: Cuatro Ejes para Comprender el Cambio* (pp. 135–168). Vicepresidencia del Estado/Fundación Boliviana para la Democracia Multipartidaria.
Tussie, D. (2009). Latin America: Contrasting motivations for regional projects. *Review of International Studies*, *35*(S1), 169–188. https://doi.org/10.1017/S026021050900847X
Uc, P. (2019). *Tinku y Pachakuti: Geopolíticas Indígenas Originarias y Estado Plurinacional en Bolivia*. CLACSO.
Van Cott, D. L. (2005). *From movements to parties in Latin America: The evolution of ethnic politics*. Cambridge University Press.
Vivares, E., & Dolcetti-Marcolini, M. (2016). Two regionalisms, two Latin Americas or beyond Latin America? Contributions from a critical and decolonial IPE. *Third World Quarterly*, *37*(5), 866–882. https://doi.org/10.1080/01436597.2015.1109438
Walsh, C. (2009). Estado Plurinacional e Intercultural Complementariedad y Complicidad hacia el 'Buen Vivir.'. In A. Acosta, & E. Martínez (Eds.), *Plurinacionalidad: Democracia en la Diversidad* (pp. 161–184). Ediciones Abya-Yala.
Wendt, A. (1999). *Social theory of international relations*. Cambridge University Press.
Yashar, D. J. (2005). *Contesting citizenship in Latin America: The rise of indigenous movements and the post-liberal challenge*. Cambridge University Press.
Zegada, M. T., Arce, C., Canedo, G., & Quispe, A. (2011). *La Democracia desde Los Márgenes: Transformación en el Campo Político Boliviano*. Muela del Diablo/CLACSO.

Critical Latin American agroecology as a regionalism from below

Peter M. Rosset, Lia Pinheiro Barbosa, Valentín Val and Nils McCune

ABSTRACT

Latin America has long been a hot bed for social movement organization and innovation, and for dialogue among different types of knowledge (*'dialogo de saberes'*). This has included dialog between academic knowledges framed by Western science, popular and ancestral peoples knowledges and wisdoms, and so-called *critical thought* from global and Latin American revolutionary traditions. From these conditions, we postulate that a specifically Latin American agroecology has emerged from these dynamics, as a sort of *regionalism from below*. While dominant academic writing recognizes that agroecology is simultaneously a science (in the Western sense), a movement, and a practice, it is the emergent Latin American version that is the most politically charged and popularly organized. We postulate that the joint forces of Latin American rural movements, intellectuals and scientists have uniquely forged a significant form of regional integration and regionalism *from below*, and that an agroecological variant of *Critical Latin American Thought* underpins this regionalism. This contribution uses a survey of selected Latin American agroecologists to illustrate this regionalism and its conceptual content.

Introduction

Contemporary discussions of Latin American regional integration – and regionalisms – tend to focus on one of two major perspectives, which in turn reflect distinct positions on the emerging planetary ecological and social crisis. One paradigm – that of development – emerges from Western epistemologies, focusing on the creation of common markets, cartesian science and the increasingly prominent role of the region for commercial and financial capital, in conjunction with reviving the traditional role as provider of raw materials and consumer of manufactured goods (ex. Malamud, 2018). Meanwhile, another paradigm – the 'critical' paradigm – is highly skeptical of Western development discourse, and instead sheds light upon the epistemological diversity of the 'many worlds' within Latin America (Escobar, 2019). This second paradigm is part and parcel of long-standing processes of Latin American integration – and the construction of regionalisms – 'from below' (Muni, 1985), based on social movements and accompanying intellectuals from both inside and outside of academia who are critical of 'the system' and of hegemonic forms of thought (see the introduction to this special issue (Lubbock & Vivares, 2022)). The glue that holds these regionalisms together is 'Critical Latin American Thought' (Bravo, 2010; Paikin et al., 2016).

We describe and contextualize herein the construction of a specifically Latin American *agroecology* regionalism 'from below' in the context of the dispute in rural areas between the development and critical paradigms of Latin American thought. We challenge the conventional telling of the history of agroecology, which, according to European authors, is simultaneously a 'science, practice, and social movement', heavily weighted toward the first (Western science), with a technological take on the second (farming practice), and only recently some mention of the last (movement) (Wezel et al., 2018). Rather than these non-exhaustive, non-exclusive and contested categories, this article will employ a historical and sociocultural frame to characterize the agroecological phenomenon among the land and peoples of the Americas. This 'peoples' regionalism' has one major pillar in peasant and indigenous social movements and cosmovisions, and the other in the Latin American academic, scientific and technical world, which uniquely interacts on a continual basis with the former, producing what we have chosen to name 'Latin American critical agroecological thought', which we believe is the essence of this unique regionalism (see also Galt, 2016).

Latin American agroecology: decolonization, self-determination, construction of territories

In recent decades, Latin America and the Caribbean and their social movement thought have been increasingly looked to as the region of the world with the potential to offer solutions to the world-ecology debacle of the globalized capitalist system (Berrón et al., 2013). In Latin America in the late 1980s, diverse popular mobilizations shook the foundations of the emerging free-market triumphalism. Many of these mobilizations broadened the conventional class struggle frame, with some of the most encouraging and successful challenges to neoliberal hegemony born out of diverse epistemes, particularly the indigenous and peasant struggles against the destruction of Mother Earth and the privatization of common goods (Barbosa, 2019b). A particular focus of this reaction has been against the numerous negative impacts of the so-called Green Revolution (monoculture, commercial seeds, agrichemicals, heavy farm machinery, etc.) imposed by dominant global institutions on Latin America (and other continents) and against which peasants and indigenous people (first) and scientists (later) reacted, putting forward agroecology as a key alternative, and as a reassertion of the inseparable bond of nature and culture (Holt-Giménez, 2006; Patel, 2013; Rosset & Altieri, 2017).

In this essay, we demonstrate the existence of a specifically Latin American agroecology, as part of the emergence of Latin American regionalism infused with specifically *Latin American Critical Thought*. If *critical thought* is that which questions established wisdom and authority, then in the case of Latin America this takes the form of questioning Eurocentrism and more recently neoliberalism (Lander, 2002). As Bialowsky et al. (2014, p. 70) explain:

> Debates of critical thought have blossomed in Latin America over the past decade. Although they are influenced by the scientific accumulation of Western social sciences, they produce a fusion with them, with a shifting of contents and epistemological bases. Currently they are defined in resistance to the hegemony of neoliberal thought which still defines a major part of the Academy and the institutions of scientific production, their forms of control, [and] the rift between the natural and social sciences and humanities .... In this context we can analyze the continental circulation of critical thought ... and its epistemological validity for interpreting social movements and the collective intellect of Latin America.

We argue that in the Latin American context there is a greater emphasis on critical political, social and cultural content than is the case in other continents. To address this affirmation, in what follows we first offer an overview of the origins, history and characteristics of Latin American critical thought. We then briefly define agroecology, and offer a brief history of it in Latin America in contrast to Europe and North America, with emphasis on the role of social movements and on the somewhat unique nature – among scientific academies – of the Latin American Scientific Society for Agroecology (SOCLA). We then examine the responses of twenty selected Latin American agroecologists[1] – from both the Academy and from grassroots social movements – to a survey we conducted on their opinions concerning the characterization of a specifically Latin American agroecology.

We show that agroecology in Latin America carries historical, social, cultural and political connotations which it does not necessarily carry in other continents, though it may be that these meanings charged with social movement perspectives and deeper counterhegemonic meanings are just now beginning to spread across the globe, for example in La Via Campesina (Martínez-Torres & Rosset, 2014; Val et al., 2019). We also find that agroecology is part of and contributes to Latin American critical thought by being anti-colonial and decolonizing, and more autonomist than much of the debate on the Left (Rosset & Barbosa, 2021). Thus, Latin American agroecological regionalism as represented by critical agroecological thought is contributing to a novel form of Latin American regionalism from below.

From Latin American thought to Latin American agroecological thought

While never questioning the conventional narrative of 'discovering America', classic European critical thought indeed recognized the primary role of the European invasion of the Americas as providing the original wealth that allowed for credit and resources to flow into emerging capitalist economies. Only the mass slaughter, rape and enslavement in mines of the large indigenous population, as well as the commercial hunting, kidnapping and forced agrarian labour of tens of millions of Africans, permitted the 'rosy dawn' of capitalism (Marx, 1867/1990, p. 823). While this conception of primitive accumulation acknowledges the genocidal origins of the dominant world-system (Wallerstein, 1974), it does not, on its own, address the impact of genocide upon the knowledge systems, or epistemes, of the peoples in what would come to be known as the Americas. In the Valladolid debate of 1550, Spain's leading theologists argued about whether the indigenous of America had souls. Leading philosopher Juan Gines de Sepulveda, with support from the emerging landholding colonist class, argued for continued war and maximum exploitation of the indigenous population. Dominican friar Bartolome de las Casas, with support from a Spanish throne concerned with the growing power of colonist landowners, argued that the *encomienda* system of slavery and gruesome torture was unjust, the native peoples should be Christianized, and Africans should instead be brought as slaves to the Americas. Given this remarkably narrow range of thought in the dominant European law, philosophy, geography and history of Conquest, it is no surprise that the post-genocide, post-epistemicide and post-colonial emergence of Latin American thought would require centuries to be heard (Castro-Gómez, 2005; Dussel, 2010).

Before the Conquest, the original peoples who inhabited the continent had different names to designate the different territories that make up what we know today as Latin America: *Tawantinsuyo* (the region that today comprises Bolivia, Ecuador and Peru), *Anauhuac* (today's Mexico and Guatemala), *Pindorama* (the Tupi name for Brazil), etc. The Kuna people[2] called the region we know today as Latin America *Abya Yala*, which in the Kuna language means *flowering land, mature land, living land* (Albó & Barrios, 1993). These territories were inhabited by a wide range of civilizations with their own epistemes and ontologies originating in cosmogonies, linguistic matrices that provided them with complex conceptual frameworks, and a *modus vivendi* based on an intimate relationship between human life and the plurality of living and non-living beings existing in the cosmos, as attested to by pre-Hispanic historiography (Barrera-Vázques & Rendón, 1963; de la Garza, 2012; Mann, 2005; Rivera-Cusicanqui, 2015).

The *idea* of *America* has existed since the times of the Conquest, as a sort of permanent dialectic between the Old World and the New World, part and parcel of a European ideation that demarcates the emergence of a new part of the world, different from Europe, Asia and Africa (Ardao, 1980). The term *New World* has been used in writings and maps for centuries, for classifying and qualifying purposes, a descriptive or explanatory condition which denotes a world that is discovered and revealed before European eyes. The idea of *Latin America* emerged in the eighteenth century to designate the Americas characterized by the Spanish, French and Portuguese languages, and cannot be explained outside of its dialectical relationship with Anglo-Saxon America, given that 'they are related concepts, although by opposition; they could not appear and develop but together, through their contrasts' (Ardao, 1980, p. 24).

Within the framework of the social and political history of the region, the question of Latin American *identity* has always been present in Latin American critical thought (Sambarino, 1980), as famously articulated by José Martí, whether through his expression of the ethical-political desire for the unity of *Nuestra América* ['Our America'] (Martí, 1974), or as a theoretical-methodological entry point to interpret the process of socio-historical formation and the paths of decolonization of thought (Martí, 2005, 2009). The years that Martí spent in Mexico (1875–1876) and Guatemala (1877–1878) were fundamental to his elaboration of the concept of *Nuestra América*,[3] helping him to develop a consciousness and definition of Latin American autochthony, especially through contact with the indigenous cultures of these countries. In his text *The New Codes* (1877)[4] he developed initial elements of his conception of *Nuestra América*, positing the existence of a new identity, as a fruit of the Conquest:

> With the natural and majestic work of American civilization interrupted by the conquest, a new strange people was created with the arrival of the Europeans. Not a *Spanish* people, because the new sap rejects the old body; and not *indigenous*, because it has suffered the intervention of a devastating civilization; two words that, in their antagonism, constitute a process. A *mestizo* people was created such that, with the reconquest of its freedom, it develops and restores its own soul.

Inspired by the liberal ideas of the conformation of nation states, Martí elaborated his conception of Latin American identity based on three essential ideas (Rodríguez, 2007): (1) Latin America is constituted by new peoples; (2) there is a particular Latin American character, with its own spiritual qualities and social psychology; (3), therefore Latin American particularities and specificities require their own analysis and their own solutions.[5]

In the twentieth century, Mariátegui (1928) argued that all theses that ignored the indigenous problematic or abstractly reduced it to an ethnic and moral question were doomed to be but 'sterile theoretical exercises'. In his theoretical-analytical conceptualization of an *Indo-American socialism*, as distinct from a European socialism, the Peruvian thinker identified germinal elements in the historical process of Peru, linked to the survival of peasant and indigenous communal traditions in the face of developing capitalism. This, he argued, created a different specificity in regard to the nature of the contradiction between labour and capital predominant in Europe. In the perspective of an Indo-American socialism, he emphasized that the historical overcoming of the indigenous problematic should be the task of indigenous people themselves, as a historical-political and revolutionary subject distinct from a European-style working class (Mariátegui, 1982, pp. 185–186).

If at first the concept of a Latin American identity was born in the spirit of liberal republican intellectuals or Latin American revolutionary Marxists, such as Martí and Mariátegui, that same identity has another face, that of the original peoples and peasants, with their historical struggles marked by both legacies of and ruptures with conventional Eurocentric conceptions of the *political project* and the *political subjects* of a revolutionary process, affirming a different epistemic paradigm for their way of being, thinking and living (Barbosa, 2017). According to the Colombian sociologist, Orlando Fals-Borda (2008), this means that the indigenous-influenced Latin American episteme is *Sentipensante* – that is, both thought and felt – adding the heart (*corazón*) to the thought process, in contrast the almost exclusively *rational thought*-based European episteme.[6] Here, the heart constitutes the epistemic and ontological nucleus of a *rationality* proper to the epistemologies of the peoples of Latin America, the *feelings, word, political action* proper to this rationality, delineated as a different paradigm of thought and construction of knowledge, one that is closely linked to the defense of territories and of nature ('Mother Earth' or *Madre Tierra*), in a communal and agroecological sense (Barbosa, 2019a). As opposed to the endless dualisms that characterize reductionist European thought, epistemes native to the American continent tend to strive for unity, integrating reason, feeling, practice and reciprocity among active subjects, from the soil to the cosmos.

The *sentipensante* perspective establishes a different relationship with nature and the reproduction of life. Here we find the seeds of what we call *Latin American Agroecological Thought*, especially when based on the concrete experiences of peasant and indigenous peoples' movements and organizations, as they recover their collective historical memory of Abya Yala in the reconstruction of their own history, no longer as the soulless primitives in the eyes of the European colonizer, but as peoples endowed with their own, often millenary, wisdoms and knowledges. It is no coincidence that for the organizations of Latin America, the origins of the global peasant movement, La Via Campesina, are found in the 500th anniversary of Christopher Columbus' arrival to Abya Yala. In response to the official celebrations organized by the governments of several Latin American countries, as well as the USA, the European Community, Japan and Israel, a *Continental Campaign of 500 Years of Indigenous, Black and Popular Resistance* was formed between 1988 and 1991, which organized simultaneous actions of resistance across the continent and formed the regional structures (North, Central America, Andes, Southern Cone and Caribbean) that would become the basis for the Latin American Coordination of Rural Organizations (CLOC – *Coordinadora Latinoamericana de Organizaciones del Campo*), the continental expression of La Via Campesina in Latin America.

Today we can observe the theoretical-political claim to Abya Yala made by peasant, indigenous and Afro-Latin movements in the region, employed to express a geographical, socio-cultural and political territorial unity. This phrase was used in its political sense in 2004, within the framework of the *II Continental Summit of the Indigenous Peoples and Nationalities of Abya Yala*, held in Quito, Peru. In the Quito Declaration, they stated:

> We are the original peoples of *Abya Yala*. Our ancestors, our grandparents taught us to love and venerate our bountiful *Pacha Mama*, to live in harmony and freedom with the natural and spiritual beings that co-exist in her. Our own political, economic, social and cultural institutions are an inheritance from our ancestors and are the basis for the construction of our future.[7]

At the *III Continental Summit of Indigenous Nationalities and Peoples of Abya Yala*, held in Iximche, Guatemala, in 2007, they explicitly convened themselves as *Abya Yala* and formed a Continental Coordination of the Indigenous Nationalities and Peoples of *Abya Yala*, understood as:

> [...] a permanent space for liaison and exchange, where experiences and proposals can converge, so that together we can confront the policies of neoliberal globalization and fight for the definitive liberation of our sister peoples, of Mother Earth, of territory, of water and of all our natural heritage in order to live well (*vivir bien*).[8]

We are witness to a processes of political-identity construction and resignification of *Abya Yala*, where discursive practices and political positions play a relevant role in the decolonization of thought, recovering *other* paradigms that are positioned in the critique of the paradigm of modern Western capitalism and its associated thought. These discursive practices have helped fuel the expansion of indigenous and peasant resistance in Latin America, in the defense of their territories as they are confronted with new patterns of the capital accumulation, characterized by the deepening of the extractivist model based on accumulation by dispossession (Harvey, 2004), as seen in large-scale mining concessions, the privatization of water, and the energy industry, among others.

It is important to note that increasingly these organizations and movements articulate a political discourse based on matrices that structure *other* intersubjective rationalities with their territories. In essence, this constitutes a critique of the reproduction of life under the hegemony of capital, which can be understood as what Barbosa (2016) has called the *Epistemic Paradigm of the Countryside*. Some concepts are central to these rationalities and to this epistemic paradigm of the countryside, such as *Sumak Kawsai* (from equatorial *quéchua*) or *Sumak Qamaña* (from the Bolivian *aymara*) or *Buen Vivir* (*living well*), understood as an essential principle of the rights of humans and of Nature, in contrast to the perspective of 'living better' defended by modern capitalism (Giraldo, 2014; Lalander & Lembke, 2018; Royero-Benavides et al., 2019).

Within this framework, we can imagine a critical *Latin American agroecological thought* that is structured on three perspectives. The first is articulated to an epistemic understanding of territory (Barbosa, 2018), in which it is a locus of resistance and conformation of an *identitary ethos*, incorporated into the political narrative of Latin American indigenous and peasant movements, in the defense of land, nature, common goods and the recognition of territory as a space for the reproduction of life, as well a place of creation and resignification of socio-cultural and power relations. This appropriation of territory directly challenges that which prevailed at the time of the Conquest, under the eyes of the conqueror, that is to say, of an 'empty' land, a no man's land, an uninhabited territory, therefore open to colonization, exploitation, and unlimited appropriation (Barbosa, 2018, 2019a). These movements and currents of thought see territories as inhabited, or even as spaces of co-habitation among peoples and between human beings and nature (Giraldo, 2018).

The second has to do with the biocultural memory of traditional knowledges and wisdoms (Toledo & Barrera-Bassols, 2008), which often underlie efforts to preserve native seeds, to conserve soils, to make sustainable use of water, to recover ancestral agroecological practices, among other ancestral knowledges, and which underpins this conception of Agroecology (Guzmán Luna et al., 2019). The third is directly linked to the rural social movement use of agroecology as a banner of collective struggle and (re)construction and as a political project in the defense of its territories and food sovereignty (Barbosa & Rosset, 2017).

These three axes of a possible Latin American Agroecological Thought can be seen in different peasant and indigenous peoples' organizations and movements throughout the continent. For example, the organizations of the CLOC, the Latin American part of La Via Campesina (LVC), articulate an agroecological peasant pedagogy (Barbosa & Rosset, 2017) based on epistemes that dialogue inside CLOC/LVC (Rosset, 2015). Elsewhere we have described the origins and functioning of CLOC/LVC (Barbosa & Rosset, 2017; Martínez-Torres & Rosset, 2010, 2014; Rosset & Martínez-Torres, 2012), and we recently examined the continental network of peasant agroecology schools and peasant-indigenous universities that they have constructed, which serve to consolidate this Latin American vision of peasant agroecology as a dispositive for the collective transformation of reality (Rosset et al., 2019; Val et al., 2019). Remarkably, and fairly unique to Latin America, agroecological scientists share many of the elements of the critical social movement vision of agroecology, as exemplified by the discourses commonly expressed in the Latin American Scientific Society for Agroecology (SOCLA)[9] (Altieri, 2008; Altieri & Nichols, 2017). Since its first academic congress held in Medellín, Colombia in 2007, and biannually around the continent since, SOCLA congresses have consistently featured hundreds and sometimes thousands (the two times they were held in Brazil) of academics, researchers and technicians, along with dozens and sometimes hundreds of peasant farmers and rural social movement representatives and organic intellectuals,[10] generating a rich debate and 'dialogue of knowledges' (Artacker, 2019; Martínez-Torres & Rosset, 2014) between the two sectors, who can be thought of as the two 'parents' of contemporary Latin American critical agroecology as a distinct regionalism from below.[11]

What is agroecology?

Agroecology stems from the accumulation of knowledge about nature through indigenous and traditional farming and food production systems over millennia [see the lifelong work of leading Latin American agroecologist Miguel Altieri, from Altieri (1987) to Rosset and Altieri (2017), with many works in between]. Using their intricate local knowledge, traditional peasant farmers have maintained high levels of biodiversity associated with their farming systems, developing agroecosystems that cycle nutrients through closed systems, maintain soil fertility and requiring very few external inputs (Gliessman, 2014). In its contemporary usage, agroecology is variously known as the *science* that studies and attempts to explain the functioning of agroecosystems, primarily concerned with biological, biophysical, ecological, social, cultural, economic and political mechanisms, functions, relationships and design; as a set of *practices* that permit farming in a more sustainable way, without using dangerous chemicals; and as a *movement* that seeks to make farming more ecologically sustainable and more socially just (Rosset & Altieri, 2017; Wezel et al. 2009).

Agroecology as a science and a movement has been built upon the rejection of the main tenets of the Green Revolution, namely that crop genetics and the application of purchased synthetic chemicals to monoculture plantations is the most efficient way to produce food (Rosset & Altieri, 2017). The basic assumptions of high-input, industrial agriculture have led to enormous negative externalities, in terms of resource depletion, air, land and water pollution, and greenhouse gas emissions, at the same time as they have concentrated power over food systems in the hands of a few large corporations, and contributed to the deterioration of the health of farm workers and consumers. Perhaps most conclusive, even on its own terms of ending hunger, the Green Revolution has failed – around 900 million people continue to suffer from malnutrition, even as half a billion now suffer from diet-induced obesity (Patel, 2012).

Resisting the homogenizing ethos of industrial agriculture, agroecology aspires to mimic nature by organizing food systems around the principles of diversity, energy efficiency, and mineral recycling. This means, in practice, the use of local resources, including knowledge, and the development of complex feedback relationships among agroecosystem components (Rosset & Altieri, 2017).

Agroecology in Latin America

In Latin America and the Caribbean, agroecology has long-existed on the margins of the *latifundio*, or landlord estate, a feudal system established by colonial powers (Hecht, 1999). Much of the New World endured slave agriculture for centuries, during which indigenous and African peoples were forced to work in monoculture plantation *latifundios*. The peasant farming in resistance, as well as the small areas that enslaved workers dedicated to food production, relied on local resources, seed saving, and complex intercropping. These historical experiences of a hegemonic 'their agriculture' in contrast to an 'our agriculture' of everyday resistance deeply inform the relationship that peasants, indigenous peoples, rural proletarians, and Afro-descendent populations in Latin America maintain with agricultures (La Via Campesina, 2013).

It is precisely this history that has led agroecology to insert itself as 'the scientific, methodological, and technological basis for a new 'agrarian revolution'' in Latin America (Altieri & Toledo, 2011, p. 587). As twentieth century struggles against *latifundio* have led to renewed land access via land occupations and the conquest of limited land reforms, tillers have reclaimed their knowledge systems as well. Agroecology in Latin America tends to explicitly address the socioeconomic structure within which agriculture exists by acknowledging the need to transcend *latifundio* property relations. At the same time, it can be argued that Latin American agroecology challenges the '*latifundio* of the mind' that remains tied to Eurocentric categories of analysis and Cartesian reductionism (McCune et al., 2017). As such, the biocultural relationship between people and territory transcends both exclusion and exploitation: popular sectors that gain or defend land access enact a productive model that contrasts with that of agrarian capitalism.

Agroecology is understood in popular movements as the recovery of ancestral knowledge associated with food production, as well as access to the productive means needed for this knowledge to contribute to the collective right to build and defend food systems, a right also known as food sovereignty. In Latin America, agroecology is largely seen as being part of a relationship that involves knowledge, land, and political power (Borsatto & Carmo, 2012; Leff, 2002). In this sense, SOCLA has played a unique role in galvanizing alliances that not only including popular actors, but in many cases are inspired by and even led by the methodological proposals of these actors (Ferguson & Morales, 2010). As such, academic approaches toward agroecology in Latin America tend to respond to demands to democratize knowledge and learning institutions themselves. The co-evolution of the agroecology movement in Latin America and the anti-neoliberal agenda has produced rich experiences in agroecology as a form of resistance to capitalist relationships.

The pioneering work of Mexican agronomist and ethnoecologist Efraím Hernández Xolocotzi, who sent Chapingo University students to learn from indigenous peasant farming techniques, was complemented in the 1970s by Stephen Gliessman and his team, who systematized the ecological basis of traditional agricultural systems of Tabasco (Altieri & Nichols, 2017). By the 1980s, agroecology existed as a scientific discipline with transdisciplinary, participatory and action-oriented tendencies (Méndez et al., 2013). The peasant-to-peasant agroecological movement gained traction as a horizontal method for taking agroecological practices to scale in Guatamala, México, Nicaragua and other Mesoamerican countries during the same time period (Holt-Giménez, 2006). By the mid-1990s, many reported on the agroecological transformation of Cuban agriculture as a creative response to the Special Period that began when the Soviet Union fell and the US blockade was tightened (summarized in Funes et al., 2002). The capacity of Cuba to show that a national-level transition to agroecology was possible, further consolidated the Latin American understanding of agroecology as a form of resistance to neoliberal globalization.[12] The consolidation during the 1990s and early 2000s of the Latin American Coordination of Rural Organizations (CLOC) and La Via Campesina International (LVC), with their demands for food sovereignty, and against free trade agreements, provided further momentum to a conception of agroecology as a class project of the global peasantry in opposition to capitalist relations in the countryside (Altieri & Toledo, 2011; McCune & Sánchez, 2019). As opposed to apolitical Northern notions of agroecology as the productive techniques (and scientific basis) of market-friendly 'organic' or local agriculture, agroecology in Latin America carries historical, social and political weight (Ferguson & Morales, 2010). Remarkably, academic configurations such as SOCLA, rather than repressing these broader connotations of agroecology in Latin America, have synthesized and translated them, deepening the global discussion of agroecology (Altieri, 2008).

Responses to our survey: what is Latin American agroecology?

We posed this question in a survey of twenty Latin American agroecologists, both from academia and from rural social movements in the region. The majority, more than 75%, argued in favour of the existence of a Latin American agroecology (LAa) and described its characteristics. Although not an exhaustive sample, this percentage, as well as the coincidences in the characteristics highlighted by the interviewees, are highly significant. It also seems that even those who do not adhere to the idea of a particularly Latin American agroecology recognize the same set of distinctive characteristics of agroecological thought in the region.

In general, the main features identified by the agroecologists consulted that would characterize Latin American agroecology can be summarized into 3 mutually related axes: (1) *Agri*-culture and ancestralism: deep roots in traditional *agri*-cultures and co-evolution between human beings and their environment; (2) Organization and common horizons of struggle: The articulation in a social movement of resistance and construction of alternatives in the search for independence, autonomy and socially, economically and environmentally sustainable modes of production and reproduction; and (3) Formation and dialogue of knowledge: the emphasis of the organizations in the formation of technicians/cadre in agroecology and the dialogue of knowledge between the ancestral/vernacular/local knowledge and that of technicians/scientists/academics (Toná & Guhur, 2009). We develop each of these as follows:

Agri-*culture and ancestrality*

One question that appears in almost all the answers is the ancestral relationship between human beings and their environment. The sustainable management of agroecosystems through an agricultural practice that conserves biodiversity and the natural commons is a consequence of a long *agri*-cultural tradition (i.e. the South American *chacra*, the Mesoamerican *milpa*) of co-evolution and co-creation of landscapes. In the words of the Argentine agroecologist Walter Pengue (*Universidad Nacional de General Sarmiento*): '*Agroecology in Latin America involves not only agricultural issues, but is framed by humanity and in its environment, its landscapes and the configuration that has been historically given to the same (…)*'. In the same vein, Marta Chiappe, an agroecologist at the University of the Republic (Uruguay), affirms that in Latin America '*there is a greater identification of agroecology with ancestral agrarian practices that form part of its cultural identity than in countries or regions where agroecology appears as an alternative to conventional production*'.[13]

From the production point of view, it is pointed out that the origin of Latin American agroecology is linked to the need for farmers to reduce their dependence on external inputs (mainly energy, fertilizers and pesticides – called *agrotoxics*) and to reduce their costs of production in the face of endemically unstable and generally unfavourable marketing conditions for peasants and family farmers in the region. For some, this is the very origin of a Latin American agroecology: '*I believe that Agroecology is of Latin American origin (…) and was born as an approach or paradigm by which to reduce the dependence of Latin American farmers on inputs, and as a consequence allow them to produce quality food,*' says Santiago Sarandón of the National University of La Plata (Argentina) and new president of SOCLA.

Likewise, many people highlighted the endogenous peasant-indigenous character of the development of Latin American agroecology; arguing that its power lies in the fact that it emerges from the territories and communities, and not as a proposal external to them. In the words of Bolivian agroecologist Georgina Catacora-Vargas, vice president of SOCLA: '*Latin American agroecology is characterized by being peasant based, based on traditional knowledge, biodiverse and integrated into proposals for food sovereignty.*'

In short, and as Lorena Soto Pinto of *El Colegio de la Frontera Sur* (Mexico) very clearly puts it, agroecology in Latin America is '*an agroecology based on culture, on what people have been doing for thousands of years*'. As will be seen throughout this text, these arguments are repeated in almost every intervention, even among those who do not believe in the existence of a Latin American agroecology.

Organization and common horizons of struggle

The vast majority of agroecologists interviewed referred to the high degree of politicization and organization of Latin American rural populations. Moreover, they affirm that this is a fundamental and characteristic aspect of Latin American agroecology. In Latin America, agroecology has been constructed in a context of struggles for land and territory, gradually becoming a tool of resistance to the attacks of territories promoted by neoliberal globalization, as well as a device for the territorialization of alternative projects *for life* (i.e. *Sumak Kausay, Buen Vivir*).

As Marlen Sánchez, a young woman agroecologist from the Association of Rural Workers of Nicaragua (ATC) and the *IALA Mesoamerica* (CLOC-VC) clearly states, '*Latin American agroecology brings to the debate the structural violence suffered by peasants and indigenous peoples; the militarization of their lands, territories and the dispossession of natural goods …* '. In the same sense, the Mexican academic Jaime Morales characterizes the agroecology of *Nuestra América* based on its articulation with social movements: '*(…) with a strong content of local knowledge, rooted in grassroots experiences and as part of broader struggles. It has a very clear political dimension. It transcends technical aspects, serves marginalized and vulnerable sectors, and is aimed at family and peasant agriculture*'.

Agroecology in this context is central to the (re)emergence of a socio-historical project that, from the recovery of ancestral knowledge and worldviews and dialogue with other ontologies and epistemes, articulates a new horizon of meanings outside the frameworks of modern-capitalist globalization (Rosset et al., 2019; Val et al., 2019). In this framework, agroecology, agrarian reform and food sovereignty are part of the same horizon of struggle (Martínez-Torres & Rosset, 2014; Rosset, 2013; Rosset & Martínez-Torres, 2012). In the words of Walter Pengue '*Agroecology in Latin America (…) implies a revolutionary social process, which has fully understood that the human being is nothing without the land he treads on, and therefore, agroecology and agrarian reform clearly go hand in hand.*'

Another question that emerges from the opinions of Latin American agroecologists revolves around the public policies for agroecology deployed in the region. Professor Irene Cardoso of the Brazilian Association of Agroecology (ABA) provides an account of this demand of the Latin American agroecological movement when she affirms that '*it expresses itself in the struggle, even for public policies, for the transformation of agro-food systems*'. Some of the interviewees also suggest that in Latin America '*agroecology has greater recognition in national regulatory frameworks, compared to other regions*' (Georgina Catacora-Vargas).

On the other hand, there are those who believe that it is precisely the lack of public policies and, in general, the non-presence of the State, that has promoted more autonomous and self-governing processes in Latin American agroecology. Professor Tomás León-Sicard of Colombia inscribed himself in this tendency when he affirmed that '*the very existence of the peasantry, of the "roots" and Afro communities, and of the indigenous nations that still fight for their territories, becomes a characteristic of our agroecology, not inscribed in other latitudes (…). Add to this the fact that we practice it in very varied soils, in different climates (…), with precariousness in property rights, subsistence economies and deficiencies in public policies*'.

Finally, there seems to be a tacit consensus that an important characteristic of the Latin American agroecological movement is its capacity to develop multi-level organizational processes (from local communities to continental processes), in dialogue and articulation with broad sectors (academia, environmental movements, NGOs, consumer organizations, urban social movements, neo-rural movements, etc.) (Martínez-Torres & Rosset, 2014; Val et al., 2019).

Thus, in Latin America, agroecology is emerging as a broad and inclusive regionalism towards the transformation of agrifood systems, as well as of social and environmental relations. This profoundly revolutionary aspect is clearly expressed in the characterization of José Maria Tardin, agroecologist and militant of the Landless Workers' Movement (MST) of Brazil, for whom Latin American agroecology is based on '*the multiplicity of cultural ethnic foundations expressed in the cosmovisions and praxis of the continent's ancestral peoples (…) and enslaved Afro-descendants. A second aspect is that within the peoples' social movements of the countryside, articulated in the CLOC/VC, agroecology is constitutive of the struggles and projects of human emancipation, is radically anti-capitalist and anti-patriarchal, and is of socialist orientation*'.

Training/formation *and diálogo de saberes*

Closely related to the previous block are the processes of training and formation[14] – especially among youth – of professionals/technicians/cadre in agroecology. Proof of this is the enormous variety of proposals, approaches, methodologies and practices in agroecological training that have emerged in recent years. Among them, the Latin American Institutes of Agroecology (IALAs), which CLOC-VC peasant universities in several countries of the region (Rosset et al., 2019), stand out. The training processes in this type of schools reinforce the holistic sense of agroecology (as a system of production, of struggle and of life), while at the same time contributing – from this holistic perspective – to the symbolic and material construction of Latin American agroecology (Rosset et al., 2019; Rosset & Martínez-Torres, 2012; Val et al., 2019).

This has also been a recurrent theme in the interviews and is clearly summarized in the argument '*Latin American agroecology is distinctive because it is simultaneously a social process, a science and a practice to promote healthy food systems, for which it relies on solidarity and spiritual relations with Mother Earth, through peasant to peasant processes, dialogical education based on processes of research-action-participation-systematization as a strategy for the collective construction of knowledge, in which scientific knowledge interacts with the current and ancestral knowledge of farmers*'.

As can be seen in many of the responses, there is a strong link between the local, vernacular and ancestral knowledge of indigenous and peasant communities and technical, scientific and academic knowledge, and their mutual feedback from the exchange of experiences and the *diálogo de saberes* (Martínez-Torres & Rosset, 2014).

We conclude this section with a phrase from the response of the political agroecologist Omar Felipe Giraldo of *El Colegio de la Frontera Sur* (Mexico), which articulates clearly and relates the proposed blocks in a clear and elegant way: '*Latin American agroecology has been forged in the context of struggles to resist the deterritorialization of neoliberal globalization and at the same time plant the seeds of re-existence and* Buen Vivir, *in which the popular sectors of the countryside and the cities (...) are recovering ancestral knowledge, constructing new knowledge situated in their own worldviews, in dialogue with Science, while reaffirming their cultural identities. In short, it is the defense of territory, which includes autonomy and self-determination, decolonization and depatriarchalization, all for* Buen Vivir.'

Agroecolog(ies) from south to north

When asked about the differences between a Latin American agroecology and other agroecologies, the answers were remarkably similar. Here again, the connection between Latin American agroecology, traditional agriculture and peasant-indigenous worldviews, as well as the strong link with social and political movements, was highlighted. In relation to the ancestral cultural traditions, the words of Dana Avila of the IALA María Cano of Colombia (CLOC/LVC) make this clear, when she affirms that agroecology in Latin America '*is based on two principles: indigenous cosmovision, and communal or collective work. It is deeply nourished by cultural and spiritual elements that are interwoven with the practices of everyday life, while in other latitudes of the planet it is more linked to productive processes without the ancestral and spiritual aspect*'.[15]

Similarly, her compatriot Tomas Enrique León-Sicard of the National University of Colombia affirms: '*I am absolutely sure that there is a profoundly Latin American agroecology, not only in the field of science, in social movements or in farming practice, but ultimately in a series of attitudes and values that can be called the "symbolic framework of agroecology"*.' The political dimension as a characteristic feature of agroecology in Latin America contrasts sharply with the perceptions the respondents hold concerning other agroecologies. The agroecologies practiced in the industrial north (mainly in Europe and the United States) are perceived as a set of agronomic practices and technical developments detached from the political, social and cultural dimensions of agroecology (Wezel et al., 2018). These northern agroecologies are seen more as a market-driven transition of family farmers to organic production to meet the demands of the healthy food market.[16]

Professor Manuel Parra of *El Colegio de la Frontera Sur* in Mexico and Walter Pengue of the *Universidad Nacional de General Sarmiento* in Argentina express themselves along similar lines of thought, though from the northern and southern extremes of the Latin American academy. The Mexican agroecologist explains the differences of contexts: '*Latin American Agroecology is commonly associated with peasant agriculture. But in the US or Europe the contexts are very different, in terms of the scale of production, forms of organization, markets, and culture.*' For his part, the Argentine researcher warns about the risks of a depoliticized agroecology: '*(...) the European view of agroecology, which is much more limited to the production processes of organic production (...), and to some newer perspectives that seek to impose so-called* smart agriculture *and* ecological intensification *(which use essentially agroecology as a battering ram), seek only to achieve "efficiencies" in the agricultural system. This empties agroecology of content, of the farmers, of their land, and of the food they produce*'.

Final reflections: Latin American critical agroecological thought as a regionalism from below

If agroecology is reduced to a scientific approach uniting ecology with agronomy (and even with sociology and anthropology), then everywhere it will be just another 'improved seed' bringing exogenous concepts to new lands – ultimately conforming to the dominant food regime (Levidow et al., 2014). However, in Latin America, agroecology is understood more broadly, as ways of resistance and survival of food and farming cultures, in which agroecosystems are biocultural repositories of traditional knowledge systems and agroecologists are agitators for structural change. Many in Latin America see agroecology as a way of *being*, *living* and *producing* (da Silva, 2014), a way of *being* and of *being in* territories (Giraldo, 2018; Royero-Benavides et al., 2019).

When these elements come into present-day dialogue with academic research, NGO networks and anti-capitalist movements, the possibilities shift, as agroecology becomes a critical contribution of Latin American indigenous, peasant and African diaspora peoples, particularly women, to the construction of alternatives to the dominant capitalist system of social reproduction (Giraldo, 2018; Val et al., 2019).

Critical agroecological thought has accompanied the last four decades of capitalist restructuring and counterhegemonic initiatives in Latin America. In Cuba, for example, agroecology passed from being a minority scientific tendency in the Cuba of the 1980s to the offensive during the Special Period beginning in 1990s, and has proven itself capable, in the hands of a peasantry with access to land, education, health care and markets, of feeding the Cuban people in a sovereign fashion, in line with the revolutionary and socialist 'sense of struggle' (Rosset et al., 2011; Machín Sosa et al. 2013). Across the continent, agroecology is present in the anti-capitalist organizing struggles of Latin America, but it also is a radicalizing element within these struggles; a 'revolution within the revolution', as former Cuban ANAP president Orlando Lugo Fonte put it (Machín Sosa et al. 2013). In Puerto Rico, agroecological peasant economies are a form of decolonization and resistance to capitalism's climate crisis (McCune et al., 2019). Latin American agroecologists and social movements emphasize the linked struggles for self-determination, self-sufficiency, autonomy, and change from below (Giraldo, 2018). This perspective has provided vitality to – and deepened debate within – regional integration processes in Latin America. With its ability to generate dialogue (Martínez-Torres & Rosset, 2014), and having survived conventional scientific institutions and the realpolitik of 'friendly' governments, anti-peasant centralized planning, neoliberal reforms, repression, and incipient neofascism, we believe that Latin American critical agroecological thought is the underpinning of an increasingly important regionalism. We close with reference to Giraldo and Rosset (2018), Nicholls (2014, 2015) and Val et al. (2019), who describe how CLOC, LVC and SOCLA were the foundations of a powerful global civil society dispositive in pushing the Food and Agricultural Organization of the United Nations (FAO) to finally take agroecology seriously, and were able to influence the global agroecological process conducted by FAO to take seriously the politicized Latin American vision of agroecology, in what is a growing dispute with other actors (institutions, the private sector, etc.) over the definition of agroecology as more political or as more technical (Giraldo & Rosset, 2018). This ongoing struggle is a clear demonstration that

Latin American critical agroecology and its underlying thought are representative of a real and powerful regionalism from below.

Notes

1. Following Rosset and Altieri (2017, p. 1) we use the word 'agroecologists' to refer to a mixed bag of agroecological researchers, academics, non-governmental organizations (NGOs) the promote agroecology, ecological farmers, agroecological peasants and agroecology activists, who together conform the agroecology movement.
2. Currently located on the Caribbean coast of Panama, the Kuna people originated in the Sierra Nevada of northern Colombia and inhabited the region of the Gulf of Urabá and the Darien mountains.
3. His classic essay *Nuestra América* was first published on 30 January 1891, in the Mexican newspaper *El Partido Liberal.*
4. First published in Guatemala in 1877.
5. According to Rodríguez (2007), these three ideas appear in different writings of José Martí and not as a specific reflection on the question of identity.
6. Fals-Borda (2008) identified the concept of *sentipensante* when he heard it in fishing villages of the Colombian Atlantic Coast: 'we believe, in reality, that we act with the heart, but we also use the head. And when we combine the two, we are sentimental.' See: https://www.youtube.com/watch?v=LbJWqetRuMo.
7. Available at http://www.cumbreindigenabyayala.org/.
8. Available at https://www.ocmal.org/3740/.
9. hsoclaglobal.com/.
10. Personal observation by the authors.
11. NGOs and their networks like CLADES and MAELA have also played a central role (Altieri & Nichols, 2017; Altieri & Toledo, 2011), but for the sake of simplicity we lump them (with the their largely professional, technical staffs) here with the scientists and technicians ('*técnicos*') represented in SOCLA.
12. It should be pointed out that while the Cuban government has admirable public policies in favour of agroecology, these were mostly the result of pressure from below (Rosset et al., 2011; Rosset, 2016).
13. Direct quotes that are from the survey responses (translated by the authors) are presented in italics.
14. Latin American social movements use the word 'formation' to refer to those types of training that include a transversal political and organizing component.
15. It should be noted that there are also attempts by peasant organizations in other continents to link agroecology with ancestrality (see for example the case of Zimbabwe, discussed by Rosset, 2013), though the argument is more fully developed in Latin American organizations. Another feature more common in Latin America than in other regions is the linking of agroecology with more radical and socialist traditions (Martínez-Torres & Rosset, 2014).
16. Although this is a relatively small sample of the Latin American agroecological universe, the little recognition of and connection with the agroecological movements of other regions of the global South, mainly Asia and Africa, is notable. The few references that were provided to other regions came from people linked to rural social movements (CLOC, LVC), who in general showed a broader and more integral view of agroecology as a social movement and alternative mode of production and way of life.

Disclosure statement

No potential conflict of interest was reported by the author(s).

Funding

This work was supported by the Fundação Cearense de Apoio ao Desenvolvimento Científico e Tecnológico [PVE grant awarded to P. Rosset]; and by the Consejo Nacional de Ciencia y Tecnología [Graduate Fellowship awarded to V. Val].

ORCID

Peter M. Rosset http://orcid.org/0000-0002-1253-1066
Lia Pinheiro Barbosa http://orcid.org/0000-0003-0727-9027
Valentín Val http://orcid.org/0000-0003-3680-3385
Nils McCune http://orcid.org/0000-0001-9040-9595

References

Albó, X., & Barrios, R. (1993). *Violencias encubiertas en BoliVia.* CIPCA.

Altieri, M. A. (1987). *Agroecology: The scientific basis of alternative agriculture* (1st ed.). Westview Press.

Altieri, M. A. (2008). El papel estratégico de la Sociedad Científica Latinoamericana de Agroecología (SOCLA) frente a los desafíos y oportunidades para una agricultura sustentable en la América Latina y el Caribe del siglo XXI. *Agroecología, 3*, 87–96.

Altieri, M. A., & Nichols, C. (2017). Agroecology: A brief account of its origins and currents of thought in Latin America. *Agroecology and Sustainable Food Systems, 41*(3–4), 231–237. https://doi.org/10.1080/21683565.2017.1287147

Altieri, M. A., & Toledo, V. (2011). The agroecological revolution in Latin America: Rescuing nature, ensuring food sovereignty and empowering peasants. *The Journal of Peasant Studies, 38*(3), 587–612. https://doi.org/10.1080/03066150.2011.582947

Ardao, A. (1980). *Génesis de la idea y el nombre de América Latina.* Centro de Estudios Latinoamericanos Rómulo Gallegos.

Artacker, T. (2019). *Academia y organizaciones sociales debaten sobre Agroecología.* Observatorio de Cambio Rural. https://ocaru.org.ec/index.php/comunicamos/noticias/item/9253-academia-y-organizaciones-sociales-debaten-sobre-agroecologia

Barbosa, L. P. (2016). Educación, resistencia y conocimiento en América Latina: por una teoría desde los movimientos sociales. *Revista De Raíz Diversa, 3*(6), 45–79. http://dx.doi.org/10.22201/ppela.24487988e.2016.6.58425

Barbosa, L. P. (2017). Legados e rupturas da Revolução Soviética desde as lutas sociais na América Latina. *Tensões Mundiais, 13*(24), 107–138. https://doi.org/10.33956/tensoesmundiais.v13i24.361

Barbosa, L. P. (2018). Epistemologia de *nosotras*, Feminismos e Teoria da Selva na construção do conhecimento: aporte das mulheres Zapatistas. *Revista Brasileira de Educação do Campo, 3*(4), 1128–1155. https://doi.org/10.20873/uft.2525-4863.2018v3n4p1128

Barbosa, L. P. (2019a). Estética da Resistência: arte sentipensante e educação na *práxis* política dos movimentos camponeses e indígenas latino-americanos. Dossiê Educação, Arte e Política: experiências, alternativas e resistências. *Revista Conhecer, 10*(23), 29–62.

Barbosa, L. P. (2019b). Paradigma epistêmico do campo e a construção do conhecimento na perspectiva dos movimentos indígenas e camponeses na América Latina. In A. Ramos dos Santos, J. M. da Silva Oliveira, & L. Andrade Coelho (Eds.), *Educação e Movimentos Sociais: Análises e Desafios* (Vol. 4) (pp. 279–300). Paco Editorial.

Barbosa, L. P., & Rosset, P. M. (2017). Educação do Campo e Pedagogia Camponesa Agroecológica na América Latina: aportes da La Via Campesina e da CLOC. *Educação & Sociedade*, *38*(140), 705–724. https://doi.org/10.1590/es0101-73302017175593

Barrera-Vázques, A., & Rendón, S. (1963). *El libro de los libros de Chilam Balam*. Fondo de Cultura Económica.

Berrón, G., Chavez, J. J., Olivet, C., & Rodríguez, G. (2013). *Rethinking regionalisms in times of crises*. Instituto Eqüit.

Bialowsky, A. L., Lusnisch, C., & Bossio, C. (2014). Más allá del neoliberalismo. Pensamiento crítico latinoamericano y movimientos al intelecto colectivo. *Revista Horizontes Sociológicos*, *2*(4), 70–88.

Borsatto, R. S., & Carmo, M. S. D. (2012). Agroecologia e sua epistemologia. *Interciencia*, *37*(9), 711–716.

Bravo, N. (2010). Movimientos Sociales y acción colectiva como bases de la filosofía latinoamericana. *POLIS*, *27*(1), 1–13. https://doi.org/10.1163/20512996-90000160

da Silva, V. I. (2014). *Classe camponesa: modo de ser, de viver e de produzir*. Padre Josimo.

de la Garza, M. (2012). *El legado escrito de los Mayas*. Fondo de Cultura Económica.

Dussel, E. (2010). Transmodernidad e interculturalidad. Interpretación desde la Filosofía de la Liberación. In A. Mondragón & F. Monroy (Coords.), *Interculturalidad. Historias, experiencias y utopías* (pp. 39–70). Plaza y Valdes.

Escobar, A. (2019). Desde abajo, por la izquierda, y con la Tierra: la diferencia de Abya Yala/Afro/Latino/América. In J. Tobar (Ed.), *Diversidad Epistémica y Pensamiento Crítico: Sumak – Kawsay, Ontología Política e Interculturalidad* (pp. 41–63). Universidad de la Cauca.

Fals-Borda, O. (2008). *Una sociología sentipensante para América Latina (antología)*. CLACSO/Siglo del Hombre Editores.

Ferguson, B., & Morales, H. (2010). Latin American agroecologists build a powerful scientific and social movement. *Journal of Sustainable Agriculture*, *34*(4), 339–341. https://doi.org/10.1080/10440041003680049

Funes, F., García, L., Bourque, M., Pérez, N., & Rosset, P. (2002). *Sustainable agriculture and resistance: Transforming food production in Cuba*. Food First Books.

Galt, R. E. (2016). The relevance of regional political ecology for agriculture and food systems. *Journal of Political Ecology*, *23*(1), 126–133.

Giraldo, O. F. (2014). *Utopías en la era de la supervivencia. Una interpretación del Buen Vivir*. Editorial Itaca. 220 p.

Giraldo, O. F. (2018). *Ecología política de la agricultura. Agroecología y posdesarrollo*. ECOSUR.

Giraldo, O. F., & Rosset, P. M. (2018). Agroecology as a territory in dispute: Between institutionality and social movements. *Journal of Peasant Studies*, *45*(3), 545–564. https://doi.org/10.1080/03066150.2017.1353496

Gliessman, S. R. (2014). *Agroecology: The ecology of sustainable food systems*. CRC Press.

Guzmán Luna, A., Ferguson, B. G., Giraldo, O., Schmook, B., & Aldasoro Maya, E. M. (2019). Agroecology and restoration ecology: Fertile ground for Mexican peasant territoriality? *Agroecology and Sustainable Food Systems*. https://doi.org/10.1080/21683565.2019.1624284

Harvey, D. (2004). The 'new' imperialism: Accumulation by dispossession. *Socialist Register*, *40*, 63–87.

Hecht, S. (1999). La evolución del pensamiento agroecológico. In M. A. Altieri (Ed.), *Agroecología: Bases científicas para una agricultura sustentable* (pp. 15–30). Editorial Nordan-Comunidad.

Holt-Giménez, E. (2006). *Campesino a Campesino: Voices from Latin America's farmer to farmer movement for sustainable agriculture*. Food First Books.

La Via Campesina. (2013). *From Maputo to Jakarta: 5 years of agroecology in La Via Campesina*. International Commission on Sustainable Peasant Agriculture of La Via Campesina.

Lalander, R., & Lembke, M. (2018). The Andean catch-22: Ethnicity, class and resource governance in Bolivia and Ecuador. *Globalizations*, *15*(5), 636–654. https://doi.org/10.1080/14747731.2018.1453189

Lander, E. (2002). Pensamiento crítico latinoamericano: la impugnación del Eurocentrismo. *Revista de Sociología*, *15*, 13–25.

Leff, E. (2002). Agroecologia e saber ambiental. *Agroecologia e Desenvolvimento Rural Sustentável, 3*(1), 36–51.

Levidow, L., Pimbert, M., & Vanloqueren, G. (2014). Agroecological research: Conforming – or transforming the dominant agro-food regime? *Agroecology and Sustainable Food Systems, 38*(10), 1127–1155. https://doi.org/10.1080/21683565.2014.951459

Lubbock, R., & Vivares, E. (2022). The reconfigurations of twenty-first century Latin American regionalism: Actors, processes, contradictions, and prospects. *Globalizations, 19*(4), 519–535. https://doi.org/10.1080/14747731.2021.2011588

Machín Sosa, B., Roque Jaime, A. M., Ávila Lozano, D. R., & Rosset, P. M. (2013). *Agroecological revolution: The farmer-to-farmer movement of the ANAP in Cuba.* ANAP and La Via Campesina. https://Viacampesina.org/en/agroecological-revolution-the-farmer-to-farmer-movement-of-the-anap-in-cuba/

Malamud, A. (2018). Overlapping regionalism, no integration: Conceptual issues and the Latin American experiences. *Política Internacional, 3*(6), 46–59.

Mann, C. C. (2005). *1491: New revelations of the Americas before Columbus.* Alfred A. Knopf.

Mariátegui, J. C. (1928). *Siete ensayos de interpretación de la realidad peruana.* ERA.

Mariátegui, J. C. (1982). *Obras. Tomo II.* Casa de las Américas.

Martí, J. (1974). *Páginas Escogidas.* Ediciones Políticas / Editorial de Ciencias Sociales.

Martí, J. (2005). *Nuestra américa.* Fundación Biblioteca Ayacucho.

Martí, J. (2009). *Nuestra América combate.* Centro de Estudios Martinianos.

Martínez-Torres, M. E., & Rosset, P. M. (2010). La ViaCampesina: The birth and evolution of a transnational social movement. *Journal of Peasant Studies, 37*(1), 149–175. https://doi.org/10.1080/03066150903498804

Martínez-Torres, M. E., & Rosset, P. M. (2014). *Diálogo de saberes* in La Via Campesina: Food sovereignty and agroecology. *The Journal of Peasant Studies, 41*(6), 979–997. https://doi.org/10.1080/03066150.2013.872632

Marx, K. (1990). *Capital: A critique of political economy.* Penguin Classics (Original work published 1867).

McCune, N. M., Perfecto, I., Avilés-Vázquez, K., Vázquez-Negrón, J., & Vandermeer, J. (2019). Peasant balances and agroecological scaling in Puerto Rican coffee farming: Crisis, coffee, and agroecological scaling in Puerto Rico. *Agroecology and Sustainable Food Systems, 43*(7–8), 810–826. https://doi.org/10.1080/21683565.2019.1608348

McCune, N. M., Rosset, P., Cruz, T., Morales, H., & Saldivar, A. (2017). The long road: Rural youth, farming and agroecological formación in Central America. *Mind, Culture, and Activity, 24*(3), 183–198. https://doi.org/10.1080/10749039.2017.1293690

McCune, N., & Sánchez, M. (2019). Teaching the territory: Agroecological pedagogy and popular movements. *Agriculture and Human Values, 36*(3), 595–610. https://doi.org/10.1007/s10460-018-9853-9

Méndez, E., Bacon, C. M., & Cohen, R. (2013). Agroecology as a transdisciplinary, participatory, and action-oriented approach. *Agroecology and Sustainable Food Systems, 37*(1), 3–18. https://doi.org/10.1080/10440046.2012.736926

Muni, S. D. (1985). SARC: Building regionalism from below. *Asian Survey, 25*(4), 391–404. https://doi.org/10.2307/2644225

Nicholls, C. (2014). *Reflexiones sobre la participación de SOCLA en el Simposio Internacional de Agroecología para la seguridad Alimentaria y Nutrición en FAO, Roma.* SOCLA.

Nicholls, C. (2015). *SOCLA reflexiones sobre la Consulta Multisectorial sobre Agroecología en Asia y el Pacífico, organizada por la FAO.* SOCLA.

Paikin, D., Perrotta, D., & Porcelli, E. (2016). Pensamiento latinoamericano para la integración. *Cultura y Educación, 15*(1), 49–80.

Patel, R. (2012). *Stuffed and starved: The hidden battle for the world food system.* Melville House.

Patel, R. (2013). The long green revolution. *Journal of Peasant Studies, 40*(1), 1–63. https://doi.org/10.1080/03066150.2012.719224

Rivera-Cusicanqui, S. (2015). *Sociología de la imagen. Miradas ch'ixi desde la historia andina.* Tinta Lemón.

Rodríguez, S. (2007). *Inventamos o erramos.* Editores Latinoamérica.

Rosset, P. M. (2013). Re-thinking agrarian reform, land and territory in La Via Campesina. *Journal of Peasant Studies, 40*(4), 721–775. https://doi.org/10.1080/03066150.2013.826654

Rosset, P. M. (2015). Epistemes rurales y la formación agroecológica en La Via Campesina. *Ciencias y Tecnología Social, 2,* 1–10.

Rosset, P. (2016). Las recetas no funcionan, lo que se propone son principios. *Revista Biodiversidad, 90,* 5–10.

Rosset, P. M., & Altieri, M. A. (2017). *Agroecology: Science and politics*. Fernwood Publishing.

Rosset, P. M., & Barbosa, L. P. (2021). Autonomía y los movimientos sociales del campo en América Latina: un debate urgente. *Aposta. Revista de Ciencias Sociales*, *89*, 8–31.

Rosset, P. M., Machín Sosa, B., Roque, A. M., & Ávila, D. R. (2011). The Campesino-to- Campesino agroecology movement of ANAP in Cuba: Social process methodology in the construction of sustainable peasant agriculture and food sovereignty. *Journal of Peasant Studies*, *38*(1), 161–191. https://doi.org/10.1080/03066150.2010.538584

Rosset, P. M., & Martínez-Torres, M. E. (2012). Rural social movements and agroecology: Context, theory, and process. *Ecology and Society*, *17*(3), 3. https://doi.org/10.5751/ES-05000-170317

Rosset, P., Val, V., Barbosa, L. P., & McCune, N. (2019). Agroecology and La Via Campesina II. Peasant agroecology schools and the formation of a sociohistorical and political subject. *Agroecology and Sustainable Food Systems*, *43*(7–8), 895–914. https://doi.org/10.1080/21683565.2019.1617222

Royero-Benavides, B., Rosset, P. M., Alvarez-Avila, M. C., Gallardo-Lopez, F., & Mariaca-Méndez, R. (2019). Desarrollo y buena vida en la mixteca alta: el caso de una organización campesina oaxaqueña. *Agricultura, Sociedad y Desarrollo*, *16*(1), 19–41. https://doi.org/10.22231/asyd.v1i1.979

Sambarino, M. (1980). *Identidad, tradición, autenticidad: tres problemas de América Latina*. Centro de Estudios Latinoamericanos Rómulo Gallegos.

Toledo, V. M., & Barrera-Bassols, N. (2008). *La memoria biocultural. La importancia ecológica de las sabidurías tradicionales*. Icaria Editorial.

Toná, N., & Guhur, D. M. P. (2009). O Diálogo de Saberes, na Promoção da Agroecologia na Base dos Movimentos Sociais Populares. *Revista Brasileira de Agroecologia*, *4*(2), 3322–3325.

Val, V., Rosset, P. M., Zamora Lomelí, C., Giraldo, O. F., & Rocheleau, D. (2019). Agroecology and La Via Campesina i. The symbolic and material construction of agroecology through the dispositive of 'peasant-to-peasant' processes. *Agroecology and Sustainable Food Systems*, *43*(7–8), 872–894. https://doi.org/10.1080/21683565.2019.1600099

Wallerstein, I. (1974). The rise and future demise of the world capitalist system: Concepts for comparative analysis. *Comparative Studies in Society and History*, *16*(4), 387–415. https://doi.org/10.1017/S0010417500007520

Wezel, A., Bellon, S., Doré, T., Francis, C., Vallod, D., & David, C. (2009). Agroecology as a science, a movement and a practice. A review. *Agronomy for Sustainable Development*, *29*(4), 503–515. https://doi.org/10.1051/agro/2009004

Wezel, A., Goette, J., Lagneaux, E., Passuello, G., Reisman, E., Rodier, C., & Turpin, G. (2018). Agroecology in Europe: Research, education, collective action networks, and alternative food systems. *Sustainability*, *10*(4), 1214. https://doi.org/10.3390/su10041214

Index

For Product Safety Concerns and Information please contact our EU representative GPSR@taylorandfrancis.com
Taylor & Francis Verlag GmbH, Kaufingerstraße 24, 80331 München, Germany

www.ingramcontent.com/pod-product-compliance
Ingram Content Group UK Ltd.
Pitfield, Milton Keynes, MK11 3LW, UK
UKHW052211190926
475702UK00006B/968

* 9 7 8 1 0 3 2 3 2 9 9 2 5 *